Praise for *Ransomware and Cyber Extortion*

"*Ransomware and Cyber Extortion* is a ma[...]te[...]n[...] lead both technical and non-technical readers alike on [...] journey through the comple[...] and sometimes dark world of cyber extortion. The encore of practical advice and guidance on preventing ransomware can help organizations of all sizes."
—Russ Cohen, Head of Cyber Services US, Beazley Group

"Davidoff and team have built a magisterial and yet still approachable guide to ransomware. This just became the definitive and classic text. I've been writing about some of these attacks for years and still was blown away by how much more they taught me. I'll hand this to every infosec newcomer and senior consultant from now on."
—Tara Wheeler, CEO, Red Queen Dynamics

"Ransomware attacks are no longer encrypt-and-export incidents; they have evolved into sophisticated, multipronged attacks that require a multidisciplinary response of forensic, technical, and compliance expertise and savvy cybercrime negotiation skills. Sherri Davidoff, Matt Durrin, and Karen Sprenger are that 'Dream Team' and concisely help the reader understand how to prepare for and respond to ransomware attacks. This book is a must-read for every member of an internal or external incident response team."
—Jody R. Westby, CEO, Global Cyber Risk LLC, Chair, ABA Privacy & Computer Crime Committee (Section of Science & Technology Law)

"A thoroughly delightful read, *Ransomware and Cyber Extortion* takes the topic everyone is talking about and deconstructs it with history and actionable guidance. A must-read before you next brief your board or peers on your own incident response plans."
—Andy Ellis, CSO Hall of Fame '21

Ransomware and
Cyber Extortion

Ransomware and Cyber Extortion

Response and Prevention

Sherri Davidoff
Matt Durrin
Karen Sprenger

✦Addison-Wesley

Boston • Columbus • New York • San Francisco • Amsterdam • Cape Town
Dubai • London • Madrid • Milan • Munich • Paris • Montreal • Toronto • Delhi • Mexico City
São Paulo • Sydney • Hong Kong • Seoul • Singapore • Taipei • Tokyo

Cover illustration by Jonah Elgart, bolognasalad.com

Screenshots by LMG Security have been reprinted with permission.

Definition icon courtesy of Colorlife/Shutterstock
Head's Up icon courtesy of iDesign/Shutterstock
Tip icon courtesy of maya_parf/Shutterstock

For information about buying this title in bulk quantities, or for special sales opportunities (which may include electronic versions; custom cover designs; and content particular to your business, training goals, marketing focus, or branding interests), please contact our corporate sales department at corpsales@pearsoned.com or (800) 382-3419.

For government sales inquiries, please contact governmentsales@pearsoned.com.

For questions about sales outside the U.S., please contact intlcs@pearson.com.

Visit us on the Web: informit.com/aw

Library of Congress Control Number: 2022942883

ISBN-13: 978-0-13-745033-6
ISBN-10: 0-13-745033-8

2 2022

Pearson's Commitment to Diversity, Equity, and Inclusion

Pearson is dedicated to creating bias-free content that reflects the diversity of all learners. We embrace the many dimensions of diversity, including but not limited to race, ethnicity, gender, socioeconomic status, ability, age, sexual orientation, and religious or political beliefs.

Education is a powerful force for equity and change in our world. It has the potential to deliver opportunities that improve lives and enable economic mobility. As we work with authors to create content for every product and service, we acknowledge our responsibility to demonstrate inclusivity and incorporate diverse scholarship so that everyone can achieve their potential through learning. As the world's leading learning company, we have a duty to help drive change and live up to our purpose to help more people create a better life for themselves and to create a better world.

Our ambition is to purposefully contribute to a world where:

- Everyone has an equitable and lifelong opportunity to succeed through learning.
- Our educational products and services are inclusive and represent the rich diversity of learners.
- Our educational content accurately reflects the histories and experiences of the learners we serve.
- Our educational content prompts deeper discussions with learners and motivates them to expand their own learning (and worldview).

While we work hard to present unbiased content, we want to hear from you about any concerns or needs with this Pearson product so that we can investigate and address them.

- Please contact us with concerns about any potential bias at https://www.pearson.com/report-bias.html.

To my husband and best friend, Tom.
– Sherri

To my caring, loving, and PATIENT wife Karah.
– Matt

To my mom, my dad, and my sister, for love and support
through all of my adventures.
– Karen

Contents

I want to devise a virus
To bring dire straits to your environment
Crush your corporations with a mild touch
Trash your whole computer system and revert you to papyrus
    —Deltron 3030, "Virus," May 23, 2000

Preface

No one realized when the hip hop song "Virus," was released in 2000 that it would turn out to be prophetic. Featuring a protagonist (Deltron Zero) who wanted to "develop a super virus," the lyrics describe his plans to infect and destroy computers around the world: "Crush your corporations with a mild touch / Trash your whole computer system and revert you to papyrus."[1]

More than two decades later, ransomware has reached epidemic proportions, shutting down hospitals, schools, law firms, municipalities, manufacturers, and organizations in every sector. Victims around the globe are routinely infected and forced to revert to pen and paper (for those lucky enough to still maintain supplies).[2,3] Worse, cyber attackers have discovered that threatening to publish information can give them similar leverage, leading to enormous—and purposeful—data leaks.

Today, data is wielded as a weapon. By threatening the confidentiality, integrity, and availability of data, criminals reap profits and force victims to bend to their will. After years of escalating ransomware attacks, brazen data publication, and a daily barrage of new victims touted in the headlines, they have honed their strategies and developed a scalable, successful business model.

The impacts of cyber extortion are far-reaching. Business operations have been halted, both temporarily and in some cases permanently. Medical records have been destroyed and patients' lives put in jeopardy. Key intellectual property has been sold to competitors. Private emails and personal details are routinely dumped so that they become visible to the public eye.

Court cases resulting from ransomware and data leaks are multiplying, even as victims and insurers pour funds into victim compensation and corrective action. Law enforcement agencies around the world are working every day to dismantle cyber extortion rackets, even as the criminals themselves crow to the media that they are not afraid.

"Extortion fatigue" is real. The problem is so pervasive that people can't digest the full scope and impact. At the same time, cyber extortion is wildly underreported. After all, no victim purposefully calls the media when they find out they've been hacked. Cases are routinely negotiated quietly, in secret. As a result, the true extent of cyber extortion cannot be known but is undoubtedly far greater than any statistics indicate.

Response is crucial. The steps taken by a victim organization in the hours, days, and months after a cyber extortion attack can dramatically impact the outcome.

---

1. Deltron 3030, "Virus," *Deltron 3030*, May 23, 2000, https://genius.com/Deltron-3030-virus-lyrics.
2. www.beckershospitalreview.com/cybersecurity/georgia-health-system-reverts-to-paper-records-after-ransomware-attack-5-details.html.
3. www.forbes.com/sites/tommybeer/2020/09/28/report-big-us-hospital-system-struck-by-cyberattack-forcing-staff-to-resort-to-paper-and-pen/.

This book is a practical guide to responding to cyber extortion threats, including ransomware, exposure extortion, denial-of-service attacks, and more. Throughout the book, we'll draw heavily from real-world case studies, as well as the vast library of unpublished cases handled by the authors during their work as response professionals. Readers will emerge better prepared to handle a cyber extortion attack properly, which will help minimize damage and expedite recovery.

As highlighted throughout the book, cyber extortion is typically the last and most visible phase of an intrusion. Often, cybercriminals have access to a victim's environment or data for an extended period of time, siphoning off key information, researching the victim, and installing malware and other tools that will maximize their leverage.

By employing effective cybersecurity prevention measures throughout society, we can reduce the risk of cyber extortion and cybercrime more generally. In the last chapter of this book, we delve into the underlying causes of cyber extortion and provide recommendations for reducing this risk.

Since cyber extortion actors, tools, and tactics evolve constantly, throughout this book we emphasize response and prevention techniques that will stand the test of time.

Who Should Read This Book?

This book is intended to be a valuable resource for anyone involved in cyber extortion prevention, response, planning, or policy development. This includes

- Chief information officers (CIO) and chief information security officers (CISO) who are involved with planning, their organizations' cyber extortion response or developing prevention strategies

- Cybersecurity professionals, incident responders, forensics investigators, ransom negotiators, cryptocurrency payment processors, and anyone involved in ransomware and cyber extortion response

- Technology staff, including system administrators, network technicians, help desk workers, security teams, and other individuals responsible for responding to cyberattacks or securing their environments

- Executives who want a deeper understanding of the cyber extortion threat and effective response and prevention strategies

- Legislators, regulators, law enforcement agents, and anyone involved in establishing policy relating to cyber extortion

- Anyone interested in learning more about ransomware and cyber extortion attacks

How This Book Is Organized

This book is designed to be a practical guide for response and prevention of ransomware and cyber extortion threats. Here is a summary of our journey in this book:

- **Chapter 1, Impact:** Cyber extortionists threaten the confidentiality, integrity, and availability of information in an effort to gain leverage over a victim. The four types of cyber extortion are denial, modification, exposure, and faux extortion. Impacts of cyber extortion range from operational disruption to financial loss, reputational damage, lawsuits, and more. In addition to targeting victims directly, adversaries compromise technology suppliers such as managed services providers (MSPs), cloud providers, and software vendors.

- **Chapter 2, Evolution:** Ransomware and cyber extortion attacks have been around longer than most people realize and come in a variety of forms. In this chapter, we cover the history of ransomware and its impact on affected organizations, and then follow its evolution into the bustling criminal economy that drives it today.

- **Chapter 3, Anatomy of an Attack:** Extortion is the last phase of a cyber extortion attack. Adversaries first gain access to the victim's technology environment and then take steps to expand their access, assess the victim, and prepare prior to extortion. In this chapter, we step through the phases of a cyber extortion attack. Along the way, we identify indicators of compromise and provide response tips that can mitigate or even stop the attack in progress.

- **Chapter 4, The Crisis Begins:** The early stages of cyber extortion response significantly impact how quickly an organization recovers and is able to resume its normal operations. In this chapter, we provide insight on recognizing the common early indicators of a cyber extortion attack. We also walk through the concept of triage and explain how development of a clear and effective response strategy is critical early in the response process.

- **Chapter 5, Containment:** When a cyber extortionist strikes, quick action can reduce the damage and help speed recovery. In this chapter, we discuss techniques for halting data exfiltration and file encryption/deletion, resolving denial-of-service attacks, and locking the adversary out of the victim's environment. We end the chapter by talking about threat hunting, including methodology, sources of evidence, tools and techniques, staffing, and results.

- **Chapter 6, Investigation:** Taking the time to conduct an investigation is critical for both short- and long-term resolution of cyber extortion incidents. In this chapter, we discuss reasons for investigating, techniques for identifying the adversary, methods for scoping an attack and tracking down "patient zero," and the fundamentals of data breach investigations. We also cover evidence preservation, which has the potential to reduce the long-term damage of cyber extortion attacks.

- **Chapter 7, Negotiation:** How do you reach an agreement with criminals? This chapter is a practical guide to initiating, managing, and completing a ransom negotiation. You'll learn about haggling, proof of life, and closing the deal. We also discuss common mistakes made during cyber extortion negotiations and ways to avoid them.

- **Chapter 8, Payment:** Although paying a ransom may be undesirable or even unthinkable for some, in many cases it is the victim's chosen path forward. In this chapter, we discuss the pros and cons of paying a ransom, and then the practicalities of the payment process, including forms of payment, types of intermediaries, timing issues, and what to do after payment has been made. We also discuss payments prohibited due to sanctions and consider the due diligence that victims should conduct before any payment is made.

- **Chapter 9, Recovery:** The goal of every incident is to return to normal operations. In this chapter, we cover the process of recovery, as well as strategies for reducing the risk of data loss and reinfection, which can enable the victim to resume operations with confidence. Along the way, we also describe key improvements for your environment that can reduce future risk and increase defensive capabilities.

- **Chapter 10, Prevention:** Cyber extortion is typically the last phase of a cyberattack. Fundamentally, prevention is best accomplished by implementing a strong, holistic cybersecurity program. In this chapter, we highlight the keys to building such a cybersecurity program, and then delve into specific defensive steps that help to reduce the risk of cyber extortion attacks or mitigate their impact. We conclude by discussing broad-scale, macro changes that are needed to effectively combat the cyber extortion epidemic.

Other Chapter Elements

Throughout each chapter we have included other elements meant to highlight important information, concepts, or examples, some with graphical icons to easily identify each element:

- **Learning Objectives:** A bulleted list of the material covered in that chapter
- **Case Studies:** Real-world cyber extortion cases that demonstrate the concepts being discussed
- **Definition:** Explanations of terms that are specific to cyber extortion or cybersecurity
- **A Word About:** Discussion of a key term and how it is used in this book
- **Tip:** Actionable information for the reader
- **Heads Up!:** Useful background information for the reader

Discussion Questions

At the end of each chapter, we include a section called "Your Turn!" in which we provide the opportunity for you to create your own scenario. We then offer questions for you to consider and discuss with others. Our hope is that this section will provide you with countless opportunities to evaluate cyber extortion incidents from all angles and understand that there is no one right answer when responding to such attacks.

Checklists

At the end of this book, you will find a series of checklists meant to be used (and reused) to help you prevent, and if necessary respond to, cyber extortion. They compile information found in the book in a high-level, quick-and-easy reference format.

Stay Up to Date

For regular updates and commentary on the latest cyber extortion and ransomware developments, visit the authors' website: ransombook.com.

Adversary tactics are rapidly evolving, and best practices for response and prevention evolve with them. In this book, we present a foundation for responding to cyber extortion events and preventing these devastating attacks.

Visit the authors' website for the latest news, response tips, discussion topics, and more. As we all share information and experiences, it is our hope that our global community can work together to shine a light on cyber extortion and reduce the risk.

Register your copy of *Ransomware and Cyber Extortion: Response and Prevention* on the Inform IT site for convenient access to updates and/or corrections as they become available. To start the registration process, go to informit.com/register and log in or create an account. Enter the product ISBN (9780137450336) and click Submit. On the Registered Products tab, look for an Access Bonus Content link next to this product and follow that link to access any available bonus materials. If you would like to be notified of exclusive offers on new editions and updates, please check the box to receive email from us.

Acknowledgments

It takes a village to produce a book, and this one is no exception. We'd like to thank the many people who contributed, from concept to production and everything in between.

First and foremost, thanks to our editors Haze Humbert and James Manly, whose wealth of publishing experience and professional insights were invaluable. We especially appreciated your expert cat-herding skills, and how you patiently kept the process moving forward while giving us grace and time as we all navigated the uncharted waters of working together during the pandemic.

We are grateful to our colleagues Michael Ford and Ben Mayo, who took the time to review the book outline in the early phases to ensure we comprehensively addressed our audience's needs. Michael also provided deep and substantive feedback throughout the entire book, for which we cannot thank him enough. We'd also like to thank Pearson's excellent editing and production teams, including Julie Nahil, Menka Mehta, Aswini Kumar, and Jill Hobbs.

You *can* judge a book by its cover, and we feel so fortunate that artist Jonah Elgart lent his incredible skills to this work—researching actual pirate ship designs, sharing paintings and ideas, and even putting some "Easter eggs" into the illustration (see if you can find all three authors and the artist himself on the cover!). Thank you, Jonah, for gracing our written words with such a beautiful and thought-provoking work of art.

Cryptocurrency payment expert Marc Grens, co-founder of DigitalMint, kindly gave his time for an extensive interview and answered our many in-depth questions on the evolving cryptocurrency due-diligence and payment processes. His firsthand expertise in this area was invaluable, and we are grateful for the opportunity to bring this information to our readers.

Cyber insurance veterans Bob Wice and Frank Quinn took the time to give in-depth interviews that gave us a behind-the-scenes perspective on cyber insurance and risk management. Thank you for your trust and enabling us to share your wisdom with the readers of this book.

Ransomware and cyber extortion is a deep and quickly evolving topic. We've learned through experience by handling a variety of cases at LMG Security, with the support of our incredible team. Many thanks to all of our colleagues at LMG, particularly Derek Rowe, Madison Iler, and Dan Featherman. Thanks also to our longtime attorney (now judge) Shane Vannatta, for helping us to navigate the early days of ransomware and cyber extortion.

We are also grateful to our many colleagues who helped to shape our understanding of ransomware and cyber extortion over the years, including Scott Koller, Ryan Alter, Randy Gainer, David Sande, Marc Kronenberg, Bill Siegel, David Sherman, Katherine Keefe, Brett Anderson, Luke Green, Sue Yi, Mike Wright, Jody Westby, Sean Tassi, Peter Enko,

Dave Chatfield, Mark Greisinger, Vinny Sakore, Andrew Lipton, Michael Phillips, Marc Schein, and Michael Kleinman.

On a personal level, each of us would like to share our gratitude individually as well.

From Sherri: Many thanks to my dear little ones, Violet and Thunder, whose love and enthusiasm buoyed me every day. My husband, Tom Pohl, and my amazing friends, Annabelle Winne and Jeff Wilson, were there for me every day: cheering me on, listening, and providing wise advice. I couldn't have done this without you. I am grateful for my friends and family, especially my father, E. Martin Davidoff, my mother, Sheila Davidoff, my sister, Laura Davidoff Taylor, as well as Jessie Clark, Shannon O'Brien, Kaloni Taylor, Steve McArthur, Kevin Head, Samantha Boucher, Deviant Ollam, Kelley Sinclair, and so many others. Your constant support got me through the long journey of book writing once again. Above all, I feel so lucky to work with Karen Sprenger and Matt Durrin, my incredible co-authors! I have learned so much from you, both in the trenches while responding to extortion cases and during the process of crafting this book. No one could ask for a better team.

From Matt: I'd like to specifically thank my wife, Karah Durrin, and my daughter, Lauren Durrin, for being my quiet inspiration during the writing process. I could not have done this without your amazing and tireless support. I'd also like to thank all of the friends and family who helped me keep going throughout the journey. In addition to the people in my personal life, I'd like to extend a huge thank you to the LMG Security team for giving me the opportunity to make cybersecurity my career. It has been a wild ride, but I feel so blessed to be surrounded by such a wonderful and talented group of people. Finally, I'd like to thank my partners in crime (stopping), Sherri Davidoff and Karen Sprenger. I likely would have never discovered my passion for cybersecurity without both of you amazing women. Sherri believed in me enough to give me an opportunity to dive into the industry. Karen, in addition to being a fantastic security expert, was the person who first taught me how to properly capture a forensic hard drive image. I'm so grateful to have you both as friends and mentors. Thank you both and here's to continuing our shenanigans together!

From Karen: In addition to those listed above, I'd like to thank my mom, Genie Thorberg, my biggest champion and the person who taught me how to use a computer; my dad, Bob Sprenger, who gave equal parts love and life lessons; and my sister, Rhonda Johnson, the first and best of many strong women who led the way for me. To my partners in shenanigans, Sherri Davidoff and Matt Durrin, thank you for the love, laughter, and commitment throughout this project. Although you have not yet succeeded in turning me into a night owl, you have made a daunting task achievable and, dare I say, enjoyable. I'll look forward to swapping cybercrime news links for many years to come. I've had the great blessing of working for women-led companies at key points during my career. Thank you to Linda Wright and Desiree Caskey, who gave me my start many years ago—before I realized that women in technology were few and far between. And especially to Sherri, a particularly heartfelt thank you to you for taking a chance on me all those years ago and giving me a place to spread my wings in cybersecurity and business development. I've learned and grown so much working with you. Finally, thank you to my pack of poodles, Jasper and Gracie, who spent hours lying at my feet to keep me company throughout the whole process, and Sadie, who joined us near the end. I couldn't have done it without the three of you.

About the Authors

Sherri Davidoff (left), Matt Durrin (center), Karen Sprenger (right)

Sherri Davidoff is the CEO of LMG Security and the author of *Data Breaches: Crisis and Opportunity*. As a recognized expert in cybersecurity, she has been called a "security badass" by *The New York Times*. Sherri is a regular instructor at the renowned Black Hat trainings and a faculty member at the Pacific Coast Banking School. She is also the co-author of *Network Forensics: Tracking Hackers Through Cyberspace* (Addison-Wesley, 2012). Sherri is a GIAC-certified forensic analyst (GCFA) and penetration tester (GPEN) and received her degree in computer science and electrical engineering from the Massachusetts Institute of Technology (MIT).

Matt Durrin is the Director of Training and Research at LMG Security and a Senior Consultant with the organization. He is an instructor at the international Black Hat USA conference, where he has taught classes on ransomware and data breaches. Matt has conducted cybersecurity seminars, tabletop exercises, and classes for thousands of attendees in all sectors, including banking, retail, healthcare, government, and more.

A seasoned cybersecurity and IT professional, Matt specializes in ransomware response and research, as well as deployment of proactive cybersecurity solutions. Matt holds a bachelor's degree in computer science from the University of Montana, and his malware research has been featured on *NBC Nightly News*.

Karen Sprenger is the COO and chief ransomware negotiator at LMG Security. She has more than 25 years of experience in cybersecurity and information technology, and she is a noted cybersecurity industry expert, speaker, and trainer. Karen is a GIAC Certified Forensics Examiner (GCFE) and Certified Information Systems Security Professional (CISSP) and holds her bachelor's degree in music performance (yes, really). She speaks at many events, including those held by the *Wall Street Journal* Cyber Pro, Fortinet, the Internal Legal Tech Association, and the Volunteer Leadership Council. In her spare time, Karen considers "digital forensics" a perfectly acceptable answer to the question, "But what do you do for fun?" A lifelong Montanan, she lives in Missoula with oodles of poodles.

Chapter 1

Impact

Heck, what's a little extortion among friends?

—Bill Watterson

Learning Objectives

- Define cyber extortion and explain the four types (denial, exposure, modification, and "faux")
- Understand the impacts of cyber extortion on modern organizations
- Recognize that adversaries can leverage technology suppliers to compromise victims and conduct cyber extortion on a massive scale

---

Company X was a thriving accounting firm headquartered in a major U.S. city. Every day, its staff handled bookkeeping, financial oversight, tax preparation, and a myriad of other tasks for hundreds of clients.

Suddenly, one Monday morning, everything stopped. An early-rising staff member walked into the office and heard a frightening sound. Every computer was shouting a message: "Attention! What happened? All your files, documents, photos, databases, and other important data are safely encrypted with reliable algorithms. You cannot access the files right now. But do not worry. You have a chance!"

Scattered around the office were papers everywhere. All of the printers in the office had printed the ransom note, over and over, until the paper trays were empty. The point-of-sale systems that staff used to process credit cards had spit out the ransom notes on printed receipts, over and over, until the long reams spilled off the desks.

A chilling voicemail awaited one of the firm's partners: "Hello, Mr. [REDACTED]," stated an emotionless male voice with an Eastern European accent, "I'd like to notify you that we downloaded 500 gigabytes of data from your servers. If you're planning to just restore your data without paying for decryption, we'll sell your company's data on darknet.

"Unless you contact us ASAP, we'll notify all of your clients that we are in possession of their private data, like Social Security numbers and tax forms. We urge you to get in touch with us using the email from the text file we've placed on your desktop."

The voice paused for effect. "If we leak that data, your business will be as good as gone. We are looking forward to receiving your reply via email."

Click. With that, the voicemail ended.

The criminals demanded $1.2 million to restore access, and refrain from publishing the client data.

In the meantime, the firm was down. Databases containing client files were fully encrypted and unusable. Employees couldn't access shared folders, including client documents, firm payroll details, human resources (HR) data, and more. All of the clients that depended on them for daily bookkeeping or time-sensitive services were stuck.

Fortunately, the firm's cloud-based email was still available, too—and the criminals leveraged that. "Good morning," the criminals wrote in a follow-up email. "I think you still cannot understand what situation your company is in now. ... First of all, we will sell the personal data of your employees and customers on the market. ... [You] will be sued by both your employees and your clients." The criminals attached the partners' own personal tax returns to the email to illustrate the threat.

It quickly became clear that the criminals had hacked the firm's email accounts as well and were monitoring the victim's response. "We also saw the report that [antivirus vendor] provided you," the criminals wrote. "It contains many errors."

The criminals had a playbook. Day in and day out, they held organizations hostage using the Internet. First, they gained access to their victim's network. For Company X, the initial hack occurred in May, when an employee opened an attachment in a phishing email. The employee's computer was infected with malware—specifically, a remote access Trojan (known as a "RAT"), which gave the criminals remote access to the employee's computer.

Company X's antivirus software did not detect the infection. The criminals lurked for about three months. They occasionally logged in to the employee's computer remotely, presumably to check that their access still worked, but did little else. It is possible that during this time, these criminals simply peddled access to the hacked computer on the dark web. Hackers known as "initial access brokers" specialize in gaining access to computers. They then sell this access to other criminals, and in this way quickly turn their crime into profit. The purchasers—often organized crime groups—then take the next step of exploring the victim's network, stealing data and potentially holding them for ransom.

Suddenly, in August, criminals later identified as the Twisted Spider ransomware gang[1] remotely logged onto the employee's infected computer. Using common penetration testing tools, they stole passwords from the employee's computer, including the username and password of the managed service provider (MSP) that remotely administered the company's computers. Then, they used these credentials to take full control of Company X's network.

The Twisted Spider gang went straight for the heart: They copied all of the files from the firm's primary data repository. Then, they installed fast and effective ransomware software that encrypted all of the company's servers, including databases, application

---

1. Jon DiMaggio, *Ransom Mafia: Analysis of the World's First Ransomware Cartel* (Analyst1, April 7, 2021), https://analyst1.com/file-assets/RANSOM-MAFIA-ANALYSIS-OF-THE-WORLD%E2%80%99S-FIRST-RANSOMWARE-CARTEL.pdf.

servers, domain controllers, and more. They left workstations alone, not bothering to comb through individual accounts or computers. It was like a well-executed smash-and-grab.

The criminals knew their victims' pain points. They knew that the short-term business interruption was impactful, but even more devastating were the potential long-term consequences that could arise from angry clients who were upset that their data was stolen. The Twisted Spider hackers made sure to demonstrate that they had access to sensitive, regulated information, ranging from Social Security numbers to tax details. They explicitly reminded the victim's executives that they could be sued by employees and clients. They made it clear that they were prepared to publish the data and directly contact affected clients so as to damage the firm's reputation. This, in turn, could lead to loss of business, plus lawsuits, threatening the firm's very survival.

Company X paid the ransom—or rather, their cyber insurance firm paid the ransom, less a $25,000 deductible. The authors of this book were called to handle the negotiation and successfully obtained a hefty discount, settling the case for a little less than $600,000. Not surprisingly, Twisted Spider appeared to leverage inside information during the negotiations: Company X had an insurance policy with a ransomware sublimit of $600,000.

Once Twisted Spider verified that the money was received (in the form of cryptocurrency), the criminals provided preconfigured software to decrypt the encrypted files, and "confirmed" via chat that they had deleted the data. They even created a full list of all files that they claimed to have deleted, and shared this via email, presumably to provide the victim with documentation that could assuage client concerns or negate the need for notification. However, Company X's cyber lawyers determined that notification was required anyway, for both legal and ethical reasons.

1.1 A Cyber Epidemic

Company X was not alone in suffering such an attack. Thousands (if not millions) of organizations have been hit with cyber extortion over the past decade. What was once a novel crime has become mainstream—at great cost to society.

Cyber extortion attacks have shuttered hospitals, forced school closures, disrupted the food supply, and even caused large-scale fuel shortages. Today, ransomware attacks are also being pushed out to thousands of organizations simultaneously through the technology supply chain.

The cost of ransomware was estimated to hit $20 billion in 2021, and is predicted to balloon to $265 billion by 2031, according to research firm Cybersecurity Ventures.[2] In a global survey, 37% of organizations reported that they were hit by ransomware attacks in

---

2. David Braue, "Global Ransomware Damage Costs Predicted to Exceed $265 Billion by 2031," *Cybercrime Magazine*, June 2, 2022, https://cybersecurityventures.com/global-ransomware-damage-costs-predicted-to-reach-250-billion-usd-by-2031/.

2020,[3] although the full scale of the problem is impossible to assess because many victims do not report the crime.[4]

Propelled by their success, cybercriminals have invested in increasingly sophisticated cyber extortion technology and business models. Cyber extortion has evolved from small, one-off attacks to a bustling criminal economy, with franchises, affiliates, specialized software, and user-friendly playbooks.

Defenders need to ramp up their efforts, too. It is possible to dramatically reduce the damage of a cyber extortion crisis, or even prevent one altogether, by acting quickly and strategically in response to prodromal signs of an attack. Given that cyber extortion tactics evolve quickly, defenders' tactics must constantly adapt as well.

In this chapter, we first build a foundation by evaluating the impacts of cyber extortion and understanding how this crime has evolved. Then, we discuss key technological advancements that have facilitated the expansion of ransomware specifically, as well as other forms of cyber extortion. Modern cyber extortion gangs have adopted scalable business models that often involve affiliates and industry specialists, and increasingly leverage threats of data exposure. We conclude by analyzing the next-generation cyber extortion business model, which will provide context for the response and prevention tactics introduced throughout this book.

1.2   What Is Cyber Extortion?

Definition: Cyber Extortion

Cyber extortion is an attack in which an adversary attempts to obtain something of value by threatening the confidentiality, integrity, and/or availability of information technology resources.

Extortion is a crime that has evolved along with humanity. It refers to the act of obtaining something of value "by force, intimidation, or undue or illegal power."[5] As the Internet evolved and organizations around the world came to depend upon computing resources to operate, cybercriminals adapted old tactics to this new digital world.

---

3. Sophos, *The State of Ransomware 2021*, 2021, https://secure2.sophos.com/en-us/medialibrary/pdfs/whitepaper/sophos-state-of-ransomware-2021-wp.pdf.

4. Danny Palmer, "Ransomware Victims Aren't Reporting Attacks to Police. That's Causing a Big Problem," *ZDNet*, October 5, 2020, www.zdnet.com/article/ransomware-victims-arent-reporting-attacks-to-police-thats-causing-a-big-problem/.

5. "Extortion," Merriam-Webster, www.merriam-webster.com/dictionary/extortion.

1.2.1 CIA Triad

To create leverage, adversaries threaten one or more of the three security objectives for information and information systems, as defined by the Federal Information Security Management Act (FISMA) of 2002:

- Confidentiality
- Integrity
- Availability

Colloquially, these three objectives are known as the "CIA Triad," based on their acronym.[6] The CIA Triad was specifically designed for use by departments, vendors, and contractors of the federal government; however, it has been widely adopted by other organizations and the information security community itself. Although cyber extortion can violate any of the three CIA objectives, today's adversaries most commonly threaten confidentiality and availability.

1.2.2 Types of Cyber Extortion

Cyber extortion attacks fit into one of four categories—exposure, modification, denial, or faux:

- **Exposure:** Threatens the *confidentiality* of information resources. For example, an adversary may steal data from a victim, and threaten to either publish or sell it unless a ransom is paid.

- **Modification:** Threatens the *integrity* of information resources. An adversary can modify key elements of an organization's data, such as patient records or bank transactions, and demand a payment in exchange for restoring the original data or identifying the changes.[7] This type of attack is rare at the time of this writing, but adversaries may decide to leverage it in the future, particularly if scalable modification tools are developed.

- **Denial:** Threatens the *availability* of information resources. Ransomware attacks are the most common example of denial extortion. In these cases, an adversary encrypts a victim's files and refuses to release the decryption key unless a ransom is paid.

---

6. "Standards for Security Categorization of Federal Information and Information Systems," National Institute of Standards and Technology, Computer Security Division, Information Technology Laboratory, February 2004, https://nvlpubs.nist.gov/nistpubs/FIPS/NIST.FIPS.199.pdf.

7. "Enterprise Ransomware," CyberCube, 2022, https://insights.cybcube.com/enterprise-ransomware-report.

Distributed denial-of-service (DDoS) attacks have also been used by adversaries to create leverage for extortion.[8,9]

- **Faux:** An attack that appears to be cyber extortion, but in fact is not. For example, the destructive "NotPetya" malware masqueraded as ransomware, but was actually designed to destroy the victim's systems with no hope of recovery. (See Chapter 7 for more details on the NotPetya attacks.)

A Word About the "Adversary"

When we use the term "adversary" throughout this book, we are referring to the collection of actors involved in executing a cyber extortion attack, and not necessarily to a single actor.

Modern cyber extortion attacks often involve many different actors. For example, an "initial access broker" may gain the first entry into a victim's network, and then sell or rent access to other adversaries.[10] Sophisticated cyber extortion gangs may have employees or contractors with specialized skill sets that are employed at various stages of an attack. For simplicity, all of these actors are included when we refer to the "adversary" throughout this book.

1.2.3   Multicomponent Extortion

Increasingly, adversaries use multiple forms of extortion in combination, in an effort to increase their chances of scoring a big payday. Starting in late 2019, the Maze group pioneered the "double extortion" trend, combining both ransomware and data exposure threats. The term "double extortion" refers to the use of two cyber extortion tactics in tandem, such as denial and exposure threats. This creates greater leverage for the adversary and can result in a larger payment from the victim.

---

8. Lance Whitney, "How Ransomware Actors Are Adding DDoS Attacks to Their Arsenals," *TechRepublic*, June 2, 2021, www.techrepublic.com/article/how-ransomware-actors-are-adding-ddos-attacks-to-their-arsenals/.

9. Lawrence Abrams, "Ransomware Gangs Add DDoS Attacks to Their Extortion Arsenal," *Bleeping Computer*, October 1, 2020, www.bleepingcomputer.com/news/security/ransomware-gangs-add-ddos-attacks-to-their-extortion-arsenal/.

10. Victoria Kivilevich and Raveed Laeb, "The Secret Life of an Initial Access Broker," KELA, August 6, 2020, https://ke-la.com/the-secret-life-of-an-initial-access-broker/.

Other groups such as RagnarLocker, Avaddon, and SunCrypt have combined DDoS tactics with traditional ransomware or data exposure threats.[11,12] For example, in an October 2020 attack on a home appliances company, the SunCrypt gang launched a DDoS attack against the victim's network after initial ransomware negotiations stalled. According to a leaked transcript, the criminals wrote: "We were in the process on the negotiations and you didn't show up so further actions were taken."[13]

We will discuss the expansion of extortion tactics in more detail throughout Chapter 2.

1.3 Impacts of Modern Cyber Extortion

Cyber extortion attacks have the potential to cause severe damage to organizations. Their impacts may include operational disruption, financial loss, reputational damage, and litigation, as well as ripple effects for employees, customers, stakeholders, and the broader community.

In this section, we discuss common negative effects of cyber extortion attacks, setting the stage for discussions of response and mitigation throughout this book.

1.3.1 Operational Disruption

The short-term impacts of cyber extortion can include partial or complete disruption of normal operations. This is particularly the case when the adversary uses denial tactics, such as ransomware or DDoS attacks.

For example, Scripps Health, a California-based health system, was hit with a ransomware attack in April 2021 that disrupted access to electronic health records for nearly four weeks. During this time, many patients were diverted to other facilities, and non-urgent appointments were delayed.[14] Later that summer, hackers affiliated with the REvil ransomware gang detonated ransomware at 1,500 organizations around the world, leveraging vulnerabilities in the popular Kaseya remote management software.[15] As a result, the

---

11. Lawrence Abrams, "Another Ransomware Now Uses DDoS Attacks to Force Victims to Pay," *Bleeping Computer*, January 24, 2021, www.bleepingcomputer.com/news/security/another-ransomware-now-uses-ddos-attacks-to-force-victims-to-pay/.

12. Sean Newman, "How Ransomware Is Teaming up with DDoS," *Infosecurity Magazine*, June 18, 2021, www.infosecurity-magazine.com/opinions/ransomware-teaming-ddos/.

13. Newman, "How Ransomware Is Teaming up with DDoS."

14. "147,000 Patients Affected by Scripps Health Ransomware Attack," *HIPAA Journal*, June 3, 2021, www.hipaajournal.com/147000-patients-affected-by-scripps-health-ransomware-attack/.

15. Liam Tung, "Kaseya Ransomware Attack: 1,500 Companies Affected, Company Confirms," *ZDNet*, July 6, 2021, www.zdnet.com/article/kaseya-ransomware-attack-1500-companies-affected-company-confirms/.

Swedish grocery chain, Coop, was forced to close hundreds of stores, causing food to spoil and leading to a significant revenue loss for the company.[16]

In a recent survey, more than one-fourth of the organizations surveyed reported that they had been forced to close their organization at least temporarily following a ransomware attack,[17] and 29% were forced to cut jobs, according to security company Cybereason.[18] Downtime statistics vary widely, but in the authors' experience, partial recovery typically comes within two to five days; resumption of normal operations takes two to four weeks.

The good news (if you could call it that) is that 96% of ransomware victims were able to get some of their data back, either by restoring it from backups, using an adversary-supplied decryptor, or through another means, according to a 2021 survey conducted by security vendor Sophos. However, an important caveat applies: Victims that paid the ransom were able to recover only 65% of their data, on average. Only a mere 8% of victims surveyed were able to restore all of their data.[19] Permanent data loss can lead to errors and cause extra work for many years in the future.

Definition: Decryptor

The term "decryptor" refers to software that is used to decrypt data that was encrypted during a ransomware incident. While this term is not yet in the dictionary (as of the time this book was written), it is commonly used by ransomware response professionals, and so we will use it throughout this book. Note that ransomware decryptors can be obtained from many different sources, including free decryptors from security vendors, experimental utilities created by government or law enforcement agencies, and as software purchased from the adversary in exchange for a ransom payment.

Ransomware attacks can even put businesses *out* of business. In 2019, U.S.-based healthcare provider Wood Ranch Medical closed its doors forever after a ransomware attack encrypted all their patient data. "Unfortunately, the damage to our computer system was such that we are unable to recover the data stored there and, with our backup system encrypted as well, we cannot rebuild our medical records," wrote the practice in its final statement to patients. "We will be closing our practice and ceasing operations…"[20]

---

16. Lawrence Abrams, "Coop Supermarket Closes 500 Stores After Kaseya Ransomware Attack," *Bleeping Computer*, July 3, 2021, www.bleepingcomputer.com/news/security/coop-supermarket-closes-500-stores-after-kaseya-ransomware-attack/.

17. *Ransomware: The True Cost to Business* (Cybereason, 2021), p. 14, www.cybereason.com/hubfs/dam/collateral/ebooks/Cybereason_Ransomware_Research_2021.pdf.

18. *Ransomware: The True Cost to Business*, p. 12.

19. Sophos, *The State of Ransomware 2021*, p. 11.

20. Wood Ranch Medical, "Wood Ranch Medical Notifies Patients of Ransomware Attack," September 18, 2019, https://web.archive.org/web/20191229063121/https://www.woodranchmedical.com/.

A Word About "Ransomware"

The term "ransomware" originally referred to malicious software used to deny victims access to information resources, typically by encrypting files or devices. Over time, colloquial use of this term has broadened to include other types of cyber extortion, such as threats to publish data.

In this book, we will use the term "ransomware" specifically to refer to the malicious software used to deny access to information resources. In the broader sense, we will use the term "cyber extortion."

1.3.2 Financial Loss

Cyber extortion can have a devastating impact on a victim's financial state. Losses typically accrue because of short-term disruption to the victim's revenue generation process, expenses related to the investigation and remediation costs, and the ransom payment itself. For example, the global shipping company Maersk reported total losses between $250 million and $300 million after its IT infrastructure was suddenly wiped out in the destructive NotPetya faux ransomware attacks of 2017. The NotPetya malware destroyed the hard drives of infected computers. Although it appeared to offer a recovery option in exchange for a ransom payment, in fact the files were unrecoverable.[21]

In this section, we discuss three common causes of financial loss in cyber extortion attacks: revenue disruption, remediation costs, and ransom payments.

1.3.2.1 Revenue Disruption

Obviously, any operational interruptions can cause an immediate disruption in revenue generation. This is especially impactful for businesses that generate revenue daily (as opposed to nonprofit organizations, schools, and public entities that may be funded on an annual basis). Hospitals, retailers, professional services firms, transportation, and manufacturing companies are particularly hit hard by such disruptions. For example, Scripps Health reportedly lost $91.6 million of revenue as a result of its 2021 cyberattack, largely due to "volume reductions during May 2021 from emergency room diversions and postponement of elective surgeries."[22]

Business interruption insurance can soften the blow to a victim's wallet. Typically, this type of insurance kicks in after a waiting period (such as 24 hours), after which the insurer will cover lost revenue up to a set dollar amount. See Chapter 12 for more information on cyber insurance coverage.

---

21. Mike McQuade, "The Untold Story of NotPetya, the Most Devastating Cyberattack in History," *Wired*, August 22, 2018, www.wired.com/story/notpetya-cyberattack-ukraine-russia-code-crashed-the-world/.

22. Robert King, "May Cyberattack Cost Scripps Nearly $113M in Lost Revenue, More Costs," Fierce Healthcare, August 11, 2021, www.fiercehealthcare.com/hospitals/may-cyber-attack-cost-scripps-nearly-113m-lost-revenue-more-costs.

1.3.2.2   Remediation Costs

The costs to remediate a ransomware attack can add up quickly. Depending on the recovery strategy, necessary expenses may include hardware purchases (such as new hard drives or desktops deployed to quickly replace infected ones), software licenses, outsourced IT support, security and forensics services, and more.

The City of Baltimore reportedly spent more than $18 million recovering from its 2019 Robbinhood ransomware attack—a figure that generated significant controversy, since the ransom demand was only a fraction of this cost (the equivalent of $76,000 in Bitcoin).[23] A large percentage of the funds were originally earmarked for parks and recreation.[24] Similarly, Scripps Health reportedly spent at least $21.1 million on investigation and recovery following its 2021 attack.[25]

In 2021, the costs to remediate a ransomware attack more than doubled compared with the previous year, costing on average $1.85 million, according to Sophos.[26] The average cost of a ransomware attack when a data breach was also involved was $4.62 million, according to IBM's 2021 *Cost of a Breach* report.

1.3.2.3   Ransom Payments

Obviously, the cost of a ransom payment itself can dramatically impact a victim's finances. The average ransom payment has increased enormously in just a few short years. Many ransom payments are never disclosed, so it's impossible to know the full picture, but we can monitor trends based on information published by ransom negotiators, insurance companies, and cryptocurrency research firms.

The incident response firm Coveware reported an average ransom payment of $136,576 in the second quarter of 2021, based on an analysis of the cases in which it was involved in the payment process.[27] While this amount was down from the high reported by Coveware in 2020, it was a dramatic increase compared with the reported average ransom payment of $36,295 in the second quarter of 2019, and a mere $6,733 at the end of 2018.[28]

---

23. Ian Duncan, "Baltimore Estimates Cost of Ransomware Attack at $18.2 Million as Government Begins to Restore Email Accounts," *The Baltimore Sun*, May 29, 2019, www.baltimoresun.com/maryland/baltimore-city/bs-md-ci-ransomware-email-20190529-story.html.

24. Luke Broadwater, "Baltimore Transfers $6 Million to Pay for Ransomware Atttack; City Considers Insurance Against Hacks," *The Baltimore Sun*, August 28, 2019, www.baltimoresun.com/politics/bs-md-ci-ransomware-expenses-20190828-njgznd7dsfaxbbaglnvnbkgjhe-story.html.

25. King, "May Cyberattack Cost Scripps Nearly $113M."

26. Sophos, *The State of Ransomware 2021*, p. 12.

27. Coveware, "Q2 Ransom Payment Amounts Decline as Ransomware Becomes a National Security Priority," July 23, 2021, www.coveware.com/blog/2021/7/23/q2-ransom-payment-amounts-decline-as-ransomware-becomes-a-national-security-priority.

28. Coveware, "Ransomware Amounts Rise 3x in Q2 as Ryuk & Sodinokibi Spread," July 16, 2019, www.coveware.com/blog/2019/7/15/ransomware-amounts-rise-3x-in-q2-as-ryuk-amp-sodinokibi-spread.

Cyber insurance firm Coalition reported an average ransom demand of $1,193,159 in the first half of 2021—an increase of 170% compared with the first half of 2020. (Note that a ransom *demand* is different than a ransom *payment*; adversaries often negotiate and agree to discounts of 50% or more, particularly when higher dollar amounts are involved.) Coalition noted that "Our data only accounts for incidents where the organization filed a claim and the losses were above the organization's deductible," further skewing the average losses to the higher side.[29]

According to Chainalysis, a cryptocurrency research firm, the average ransom payment rose significantly—from $12,000 in the fourth quarter of 2019 to $54,000 in the first quarter of 2021.[30] Their data is based on payments to known ransomware-linked wallet addresses.

The authors of this book can corroborate the trend toward higher ransom demands payments. When we first began handling cyber extortion attacks in 2016, ransom demands were typically a few thousand dollars. As adversaries increased their capabilities and reach, ransom demands ballooned. As we wrote this book in 2022, we were regularly seeing ransom demands that ranged from $750,000 to $5 million. Clearly, the landscape has changed.

Heads Up! Skewed Statistics

Throughout this book, we'll share statistics related to cyber extortion. However, there are critical limitations to all existing studies on cyber extortion. In particular:

- **Underreporting:** There is no universal law requiring victims to report cyber extortion attacks (and even if there was, some would still choose to quietly attempt to sweep the incident under the rug). In some cases, the adversary deliberately publicizes a cyber extortion event. At other times, the impact is significant enough that the event becomes widely known (such as ransomware attacks on hospitals). However, many cyber extortion attacks are handled discreetly, without disclosure, and these cases may simply not be included in published statistics.

- **Statistical bias:** Many cyber extortion statistics are produced by security vendors, incident response firms, ransom negotiation specialists, and insurance companies. As a result, their sample set is limited to their own customers or customers of affiliates, and is not representative of a broad

---

29. Coalition, *H1 2021: Cyber Insurance Claims Report*, July 2021, pp. 11–13, https://info.coalitioninc.com/download-2021-h1-cyber-claims-report.html.

30. Since the Chainalysis data is based on payments to known ransomware-linked wallet addresses, early reports tended to underestimate the actual value of ransomware payments. As more addresses are linked to known criminals over time, the value of known payments tends to rise. This analysis is also limited in that only certain types of cryptocurrency are traceable (the Chainalysis research includes Bitcoin, Bitcoin Cash, Ethereum, and Tether). More and more criminals are shifting to payments in Monero, because it is much more difficult to track.

spectrum of cyber extortion victims. Trends reported may be a result of changes to the author's business, and not a result of actual changes in the cyber extortion landscape. Confusingly, vendors often try to represent their reports as using a statistically valid sampling technique, and journalists will report their data as such.

As a result, cyber extortion statistics vary wildly and their accuracy is questionable. Savvy readers should take all reports and studies on cyber extortion with a grain (or perhaps a pile) of salt.

In this book, we will share statistics from the more reputable sources, and also endeavor to point out any obvious bias or limitations in these studies. We encourage readers to carefully consider the source of any cyber extortion statistics. There may be value in the information provided, but no report can fully capture the state of cyber extortion today.

Happily, there are indications that information quality and availability may improve in the future. Recently, lawmakers and regulators have enacted stronger and more standardized reporting for cyber extortion incidents, and for cybersecurity incidents more broadly. For example, the United States' Cyber Incident Reporting for Critical Infrastructure Act of 2022 (CIRCIA) established broad reporting requirements for "covered cybersecurity incidents" that occur within "critical infrastructure." The U.S. government intends to analyze the data and publish reports and statistics regularly.[31,32]

1.3.3   Reputational Damage

Victims of cyber extortion face a loss of trust, public image, and overall reputation that may lead to increased financial loss and decreased business. According to Cybereason, 53% of victims surveyed suffered brand damage as a result of a ransomware attack.[33] This outcome is especially likely to happen when the cyber extortion incident involves theft of sensitive data, which can result in permanent loss of privacy for the data subjects, who may be employees, customers, or patients.

Criminals capitalize on the fear of reputational damage. For example, in a 2020 cyber extortion case handled by the authors, the Maze cartel emailed the victim's leadership. Here is their threatening message:

---

31. Davis Wright Tremaine LLP, "The Cyber Incident Reporting for Critical Infrastructure Act of 2022: An Overview," May 20, 2022, www.jdsupra.com/legalnews/the-cyber-incident-reporting-for-6977192.

32. Amendment to H.R. 2471, "An Act to Measure the Progress of Post-Disaster Recovery and Efforts to Address Corruption, Governance, Rule of Law, and Media Freedoms in Haiti," March 9, 2020, pp. 2464–2519, www.congress.gov/117/bills/hr2471/BILLS-117hr2471eah.pdf.

33. *Ransomware: The True Cost to Business*, p. 9.

> First of all, we will sell the personal data of your employees and customers on the market, which will already bring us a profit. Then we will inform all your clients that their private information has been compromised. … But the biggest losses for you will be from the publication of data that has been downloaded from your servers. You will be sued by both your employees and your clients. After publishing on our news site, you will incur colossal reputational losses for your business. I think that many existing clients will refuse your services. In the future, finding new customers will be problematic, since it is unlikely that someone wants to provide their personal data to a company that cannot save them.[34]

Ransomware attacks often don't make the news, particularly in industries where the public isn't directly impacted. However, today's adversaries frequently take matters into their own hands, threatening to notify data subjects even if the victim organization does not, in an effort to leverage the power of shame and embarrassment.

Modern cyber extortionists routinely launch data leak portals on the dark web, which they use to publish stolen data. More and more, cyber extortion events are widely covered by media outlets, in part due to increasingly sophisticated public relations efforts launched by adversaries. The result is greater potential damage to the victims' reputations, which empowers the adversaries.

1.3.4 Lawsuits

Lawsuits have become a routine occurrence following a cyber extortion attack. This is driven by several factors:

- *The dramatic increase in data exposure* as part of cyber extortion cases. This increases publicity surrounding the crisis and can also trigger data breach notification laws, in addition to proactive cybersecurity regulations.

- *Increasing numbers of experienced cyber attorneys and regulators* who understand relevant laws/regulations and have experience responding to data breaches, business interruption, and related "cyber" topics.

- *A proliferation of laws and regulations that specifically address data breaches, cyber extortion, and cybersecurity.* Examples include Europe's General Data Protection Regulation (GDPR), state-level breach notification laws in all 50 U.S. states, and industry-specific regulations such as the Health Insurance Portability and Accountability Act (HIPAA) and the Health Information Technology for Economic and Clinical Health (HITECH) Act. Further adding to the risk are stipulations such as ransomware guidance released by the U.S. Department of Health and Human Services, which states that victims need to "presume" that a breach has occurred "[u]nless the covered entity or business associate can demonstrate that there is a '… low probability that the PHI [personal health information] has been compromised.'"[35]

---

34. Email written by the Maze ransomware gang, August 2020.

35. "Fact Sheet: Ransomware and HIPAA," U.S. Department of Health and Human Services, Office for Civil Rights, July 11, 2016, www.hhs.gov/sites/default/files/RansomwareFactSheet.pdf.

Lawsuits may be filed by customers, patients, employees, vendors, shareholders, or any other party potentially harmed by the cyber extortion event. For example, Scripps Health experienced major disruptions to its operations and notified more than 147,000 patients that their personal information might have been stolen in its 2021 ransomware attack.[36] In the aftermath, patients filed multiple class-action lawsuits alleging that the health system was negligent and failed to appropriately manage risk.

In a growing trend, plaintiffs are citing harm beyond the potential for identity theft and breach of privacy. After Universal Health Service (UHS) was hit with a ransomware attack in September 2021, patient Stephen Motkowicz filed a lawsuit because "the data theft delayed his surgery, which caused his employer-provided insurance to lapse and required him to purchase alternative insurance at a higher premium."[37]

Litigation, of course, can be expensive, time-consuming, and trigger negative media attention for years after a cyber extortion event.

Case Study: Ripple Effects

The impacts of (and potential damage from) a cyber extortion event can be far-reaching. As an example, in May 2021, Colonial Pipeline suffered a complete service outage across its entire infrastructure that was triggered by a ransomware attack by the DarkSide ransomware group.[38] The pipeline transported 100 million gallons of fuel throughout the east coast of the United States every day, so an operational outage of any kind meant serious issues for millions of consumers and businesses.

Colonial had backups of its systems, but the restoration of services was a slow process. The organization paid 75 Bitcoin (roughly $4.5 million at the time) to obtain a decryptor, but the decryptor utility was so slow that it was essentially useless. Operations began to come back online five days after the attack started, but it was much longer before full recovery was reached.

In the meantime, gas stations that relied on Colonial Pipeline ran out of fuel and were forced to shut down. EZ Mart, a gas station in North Carolina, was one of them. According to EZ Mart's owner, Abeer Darwich, his gas station ran out of fuel

---

36. Heather Landi, "Before Attacking IT Systems, Hackers Stole Information from 147K Patients, Scripps Health Says," Fierce Healthcare, June 3, 2021, www.fiercehealthcare.com/tech/before-attacking-it-systems-hackers-stole-information-from-147-000-patients-scripps-health.

37. *Barry K. Graham, et al. v. Universal Health Service, Inc.*, Case 2:20-cv-05375-GAM, May 17, 2021, https://fingfx.thomsonreuters.com/gfx/legaldocs/bdwpkwqxqpm/HEALTH%20UHS%20DATA%20BREACH%20opinion.pdf.

38. Joe Panettieri, "Colonial Pipeline Cyberattack: Timeline and Ransomware Attack Recovery Details," MSSP Alert, May 9, 2022, www.msspalert.com/cybersecurity-breaches-and-attacks/ransomware/colonial-pipeline-investigation/.

on May 12. He called his distributor, Oliver's Oil, which told him that he could not get more fuel delivered until the pipeline was flowing again. The gas station was not fully operational for ten days, which resulted in lost revenue and potential loss of customers on a long-term basis.

After the attack, EZ Mart filed a lawsuit seeking compensation for disruption to its business, which relied on the key upstream provider. Notably, its case was strengthened because criminals did not directly shut down the Colonial Pipeline. Rather, according to court documents, the pipeline operators "elected to shut down the pipeline in whole or part not because the threat actor had reached the operational systems, but because Defendant was not sure it could continue to accurately bill for the product moving through its Pipeline."[39]

Often, impacted customers and third parties have no recourse or way to obtain compensation outside of litigation. In the case of Colonial Pipeline, the operator reportedly "acknowledged its duty to those affected by the failure, but to date has failed to offer them any compensation or remedy."[40] Affected businesses like EZ Mart, which do not have a direct contractual relationship with Colonial Pipeline, may have little recourse outside a court of law.

1.4 Victim Selection

Cyber extortion attacks may be opportunistic, targeted, or hybrid, as described in this section. Understanding the attack type can help you gauge the likelihood of advanced evasion tactics, evaluate the risk of further compromise, and predict the adversary's response to specific negotiation strategies.

1.4.1 Opportunistic Attacks

In an opportunistic extortion attack, the adversary's strategy is not crafted with a specific victim in mind. Rather, the adversary maximizes their return on investment by casting a wide net and compromising victims that individually require a relatively low investment of resources. Typically, adversaries leverage automated tools such as phishing toolkits that can distribute malicious emails en masse, credential stuffing tools, vulnerability scanning

---

39. *EZ Mart 1, LLC, on Behalf of Itself and All Others Similarly Situated, v. Colonial Pipeline Company*, Case 1:21-cv-02522-MHC, June 21, 2021, p. 7, https://dd80b675424c132b90b3-e48385e382d2e5d17821a5e1d8e4c86b.ssl.cf1.rackcdn.com/external/coloniallawsuit.pdf.

40. *EZ Mart 1, LLC, v. Colonial Pipeline Company*, p. 7.

software or services, and more. (We will discuss these entry methods in greater detail in Section 3.2.)

Victims may be any organization unlucky enough to have a vulnerability in a perimeter device, or an employee who accidentally clicks on a link in a phishing email. Organizations with slim budgets for cybersecurity are at higher risk, since they may not have the resources to patch vulnerabilities as quickly, roll out multifactor authentication, or implement comprehensive prevention measures like those described in detail in Chapter 10.

In the following case study, a veterinary clinic was completely shut down because of an opportunistic ransomware attack—without any manual interaction from the adversary.

Case Study: Veterinary Clinic

At a small veterinary clinic in Colorado, a receptionist received a DHL shipment notification and clicked on the attachment. Little did she know that it was a phishing email. When she opened the attachment, a macro executed that downloaded the GandCrab ransomware loader.

The ransomware automatically spread throughout the network. It scraped passwords from the receptionist's computer (including the Local Administrator password) and moved laterally to other systems. The ransomware software also took advantage of the Eternal Blue vulnerability, exploiting a weakness in SMB to gain access to the clinic's main file server. It locked up all computers on the network, including servers and workstations. The clinic had no backups, but if they had, the ransomware would have automatically encrypted them, too.

At the time, GandCrab was one of the top ransomware strains globally, and owed its success in part due to its "ransomware as a service" syndication model. The cybercriminals behind it essentially rented out their software, enabling would-be extortionists around the world to access their sophisticated tools for a fee.

For each computer that was encrypted, the GandCrab software automatically created a web portal on the dark web. Victims could access the portal using a Tor browser to visit the link that was listed in the ransom note. Each computer had its own ransom note. Using the portal, victims could view the ransom amount, automatically upload a (small) sample file for test decryption, access a chat feature, and more.

The ransom demand at the veterinary clinic was set at $5,000 per computer. There were 14 computers, so the cost to recover everything was $70,000. The clinic opted to purchase the key for three computers—two servers and one workstation. Happily, they didn't need to pay. Within days of the attack, the GandCrab group announced that they were "leaving for a well-deserved retirement," and shortly thereafter, a security research firm released an effective decryption tool.

The veterinary clinic was clearly hit with an opportunistic attack. The authors of this book, who were engaged as the response team, preserved the DHL shipping phishing email that had acted as the initial malware delivery vector. It turned out there were thousands of reports of this phishing email in VirusTotal, a popular malware analysis and reporting website. This was clearly a large-scale campaign that had been indiscriminately blasted out to a very large number of email addresses.

In all likelihood, the receptionist received that phishing email because her address was already on a mass spam distribution list that was bought and sold on the dark web, or she may have been included in the "Contacts" list of another organization that had been recently hacked. The adversary that attacked the veterinary clinic may have also successfully extorted dozens, hundreds, or even thousands of other organizations.

1.4.2 Targeted Attacks

In a targeted attack, the adversary focuses on compromising a specific entity. Targeted cyber extortion can take on many forms, and typically involves significant investment by the adversary, such as extensive reconnaissance, resource gathering, malware customization, and other specialized activities.

Typically, adversaries target organizations that they perceive have enough revenue to pay their desired ransom demand. In addition, adversaries often target organizations that may be critically impacted by technology outages (such as hospitals, technology providers, or manufacturing companies) or hold highly confidential and/or regulated information (such as public-sector organizations, law firms, and professional services). This gives the adversary strong leverage to use during the extortion phase.

For example, Tesla was targeted[41] in 2020 by a Russian cybercriminal gang that attempted to pay a Tesla employee to install malware for purposes of extortion. The criminals' goal was to exfiltrate Tesla's sensitive information and then extort the company for millions of dollars. In preparation, Russian agent Egor Igorevich Kriuschkov fostered a relationship with a Tesla employee using WhatsApp, and then flew to the United States to wine and dine him before making his pitch: install malware in Tesla's environment in exchange for a large payment. According to Kriuschkov's later indictment,[42] the adversaries "had to pay US $250,000 for the malware, which would be written specifically for targeting [Tesla's] computer network." In addition, the adversaries planned to pay Kriuschkov $250,000 and the employee $1 million for their assistance.

Although some adversaries deliberately target "big game," this strategy has also led to high-profile news articles and law enforcement attention, which criminals perceive as a threat. After the swift U.S. response to the Colonial Pipeline oil supply attacks, a REvil

41. Andy Greenberg, "A Tesla Employee Thwarted an Alleged Ransomware Plot," *Wired*, August 27, 2020, www.wired.com/story/tesla-ransomware-insider-hack-attempt/.

42. *United States of America v. Egor Igorevich Kriuchkov*, Case 3:20-cr-00045, September 3, 2020, www.justice.gov/opa/press-release/file/1313656/download.

affiliate cautioned, "You can hit the jackpot once, but provoke such a geopolitical conflict that you will be quickly found. It is better to quietly receive stable small sums from mid-sized companies."[43]

1.4.3 Hybrid Attacks

Many cyber extortion attacks are a hybrid of opportunistic and targeted attacks. For example, an adversary might send out thousands of phishing emails using an exploit kit and wait for victims to click on attachments. As the list of victims grows, the adversary can choose to actively engage with those who have high revenues or in specific industries such as healthcare (which has strong privacy regulations and stringent uptime requirements).

> ### A Word About "Initial Access Brokers"
>
> The adversary who encrypts a network or exfiltrates data is not always the adversary who originally compromises the victim. "Initial access brokers" operate as a partner to cyber extortion groups and exist for the sole purpose of selling access to already compromised environments. Brokers may operate as intermediaries between the adversary responsible for compromise and the cyber extortionist. Alternatively, as in cases like the infamous Emotet[44] group, they may operate as a separate cybercriminal organization.

1.5 Scaling Up

Over time, adversaries became increasingly aware that victim environments were interconnected through the technology supply chain and recognized it as a way to impact more victims with less effort. Cyber extortionists began to leverage weaknesses in the global technology supply chain to extort victims en masse, which caused widespread damage. This included leveraging managed service providers, technology manufacturers, software vulnerabilities, and cloud providers.

---

43. "Russian Hacker Q&A: An Interview with REvil-Affiliated Ransomware Contractor," *Flashpoint Intel* (blog), September 29, 2021, www.flashpoint-intel.com/blog/interview-with-revil-affiliated-ransomware-contractor.

44. "FBI, Partners Disarm Emotet Malware: Global Law Enforcement and Private Sector Take Down a Major Cyber Crime Tool," Federal Bureau of Investigation, February 1, 2021, www.fbi.gov/news/stories/emotet-malware-disrupted-020121.

1.5.1   Managed Service Providers

Managed service providers (MSPs) provide technical services, support, and products for their customers. An MSP can be a perfect conduit for cybercriminals, since by design it has access to a multitude of organizations, and frequently uses standardized remote management software to connect to and manage all of its clients' systems. An adversary with access to the MSP network could potentially use these same tools to connect to all of the targets simultaneously, steal files, or spread ransomware.

For example, on August 19, 2019, 22 Texas towns[45] were hit simultaneously with ransomware, one of the first large-scale attacks of its kind. The adversaries, who were said to be affiliated with the REvil ransomware syndicate,[46] carried out their attack by first compromising a Texas technology services firm that provided services to all 22 towns. The ransomware disrupted the cities' abilities to provide building, driver, and contractor licenses; issue birth and death certificates; accept utility payments; and more.

The adversary demanded a "collective ransom" of \$2.5 million in exchange for the decryptor.[47] Despite the massive impact on their operations, the victims reportedly did not pay the ransom, and instead recovered most of their data from backups. By September 7, 2019, about half of the towns were back to normal operations, while the rest struggled to complete their recoveries.

This type of entry vector was not new. As early as 2016, the Dark Overlord cyber extortion group conducted an attack on multiple healthcare clinics, which was later traced back to an "inadequately secured" file in the cloud that contained passwords for all of the vendor's customer networks.[48]

Over time, cyber extortionists discovered that many MSPs used identical passwords to manage all of their customer systems, and eschewed multifactor authentication, since it would have added complexity to their support processes. The criminals then ramped up their crime spree: At the end of August 2019,[49] REvil repeated its attack and compromised an MSP, encrypting the files of approximately 400 dental clinics. In November 2019,[50] the group encrypted files at 100 dental offices, by again compromising their MSP.

---

45. Bobby Allyn, "22 Texas Towns Hit with Ransomware Attack in "New Front" of Cyberassault," NPR, August 20, 2019, www.npr.org/2019/08/20/752695554/23-texas-towns-hit-with-ransomware-attack-in-new-front-of-cyberassault.

46. Jake Bleiberg and Eric Tucker, "Texas Ransomware Attack Shows What Can Happen When Whole Towns Are Targeted," *USA Today*, July 26, 2021, www.usatoday.com/story/tech/news/2021/07/26/texas-ransomware-attack-impact-cyberattack-cybersecurity-small-town-america/8090316002/.

47. Ionut Ilascu, "Hackers Want \$2.5 Million Ransom for Texas Ransomware Attacks," *Bleeping Computer*, August 21, 2019, www.bleepingcomputer.com/news/security/hackers-want-25-million-ransom-for-texas-ransomware-attacks/.

48. "Quest Records LLC Breach Linked to TheDarkOverlord Hacks; More Entities Investigate If They've Been Hacked," DataBreaches.net, August 15, 2016, www.databreaches.net/quest-records-llc-breach-linked-to-thedarkoverlord-hacks-more-entities-investigate-if-theyve-been-hacked/.

49. Brian Krebs, "Ransomware Bites Dental Data Backup Firm," Krebs on Security, August 29, 2019, https://krebsonsecurity.com/2019/08/ransomware-bites-dental-data-backup-firm/.

50. Brian Krebs, "Ransomware at Colorado IT Provider Affects 100+ Dental Offices," Krebs on Security, December 7, 2019, https://krebsonsecurity.com/2019/12/ransomware-at-colorado-it-provider-affects-100-dental-offices/.

Reputable MSPs quickly adapted, adopting multifactor authentication (if they hadn't already) and more secure password generation and storage practices. Still, they remained a target, by virtue of their key role in the technology supply chain.

1.5.2   Technology Manufacturers

Cybercriminals have long known that by gaining access to technology manufacturers, they can distribute malware far and wide. This type of attack was famously used to deploy the destructive NotPetya faux ransomware, dubbed "the most devastating cyber-attack in history" by *Wired* magazine, with estimated global damages of more than $10 billion.[51]

The NotPetya compromise began when cybercriminals gained access to an update server at a tax preparation software company, M.E.Doc, which was used by an estimated 80% of companies in Ukraine at the time.[52] In April 2017, they installed a backdoor in the company's tax preparation software, which was released to customers. Two more back-doored releases were deployed to customers in May and June. Finally, on June 27, the adversary modified the update server's configuration and redirected customer traffic to an outside server, which was used to deploy NotPetya.

As the malware detonated on victim machines, it spread rapidly to connected systems by leveraging the EternalBlue vulnerability and other methods. "To date, it was simply the fastest-propagating piece of malware we've ever seen," stated Craig William, a spokesperson at Cisco Talos, which handled the investigation. "By the second you saw it, your data center was already gone."[53]

Fast-forward to December 2020, when a customer of SolarWinds, a popular remote IT monitoring and management software, discovered a backdoor in their network, which they traced back to SolarWinds' Orion software.[54]

An investigation determined that the attackers inserted malicious code into a routine software update that SolarWinds pushed to its customers.[55] The malware had been distributed in the SolarWinds product between March and June of 2020—meaning the adversaries had the opportunity to access customer systems for at least six months before they were detected. In all 18,000 SolarWinds customers (including Microsoft, Visa, Mastercard,

---

51. Andy Greenberg, "The Untold Story of NotPetya, the Most Devastating Cyberattack in History," *Wired*, August 22, 2018, www.wired.com/story/notpetya-cyberattack-ukraine-russia-code-crashed-the-world/.

52. "Ukraine Cyber-attack: Software Firm MeDoc's Servers Seized," BBC News, July 4, 2017, www.bbc.com/news/technology-40497026.

53. Greenberg, "The Untold Story of NotPetya."

54. William Turton and Kartikay Mehrotra, "FireEye Discovered SolarWinds Breach While Probing Own Hack," *Bloomberg*, December 14, 2020, www.bloomberg.com/news/articles/2020-12-15/fireeye-stumbled-across-solarwinds-breach-while-probing-own-hack.

55. Dina Temple-Raston, "A 'Worst Nightmare' Cyberattack: The Untold Story of the SolarWinds Hack," NPR, April 16, 2021, www.npr.org/2021/04/16/985439655/a-worst-nightmare-cyberattack-the-untold-story-of-the-solarwinds-hack.

Ford, Cisco, U.S. Secret Service, U.S. Department of Defense, and Office of the President of the United States, among many others[56]) had installed the infected update.

Fortunately, SolarWinds was not publicly linked to a wave of ransomware attacks. Nevertheless, it illustrated how even today, adversaries can use technology vendors to gain a persistent foothold within their customers' environments, enabling widespread data theft and arbitrary deployment of malicious software—both common precursors of a cyber extortion attack. This tactic has the potential to facilitate cyber extortion on a mass scale in the future.

1.5.3 Software Vulnerabilities

Cyber extortionists have targeted software, using vulnerabilities in these products or the products themselves as a mass distribution vector. For example, on July 3, 2021—the day before a major national holiday in the United States—the REvil cartel executed what was, at the time, the largest single ransomware deployment in cybersecurity history.[57] The adversary exploited multiple zero-day vulnerabilities in the Kaseya VSA on-premises remote monitoring and management system, used by MSPs around the world to remotely manage customer networks.

By leveraging access to this software product, REvil was able to detonate its malicious software on more than 1,500 victim networks around the world (a total of more than 1 million individual devices, the group claimed). This included grocery stores, healthcare clinics, municipalities, and more. The criminals demanded $70 million to provide a decryptor for all of the victims. Eventually, the keys were released, reportedly due to an international law enforcement operation.[58]

Similarly, the Microsoft zero-day Exchange vulnerabilities of 2021 led to a wave of ransomware attacks—and fast. A patch released on March 2, 2021, addressed four vulnerabilities discovered in on-premises instances of Exchange. Almost immediately, cybercriminals began leveraging these vulnerabilities to install ransomware.[59] Similarly, in the aftermath of the Log4j widespread vulnerability announcement, extortionists such as Conti began exploiting vulnerable VMWare servers as an initial entry point.[60]

---

56. Mia Jankowicz and Charles R. Davis, "These Big Firms and US Agencies All Use Software from the Company Breached in a Massive Hack Being Blamed on Russia," *Business Insider*, December 15, 2020, www.businessinsider.com/list-of-companies-agencies-at-risk-after-solarwinds-hack-2020-12.

57. Associated Press, "Scale, Details of Massive Kaseya Ransomware Attack Emerge," NPR, July 5, 2021, www.npr.org/2021/07/05/1013117515/scale-details-of-massive-kaseya-ransomware-attack-emerge.

58. Dan Goodin, "Up to 1,500 Businesses Infected in One of the Worst Ransomware Attacks Ever," ARS Technica, July 6, 2021, https://arstechnica.com/gadgets/2021/07/up-to-1500-businesses-infected-in-one-of-the-worst-ransomware-attacks-ever/.

59. "Ransomware Is Targeting Vulnerable Microsoft Exchange Servers," Malwarebytes Labs (blog), March 12, 2021, https://blog.malwarebytes.com/ransomware/2021/03/ransomware-is-targeting-vulnerable-microsoft-exchange-servers/.

60. Vitali Kremez and Yelisey Boguslavskiy, "Ransomware Advisory: Log4Shell Exploitation for Initial Access & Lateral Movement," AdvIntel, December 17, 2021, www.advintel.io/post/ransomware-advisory-log4shell-exploitation-for-initial-access-lateral-movement.

In late 2021 and 2022, ransomware gangs such as Conti, BlackByte, and others began routinely exploiting Microsoft Exchange servers using the ProxyShell vulnerabilities.[61,62,63] Although Microsoft had previously released a series of patches, many victims had not successfully installed them, leaving organizations around the world vulnerable to attack.

1.5.4   Cloud Providers

As organizations around the world shifted their technology infrastructure to the cloud, many had the unspoken expectation that cloud providers would be immune to compromise—a sentiment that cloud providers themselves encouraged.

Cyber attackers have since proved them wrong. Cloud providers, as a rule, invest heavily in securing their infrastructures, but adversaries (including cyber extortionists) have repeatedly found ways to sneak through the cracks. What's more, due to cloud providers' extreme uptime requirements and potential for storing large volumes of sensitive data, they are high-value targets.

For example, Blackbaud,[64] a cloud provider whose software is used by nonprofit organizations, charitable foundations, universities, and other organizations, was hit with a ransomware attack in May 2020. The company had approximately 35,000 customers in more than 60 countries, and boasted millions of users.[65] Blackbaud's products included support for fundraising, marketing, analytics, and more—which meant their cloud platform was designed to store a vast range of sensitive information, including personal details, sensitive financial records, payment card numbers, and more.

The criminals gained access to Blackbaud's environment in February 2020, but did not detonate ransomware until May 2020. Blackbaud, in turn, did not notify customers until July—two months after the company detected the attack—when it released a statement notifying customers of a "security incident that recently occurred." The cloud provider told customers that the company's cybersecurity team had stopped a ransomware attack in progress, and stated that "the cybercriminal removed a copy of a subset of data from

61. Lawrence Abrams, "Conti Ransomware Now Hacking Exchange Servers with ProxyShell Exploits," *Bleeping Computer*, September 3, 2021, www.bleepingcomputer.com/news/security/conti-ransomware-now-hacking-exchange-servers-with-proxyshell-exploits/.

62. Bill Toulas, "Microsoft Exchange Servers Hacked to Deploy BlackByte Ransomware," *Bleeping Computer*, December 1, 2021, www.bleepingcomputer.com/news/security/microsoft-exchange-servers-hacked-to-deploy-blackbyte-ransomware/.

63. Lindsey O'Donnell-Welch, "Vulnerable Microsoft Exchange Servers Hit with Babuk Ransomware," *Decipher*, November 4, 2021, https://duo.com/decipher/attackers-infect-vulnerable-microsoft-exchange-servers-with-babuk-ransomware.

64. Sergui Gatlan, "Blackbaud: Ransomware Gang Had Access to Banking Info and Passwords," *Bleeping Computer*, September 30, 2020, www.bleepingcomputer.com/news/security/blackbaud-ransomware-gang-had-access-to-banking-info-and-passwords/.

65. Nicole McGougan, "Blackbaud Makes Good on Modern Cloud Promise," *Blackbaud Newsroom*, April 26, 2016, https://web.archive.org/web/20210116124707/https://www.blackbaud.com/newsroom/article/2016/04/26/blackbaud-makes-good-on-modern-cloud-promise.

our self-hosted environment." However, it assured customers that the stolen data did not include "credit card information, bank account information, or social security numbers."[66]

Blackbaud went on to state that it had paid the ransom, with the assurance that any stolen data subset would be deleted. It also asserted that they had "no reason to believe that any data … was or will be misused; or will be disseminated or otherwise made available publicly."[67]

The subsequent ripple effects were enormous. Hundreds—if not thousands—of Blackbaud's customers launched investigations to assess the risk to their community's data. In many cases, they determined that they were legally obligated to do so. For example, many healthcare clinics are regulated by HIPAA/HITECH, which states that "[a]n impermissible use or disclosure of protected health information is presumed to be a breach unless the covered entity or business associate, as applicable, demonstrates that there is a low probability that the protected health information has been compromised based on a risk assessment."[68] Cyber insurers grappled with the surge of investigations and claims.

On September 29, 2020, Blackbaud submitted a filing with the U.S. Securities and Exchange Commission (SEC) and disclosed that "further forensic investigation found that for some of the notified customers, the cybercriminal may have accessed some unencrypted fields intended for bank account information, social security numbers, usernames and/or passwords."[69] This new revelation further fanned the flames.

In the months that followed, a wide range of organizations publicly announced that they were impacted—including the Boy Scouts, National Public Radio (NPR), the Bush Presidential Center, universities, nonprofit organizations, and more. Approximately 100 U.S. healthcare organizations publicly reported a data breach as a result of the Blackbaud attacks, affecting at least 12 million patients.[70,71]

More than two dozen lawsuits were filed against Blackbaud, and customers that were victims of the breach were also sued by their members and patients.[72] At the time of this writing, lawsuits are still ongoing.

---

66. "Security Incident," *Blackbaud Newsroom*, updated September 29, 2020, https://web.archive.org/web/20210429203816/https://www.blackbaud.com/securityincident.

67. "Security Incident," *Blackbaud Newsroom*.

68. "HITECH Breach Notification Interim Final Rule," www.hhs.gov/hipaa/for-professionals/breach-notification/laws-regulations/final-rule-update/hitech/index.html.

69. "Blackbaud, Inc.," Securities and Exchange Commission, September 29, 2020, www.sec.gov/Archives/edgar/data/1280058/000128005820000044/blkb-20200929.htm.

70. Paul Bischoff, "Ransomware Attacks on US Healthcare Organizations Cost $20.8bn in 2020," Comparitech (blog), March 10, 2021, www.comparitech.com/blog/information-security/ransomware-attacks-hospitals-data/#How_much_did_these_ransomware_attacks_cost_healthcare_organizations_in_2020.

71. This statistic may include duplicate entries, as it is a sum of reported data subjects submitted by each individual entity.

72. "Rady Children's Hospital Facing Class Action Lawsuit over Blackbaud Ransomware Attack," *HIPAA Journal*, January 6, 2021, www.hipaajournal.com/rady-childrens-hospital-facing-class-action-lawsuit-over-blackbaud-ransomware-attack/.

The Blackbaud attack is a landmark case that illustrates how a cyber extortion attack on a single cloud provider can impact thousands of organizations and millions of individuals. Over time, cyber extortionists will likely evolve new ways to leverage cloud providers' centralized platforms, and apply increasingly advanced extortion tactics that involve direct communication with customers.

Despite the flood of public notifications in the Blackbaud case, even more notable are the thousands of Blackbaud customers that did not report the breach to their own employees, clients, and customers, but were undoubtedly affected. While U.S.-based healthcare clinics may have been legally required to "presume" a breach had occurred, conduct a risk analysis, and report, organizations in other industries were not bound by such regulations. Many cash-strapped customers may have had insufficient resources to respond to Blackbaud's notification, and simply ignored the issue.

As the cybersecurity industry and legal frameworks around the world continue to mature, expect more cloud customers to investigate and notify the public in the wake of cloud cyber extortion attacks.

1.6   Conclusion

Cyber extortion is an epidemic. In this chapter, we defined cyber extortion and then described the four types of cyber extortion that organizations may currently face. We learned that a cyber extortion attack has very real, potentially far-reaching impacts on the operations, financial well-being, and reputation of the organization experiencing it. Finally, we showed how adversaries can leverage weaknesses in the technology supply chain to launch cyber extortion attacks on a massive scale.

In the next chapter, we will trace the evolution of cyber extortion attacks, including key technological advancements that have enabled modern cyber extortion.

1.7   Your Turn!

Every cyber extortion incident is unique. The response team's options and priorities will vary depending on the victim organization's industry, size, and location, as well as the details of the incident itself.

Based on what you learned in this chapter, let's think through the potential impact of a cyber extortion incident.

Step 1: Build Your Victim

Choose one characteristic from each of the three columns to describe your victim's organization:

Industry	Size	Location
Hospital	Large	Global
Financial institution	Midsized	United States
Manufacturer	Small	European Union
Law firm		Australia
University		India
Cloud service provider		Country/location of your choice
Organization of your choice		

Step 2: Choose Your Incident Scenario

Select from one of the following incident scenarios:

A	Ransomware strikes! All of the victim's files have been locked up, including central data repositories, servers, and workstations.
B	A well-known cyber extortion gang claims to have stolen all of the victim's most sensitive data and threatens to release it unless the victim pays a very large ransom demand. The gang posts the victim's name on their dark web leaks site, along with samples of supposedly stolen data.
C	Double extortion! Both A and B occur at the same time.
D	The victim is hit with a denial-of-service attack on its Internet-facing infrastructure that slows its access and services to a crawl. The adversary threatens to continue and even escalate the attack unless a ransom is paid.

Step 3: Discussion Time

Your victim is experiencing a cyber extortion incident. Given what you know about the victim and the scenario, answer the following questions:

1. Which objective(s) of the CIA Triad does the cyber extortion attack threaten?

2. Which type of cyber extortion is your victim organization experiencing?

3. Describe the likely impacts that the cyber extortion incident may have on your victim organization in the following areas:

   a. Operations

   b. Finances

   c. Reputation

   d. Legal risk

4. The victim organization has researched typical ransom demands for the type of cyber extortion event it is experiencing and has found a very wide range, from $1,000 to $2.5 million. What is a reasonable explanation for this broad range of reported ransom demands?

5. The victim organization hears that hundreds of other organizations are currently experiencing a very similar cyber extortion attack. What is one possible explanation?

Chapter 2

Evolution

The first rule of any technology used in a business is that automation applied to an efficient operation will magnify the efficiency.

—Bill Gates

Learning Objectives

- Describe early examples of cyber extortion and how they relate to modern-day attacks
- Understand how cyber extortion has evolved, including key technical developments that enable attackers
- Recognize how the development of specialized ransomware-as-a-service software and franchise models have spurred the growth of the cyber extortion industry
- Identify the tools and resources that criminal entities are using to scale up their attacks

---

Everything old is new again, and cyber extortion is no exception. Although the mass media often treat it as a new threat, cyber extortion has actually existed for decades (and plain old regular extortion has been around since ancient times).

In this chapter, we discuss the origins and growth of cyber extortion, as well as key technologies that enabled its spread. Finally, we discuss the "Industrial Revolution" that has occurred in recent years and enabled cyber extortion to grow into the booming criminal enterprise it is today.

2.1   Origin Story

The first known example of a cyber extortion attack[1,2] was perpetrated in 1989 by a Harvard-trained evolutionary biologist named Dr. Joseph Popp, who researched the AIDS virus and was involved with the World Health Organization (WHO).[3,4] In December 1989, Popp created a 5.25-inch floppy disk labeled "AIDS Information Diskette," which he mailed to thousands of researchers using the WHO's database of names and addresses.

Unbeknownst to the recipients, the disk installed malware on the victim's computer and modified the startup file to count system reboots. When the computer had been rebooted approximately 90 times, the malware hid all folders and files, so they were invisible to the users, and also encrypted all filenames.

Affected computers displayed a "license agreement" as a file or a popup, with the following message (there were other variants as well):[5]

> Dear Customer:
>
> It is time to pay for your software lease from the PC Cyborg Corporation. Complete the INVOICE and attach payment for the lease option of your choice. If you don't use the printed INVOICE, then be sure to refer to the important reference numbers below in all correspondence. In return you'll receive:
>
> - a renewal software package with easy-to-follow, complete instructions;
> - an automatic, self-installing diskette that anyone can apply in minutes.
>
> Important reference numbers: A5599796-2695577-
>
> The price of 365 user applications is US$189. The price of a lease for the lifetime of your hard disk is US$378. You must enclose a banker's draft, cashier's check, or international money order payable to the PC CYBORG CORPORATION for the full amount of $189 or $378 with your order. Include your name, company, address, city, state, country, zip or postal code. Mail your order to PC Cyborg Corporation, P.O. Box 87-17-44, Panama 7, Panama.

Victims' computers were effectively rendered useless. Although the files were technically recoverable, many affected users did not realize this, and accidentally deleted their own data while attempting to reinstall and recover the files.[6]

---

1. Alina Simone, "The Strange History of Ransomware," Medium, March 26, 2015, https://medium .com/@alinasimone/the-bizarre-pre-internet-history-of-ransomware-bb480a652b4b.

2. Kaveh Waddell, "The Computer Virus That Haunted Early AIDS Researchers," *The Atlantic*, May 10, 2016, www.theatlantic.com/technology/archive/2016/05/the-computer-virus-that-haunted-early-aids-researchers/481965/.

3. Edward Wilding, ed., *Virus Bulletin*, March 1990, www.virusbulletin.com/uploads/pdf/magazine/1990/199003.pdf.

4. Edward Wilding, ed., *Virus Bulletin*, January 1990, www.virusbulletin.com/uploads/pdf/magazine/1990/199001.pdf.

5. Joseph L. Popp, AIDS Information Trojan author, https://sophosnews.files.wordpress.com/2012/09/aids-info-demand-500.png?w=488&h=232; "File:AIDS DOS Trojan.png," Wikimedia Commons, https://commons.wikimedia.org/w/index.php?curid=45320703.

6. Simone, "The Strange History of Ransomware."

The AIDS Trojan was a far cry from modern ransomware, and researchers were quickly able to develop tools that reversed the effects. This was possible because of a few key design flaws:

- The ransomware used symmetric key encryption, meaning the same key was used to encrypt and decrypt the data. The key was also distributed with the malware, so once researchers uncovered it, they were able to write tools that decrypted the filenames.

- The same key was used for all victim computers, so once it was recovered for one computer, all other victims could decrypt their data, too.

- The ransomware simply hid files and did not actually encrypt the contents (just the filenames). A savvy user could find and reopen their files using a different operating system, although the filenames would be scrambled.

The malware was quickly traced back to Popp, who was living in the United Kingdom at the time. He was subsequently extradited to the United States, where he stood trial. Popp claimed that the ruse was an attempt to raise money for AIDS research and was ultimately declared mentally unfit to stand trial.

A researcher named Jim Bates published a detailed technical analysis of the malware in *Virus Bulletin* and distributed two free programs to clean the malware and restore victims' files: AIDSOUT and AIDSCLEAR. Despite the AIDS Trojan's inherent flaws, the idea of ransomware was born.

2.2 Cryptoviral Extortion

In 1996, Adam Young of Columbia University and Moti Yung, who at that time worked for the IBM T. J. Watson Research Center, unveiled the concept of "cryptovirology," which they defined as the "study of the applications of cryptography to computer viruses." In their paper, these researchers presented a description of what we now see as modern ransomware: "extortion-based attacks that cause loss of access to information, loss of confidentiality, and information leakage."[7]

At the time, malware was commonly deployed for information theft purposes (i.e., stealing payment card numbers), to gain persistent remote access, or simply as a nuisance. Cyber extortion attempts at the time were rare, and when they occurred, they were not very successful (as in the case of the AIDS Trojan). Young and Yung specifically pointed out that existing attempts by malware authors to engage in extortion were inherently flawed, because they leveraged either no encryption or symmetric key encryption. In the latter case, the keys could simply be extracted from the malware.

---

7. Adam Young and Moti Yung, "Cryptovirology: Extortion-Based Security Threats and Countermeasures," www.ieee-security.org/TC/SP2020/tot-papers/young-1996.pdf.

As an alternative, Young and Yung introduced the idea of using asymmetric key encryption for purposes of extortion. In so doing, they foresaw a critical advancement that would later pave the way for the global ransomware epidemic. "We believe that it is better to investigate this aspect rather than to wait for such attacks to occur," they wrote.[8]

The researchers described a proof-of-concept virus that was designed to accomplish two things:

- Infect a computer system with a Trojan that would be difficult to detect, and likely to survive on its infected host.

- Utilize public key encryption to lock files on the computer.

Using these parameters, Young and Yung demonstrated their attack on a Macintosh SE/30 computer, utilizing RSA and TEA encryption to render the victim's data unusable. The malware generated a unique symmetric key for each infected host, which was used to encrypt the victim's files. The symmetric key was then encrypted using the malware authors' public key, and deleted from memory.

In this manner, the researchers addressed the key weaknesses of the AIDS Trojan and similar early ransomware prototypes—namely, the victim could not recover the decryption key from the malware or local system, and a unique key was used for each infected computer. This proof-of-concept virus foreshadowed modern ransomware.

2.3 Early Extortion Malware

Apparently, criminals don't always read IEEE research papers, because it was a decade before adversaries actually implemented the powerful concepts introduced by Young and Yung. In the meantime, cyber extortion evolved in fits and starts.

"In December 2004 we received the first samples of a number of files which were encrypted by an unknown encryption program," wrote Alexander Gostev, Senior Virus Analyst at Kaspersky. "There was no hint that in six [months'] time, such files would become so common that we would be receiving several dozen a day."[9]

This was the earliest known example of Gpcode, a malware strain likely of Russian origin that was designed to encrypt the victim's files. At first, Gpcode used a weak encryption algorithm apparently designed by the malware's authors, which was easy for researchers to crack. However, the authors quickly improved their malware and released stronger variants. In 2006 (a decade after Young and Yung's paper), a new variant of Gpcode emerged that incorporated strong RSA asymmetric key encryption. The future was here.

---

8. Young and Yung, "Cryptovirology," p. 1.

9. Denis Nazarov and Olga Emelyanova, "Blackmailer: The Story of Gpcode," Secure List, June 26, 2006, https://securelist.com/blackmailer-the-story-of-gpcode/36089/.

Not all cyber extortion malware incorporated this novel technique, however. "Locker" malware, also known as *lockerware*, evolved and proliferated during the same time frame, peaking around 2011–2012.[10] Typically, lockerware denied victims access to system resources by locking the screen or disabling the mouse and keyboard. The victim was presented with a ransom note that demanded a payment to regain access to the system. The underlying files were not always encrypted, and victims were typically able to restore access to their system with help from an IT professional. Reveton, also known as the "Police Trojan," was one example of lockerware that spread throughout the world. Reveton disabled user access to system resources, and made it appear that law enforcement had locked up the victim's computer. Some variants of Reveton encrypted files as well, but many versions did not.[11]

Despite the flurry of extortion malware development, the process of communicating with victims and receiving payments remained clunky. Typically, criminals left notes with email addresses or phone numbers on their victim's systems. Since these could be traced, the adversaries changed their contact information frequently, effectively abandoning some victims and leaving money on the table.

Payment methods were also risky and slow. Typically, adversaries instructed their victims to pay using alternative payment systems such as Ukash or Paysafe, wire transfers, or payment voucher systems such as MoneyPak. The earliest Gpcode strains instructed victims to send money using Yandex (a Russian electronic payment service similar to PayPal). All of these payment systems were brokered by third parties, and could potentially be monitored by law enforcement, enabling them to intercept payments and bust crime rings. It wasn't until the emergence of key technological advancements in communication and payment systems that ransomware as we know it finally took off.

2.4 Key Technological Advancements

As technology evolved, so did cyber extortion attacks. Two advancements, in particular, contributed to the modernization of this criminal activity: cryptocurrency and onion routing. These technologies enabled adversaries to engage in fast, anonymous communications and payments, thereby reducing risk and increasing reward. Underlying both technologies is asymmetric key encryption, which we will discuss first.

---

10. Kevin Savage, Peter Coogan, and Hon Lau, *The Evolution of Ransomware* (Symantec, August 6, 2015), p. 10, https://docs.broadcom.com/doc/the-evolution-of-ransomware-15-en.

11. Mariese Lessing, "Case Study: Reveton Ransomware," SDX Central, June 17, 2020, www.sdxcentral.com/security/definitions/case-study-reveton-ransomware/.

2.4.1   Asymmetric Cryptography

Asymmetric cryptography, also known as *public key cryptography*, is perhaps the most crucial technology underlying the epidemic of modern cyber extortion attacks. It is a critical component of the following:

- Modern file-encrypting ransomware
- Cryptocurrency
- Onion routing, which supports anonymous criminal communications channels, dark e-commerce sites, and data leak portals

While a full treatment of asymmetric cryptography is beyond the scope of this book, we will provide a general overview here to help you understand how ransomware evolved into such a destructive force. The same technologies have facilitated the expansion of all other forms of cyber extortion as well.

Definition: Cryptography Terms

- **Cryptography:** The process of transforming information based on an algorithm so that it is only meaningful for authorized parties.

- **Algorithm:** A series of steps used to accomplish a task.

- **Encryption:** The process of scrambling information so it cannot be accessed by anyone except authorized parties. This is accomplished using an algorithm and a key that is held by one or more parties.

- **Key:** A long sequence of numbers used as input to the algorithm. Keys are frequently stored in files on a computer or external hard drive.

- **Private key:** A key that is kept secret, and is held only by the owner.

- **Public key:** A key that can be distributed to the world.

- **Digital signature:** A block of data used to identify and authenticate the sender of a message, verify its integrity, and facilitate nonrepudiation.

- **One-way hash function (message digest algorithm):** A mathematical procedure used to transform any arbitrary message into a short, fixed-length sequence of numbers. Ideally, the resulting "hash" is unique for each message.

Given modern encryption algorithms and key lengths, attempts to guess a key today can mathematically take millions upon millions of years to achieve, even using the most powerful computers that have ever been created. This problem, referred to as "computational intractability," generally means that once a ransomware strain encrypts files, the only realistic way to recover the data is to obtain a decryption key—either by paying the adversary or through another means.

2.4.1.1 Ransomware and Symmetric Encryption

We previously discussed how early ransomware strains used *symmetric encryption* to deny victims access to their data. Symmetric cryptography relies on a single key to perform and reverse a function. For example, when encrypting data, the same key is used to encrypt as well as decrypt. This is very convenient for hard drive encryption, as a master key can be built into a hardware chip on a computer (such as on the Trusted Platform Module, or TPM chip). Symmetric key encryption can also be used to lock up files before they are stored in a data repository, such as a backup tape or cloud file share.

The benefit of symmetric key cryptography is that it is very fast. However, the reliance on a single key introduces a major drawback—namely, that all parties need to be in possession of the key to use it.

In early ransomware strains that relied on symmetric keys, the secret key was distributed with the ransomware itself. The ransomware used it to encrypt all the files on the victim's system. This created an obvious weakness: Because the symmetric key was present in the malware, and on the victim's system, it was often possible for defenders to recover the key and decrypt the victim's files without paying the adversary.

2.4.1.2 Ransomware and Asymmetric Encryption

Enter *asymmetric ("public key") cryptography*, which relies on a pair of keys. These keys are generated at the same time and perform complementary functions. For example, what one key encrypts, the other can decrypt.

The concept of asymmetric encryption is deceptively simple—and powerful. No longer did adversaries have to worry about victims unlocking their own files using a key that was distributed in the malware. In the simplest model, adversaries generated a pair of keys:

- The *public key* was distributed with the ransomware and used to encrypt the victim's data.

- The *private key* was held by the adversary, and only released to the victim after payment was received.

The downside of asymmetric encryption is that it is not as fast as symmetric key encryption. Speed was very important for cyber extortionists, who needed to encrypt large data sets as quickly as possible, before they were discovered.

2.4.1.3 A Hybrid Model Emerges

Today's ransomware strains leverage the best of both worlds, by combining both symmetric and asymmetric key encryption. Here is a typical model:

- Ransomware is distributed with the adversary's public key (or even multiple public keys, in the case of modern affiliate models; see Section 2.9.4.1).

- When a victim's computer is infected, the ransomware automatically generates a unique symmetric key, which is used to encrypt data quickly. Some ransomware strains generate a unique key for each computer, or for individual file shares, or based on any segmenting model of the adversary's choice.

- The symmetric key is then encrypted using the adversary's public key (or keys) and stored locally in a file known as a "keybag."

- After payment is made, the criminal releases a decryption utility (known as a "decryptor") that contains the appropriate private key. The decryptor is designed to use the private key to unlock the keybag and decrypt the victim's files.

In this manner, today's adversaries leverage the speed of symmetric encryption, along with the security of asymmetric encryption. There are many variations on this model, but the general concept of a hybrid encryption model for file-encrypting ransomware has become widespread.

2.4.1.4 Digital Signing and Verification

Encryption alone couldn't enable adversaries to launch extortion attacks on the massive, global scale that we see today. Fast and anonymous payment methods and communications systems were also critically important. It turned out that both of these could be achieved using asymmetric cryptography, too.

Recall that asymmetric cryptography relies on a pair of keys that perform complementary functions. For example, what one key *signs*, the other key can *verify*. How does this work?[12]

- The sender uses a *hash function* to convert a message to a short, fixed-length chunk of data ("hash").

- The sender uses their private key to encrypt the hash, using a digital signing algorithm.

- The encrypted hash is appended to the message (which is now "digitally signed") and the whole package is sent to the recipient.

---

12. "Security Tip (ST04-018): Understanding Digital Signatures," Cybersecurity & Infrastructure Security Agency, revised August 24, 2020, https://us-cert.cisa.gov/ncas/tips/ST04-018.

- To verify the digital signature, the recipient (or anyone with access to the message) uses the sender's public key, along with the *digital verification algorithm*, to decrypt the encrypted hash.

- The recipient also generates their own hash of the message and compares it to the decrypted hash. If the values match, then it confirms that the public key is correct and the message has not been modified since it was signed.

This process is fundamental to cryptocurrency and the dark web, as we will see in the following sections.

2.4.2 Cryptocurrency

Cryptocurrency is deeply intertwined with the rise of cyber extortion. In real-life kidnapping cases, criminals want payment in cash—not check or credit card—because cash payments are:

- Instantaneous
- Difficult to trace
- Nonreversible

The same is true when it comes to cyber extortion. In the early days, would-be cyber extortionists were hampered by slow and risky payment methods. Wire transfers, electronic payment systems, voucher methods, and other creative solutions could all be tracked by law enforcement and intercepted. More advanced criminals employed sophisticated money laundering schemes in order to hide their identities and remain safe—but that introduced delays and expenses.

2.4.2.1 The Birth of Bitcoin

Cryptocurrency changed all that. On October 31, 2008, a cryptographer who went by the pseudonym "Satoshi Nakamoto" posted a groundbreaking new paper to a popular cryptography mailing list. "I've been working on a new electronic cash system that's fully peer-to-peer, with no trusted third party," they wrote. With that, Bitcoin—the world's first cryptocurrency—was born.[13]

A Bitcoin is not a coin at all; it is a chain of digital signatures. Each person holds one or more public/private key pairs, which can be used to spend and receive Bitcoin. Transactions are tracked in a *blockchain*, a distributed ledger that anyone can download.

To send money, the current owner creates a new message indicating an amount of cryptocurrency and the new owner's public key, and then signs this message using their private key. This message is broadcast to the Bitcoin network and attached to the blockchain.

---

13. Satoshi Nakamoto, email to cryptography@metzdown.com, October 31, 2008, retrieved from the inbox of Sherri Davidoff on October 11, 2021.

To create new Bitcoin, *miners* (specialized software programs) work to solve a difficult mathematical puzzle. When a miner finds the correct answer, it submits it to the Bitcoin network for validation. If the answer is correct and has not previously been validated, the Bitcoin network creates a new *block* (a data entry on the blockchain) and the miner is rewarded with ownership of the newly minted Bitcoin, along with any transaction fees. Miners can also make money by validating transactions submitted by others, in which case they gain associated transaction fees.

2.4.2.2 Usage in Cyber Extortion

Once Bitcoin emerged, adversaries suddenly had the ability to receive fast, anonymous, nonreversible payments from victims. While there are many legitimate reasons to use cryptocurrency (privacy protections, political donations, etc.), it was undoubtedly the case that criminals were more willing than mainstream vendors to take risks on a new payment model.

Bitcoin is not backed by a commodity like gold or silver, but rather is a digital currency that is recognized as legal tender. No central authority manages digital currency; instead, the value is set by the market. As a result, the value of Bitcoin and other cryptocurrencies can swing wildly, which can create unexpected challenges for both victims and extortionists during the negotiation phase (see Section 8.5.3 for details).

Although Bitcoin has remained consistently popular among cyber extortionists, many adversaries accept and even prefer other cryptocurrencies. In particular, Monero has gained traction because it more difficult for law enforcement to trace, reducing risk for cybercriminals. See Section 8.2 for more details.

Definition: Cryptocurrency Terms

- **Blockchain:** A distributed digital transaction ledger that stores a record of all transactions.

- **Cryptocurrency:** A digital asset in which cryptography is used to regulate creation of new units and transfer of funds.

- **Digital coin:** A chain of digital signatures.

- **Mining:** The process of solving and validating complex mathematical equations so as to gain cryptocurrency.

- **Wallet:** Software that stores your public and private keys.

2.4.3   Onion Routing

Cyber extortionists needed fast and anonymous communication methods to facilitate negotiations, create leverage over their victims, and coordinate internally. Onion routing provided these capabilities, and many more, ultimately enabling adversaries to buy and sell tools to support their crimes, anonymously leak sensitive data, and scale their cybercriminal enterprises.

2.4.3.1 What Is Onion Routing and How Does It Work?

Onion routing is the technology that underlies darknets and the "dark web," which are used by criminals, journalists, intelligence agencies, whistleblowers, and others to facilitate anonymous communications. The concept is simple: To maintain anonymity, network traffic is passed through a series of computers so that the ultimate source and destination addresses are unknown to any one system.

Upon launching onion routing software, a user's computer establishes a *circuit*, which is simply the path that the user's traffic will take through the Internet and back. The route that the data takes through the network is encrypted in layers using the public key of each computer in the circuit.[14]

As data travels through the circuit, each computer uses its private key to decrypt the outer layer, which reveals the address of the next computer. The data is then passed along to that computer. The next computer in the circuit does the same thing, and so on, until the data reaches its destination. No computer in the circuit has the address of both the source and destination systems, thereby preserving anonymity.

Heads Up! Weaknesses of Onion Routing

There are many ways to potentially break the anonymity provided by onion routing. For example, in timing attacks, a third party with access to multiple systems in the network monitors the traffic carefully and connects a source and destination based on timing and other traffic characteristics. Information disclosure issues can also lead to identification, such as in cases where a user shares their social media information or discloses other identifying characteristics. Despite these risks, adversaries who take precautions can successfully remain anonymous for years.

2.4.3.2 The Dark Web

Onion routing is the technology that underlies the dark web, which in turn has led to a proliferation of dark e-commerce sites, criminal chat forums, data leak portals, and more.[15]

---

14. Tor Project, https://2019.www.torproject.org/about/overview.html.en.

15. Tor Project.

The "dark web" refers to a collection of web services accessible only using onion routing software.

The dark web was popularized by The Onion Routing project, or TOR for short, which was developed during the early 2000s by scientists Paul Syverson, Roger Dingledine, and Nick Mathewson.[16] TOR enables uses to offer "hidden services" such as websites, email, and chat rooms, by registering in the TOR network and obtaining a "hidden service descriptor"—that is, a 16- or 56-character domain name.[17]

Since its inception, the dark web has become a haven for the cybercriminal underworld. Prominent cyber extortion cartels like Conti, REvil, and many others rely on the dark web to collaborate, purchase access to victim networks, post stolen client data, negotiate ransom payments, and much more.

2.5   Ransomware Goes Mainstream

By 2013, the major features needed for truly modern cyber extortion were in place. Asymmetric encryption was well developed and commonly used, cryptocurrency had been launched, and the dark web was widely used. This combination allowed for a new era of cybercrime.

CryptoLocker, first identified in the fall of 2013,[18] was the first widespread malware to complete the evolution into what is considered "modern" ransomware. It incorporated the following elements:

- **Hybrid encryption model:** Local files were first encrypted with AES-256 symmetric keys, and then the symmetric keys were encrypted with a unique RSA-2048 public key downloaded from the adversary's server. The corresponding private key was held only by the adversary.[19]

- **Cryptocurrency payment option:** Victims could pay the ransom demand by sending funds to the specified Bitcoin wallet address or by using MoneyPak vouchers.[20]

Using these technologies, the criminals behind CryptoLocker were able to extort millions of dollars from their victims, while obscuring their identities for an extended period of time.

---

16. Tor Project.

17. "Hidden Service Names," https://gitlab.torproject.org/legacy/trac/-/wikis/doc/HiddenServiceNames.

18. "Original Cryptolocker Ransomware Support and Help Topic," *Bleeping Computer*, September 6, 2013, www.bleepingcomputer.com/forums/t/506924/original-cryptolocker-ransomware-support-and-help-topic/.

19. "CryptoLocker Ransomware Information Guide and FAQ," *Bleeping Computer*, October 14, 2013, www.bleepingcomputer.com/virus-removal/cryptolocker-ransomware-information#cryptolocker.

20. "CryptoLocker Ransomware Information Guide and FAQ."

Ultimately, the CryptoLocker distribution system was disrupted by Operation Tovar, an international collaboration between law enforcement, tech companies, and security researchers.[21] The new model for cyber extortion lived on, however, and was quickly expanded upon in 2014 with the release of the appropriately named Onion ransomware.

Unlike other ransomware strains that used clear-web servers for their command-and-control (C2) servers, the Onion ransomware leveraged the TOR network for C2 communications. This made its identification and takedown much more difficult for law enforcement and security teams.[22]

Ransomware attracted significant mainstream media attention in 2016 when a cyber-criminal group took over the Hollywood Presbyterian Medical Center and demanded $17,000 to unlock critical computers used by the hospital.[23] Ransomware gangs were expanding rapidly, attacking larger targets, and demanding more money—cementing ransomware's place as one of the most costly and devastating types of cyberattacks. At its peak, the ransomware strain Locky infected an estimated 90,000 computers per day.[24]

The public reactions to ransomware and cyber extortion changed significantly during this period as well. New guidance from the U.S. Office for Civil Rights made it clear that victims had to presume that ransomware infections were reportable breaches under HIPAA unless they could demonstrate otherwise.[25] In consequence, victims could no longer simply pay a ransom and sweep their malware infections under the rug. This led to an increase of insurance claims and reportable breaches linked to ransomware, particularly in the healthcare sector.

2.6 Ransomware-as-a-Service

In 2018, a prominent and strangely vocal cybercriminal gang known as "GandCrab" emerged.[26] GandCrab popularized a new ransomware-as-a-service (RaaS) model in which they maintained and licensed centralized ransomware software and gave access to other criminals in exchange for a cut of the profits.

21. Darlene Storm, "Wham Bam: Global Operation Tovar Whacks CryptoLocker Ransomware & GameOver Zeus Botnet," *Computerworld*, June 2, 2014, www.computerworld.com/article/2476366/wham-bam--global-operation-tovar-whacks-cryptolocker-ransomware---gameover-zeus-b.html.

22. *Ransomware: Past, Present, Future* (Trend Micro, 2017), https://documents.trendmicro.com/assets/wp/wp-ransomware-past-present-and-future.pdf.

23. Richard Winton, "Hollywood Hospital Pays $17,000 in Bitcoin to Hackers; FBI Investigating," *Los Angeles Times*, February 18, 2016, www.latimes.com/business/technology/la-me-ln-hollywood-hospital-bitcoin-20160217-story.html.

24. Thomas Brewster, "As Ransomware Crisis Explodes, Hollywood Hospital Coughs up $17,000 in Bitcoin," *Forbes*, February 18, 2016, www.forbes.com/sites/thomasbrewster/2016/02/18/ransomware-hollywood-payment-locky-menace/.

25. "Fact Sheet: Ransomware and HIPAA," U.S. Department of Health and Human Services, Office for Civil Rights, July 11, 2016, www.hhs.gov/sites/default/files/RansomwareFactSheet.pdf.

26. "Pinchy Spider," CrowdStrike, https://adversary.crowdstrike.com/en-US/adversary/pinchy-spider/.

Essentially, RaaS was a franchise model, which divided responsibilities into two primary roles:

- **Operators:** The individuals responsible for developing, maintaining, and upgrading the software used to infect and encrypt victims. The operators are also mainly responsible for handling the cryptocurrency payment process, infrastructure development, and other essential behind-the-scenes tasks. Often, operators delegate tasks to specialists such as malware developers.

- **Affiliates:** The individuals responsible for acquiring targets, compromising networks, and distributing the malicious software. The affiliate receives 60% to 70% of the ransom paid as a commission.

The model was a success, to say the least. Reportedly, GandCrab infected roughly 50,000 computers in its first month of existence. Each individual victim was extorted for anywhere between $400 and $700,000, with ransoms paid using a cryptocurrency called DASH.[27]

Because of this success, the GandCrab operators were able to invest significant amounts of capital into further developing their RaaS platform. Before long, new features, versions, and specific customizations began to appear that greatly improved the overall effectiveness and ease of use for affiliates. For example, the upgrades included the ability to quickly spread through a network by automatically scanning computers for common vulnerabilities and exploiting them to maximize their footprint.

On May 31, 2019, a group claiming to be the GandCrab operators proudly announced to the world that they intended to retire after successfully extorting victims for a combined total of more than $2 billion.[28] Their model had proved to be incredibly effective and profitable, ultimately lowering the technical barriers to entry and making cyber extortion accessible to less technical criminals.

The franchise model quickly became standard for other cyber extortion groups. Almost immediately after GandCrab's retirement, a ransomware variant known as "REvil" appeared that utilized an almost identical business model and some of the same code that GandCrab had incorporated.

2.7 Exposure Extortion

At the same time that ransomware was taking off, a different cyber extortion trend was gaining traction: exposure. An adversary calling themselves "The Dark Overlord" (TDO) went on a cybercrime spree in 2016, hacking into healthcare clinics, professional services

---

27. "Ransomware Knowledgebase: GandCrab Ransomware," KnowBe4, https://www.knowbe4.com/gandcrab-ransomware.

28. "REvil: The GandCrab Connection," Secureworks, September 24, 2019, www.secureworks.com/blog/revil-the-gandcrab-connection.

firms, and more. TDO stole each victim's sensitive data and threatened to publish it if they didn't pay the ransom.

In the case of Athens Orthopedic Clinic, as with many others, TDO emailed the victim and demanded payment in exchange for not publishing patient data. When the clinic did not immediately pay the ransom, TDO increased the cost and began posting batches of stolen patient data on Pastebin, along with personal notes directing the CEO to "pay up."[29]

The cyber extortionists used Twitter to taunt and threaten their victims and made a point of reaching out to journalists and releasing statements for the press. "Next time an adversary comes to you and offers you an opportunity to cover this up and make it go away for a small fee to prevent the leak," TDO wrote in one public statement, "take the offer."[30]

TDO also directly contacted the victims' patients, customers, and community members to apply even more pressure. In the case of Midwest Orthopedic Pain and Spine, they texted the daughter of one of the clinic's owners, "hi … you look peaceful … by the way did your daddy tell you he refused to pay us when we stole his company files in 4 days we will be releasing for sale thousands of patient info. Including yours."[31]

In 2017, TDO hacked the Johnston Community School District in Iowa and texted threatening messages to parents.[32] "The life of a precious young child is so precious," read one message.[33] Another was more blatant: "I'm going to kill some kids at your son's high school."[34] The district closed its schools for a day and delayed school the second day as law enforcement investigated the credibility of the threat. The gang threatened to publish student information from the Iowa district and made good on their threat when the district did not readily agree to pay.[35,36]

29. "Athens Orthopedic Clinic Patient Data Still Exposed on Leak Site," DataBreaches.net, August 17, 2016, www.databreaches.net/athens-orthopedic-clinic-patient-data-still-exposed-on-leak-site/.

30. Darlene Storm, "Hacker Selling 655,000 Patient Records from 3 Hacked Healthcare Organizations," *Computerworld*, June 27, 2016, www.computerworld.com/article/3088907/hacker-selling-655-000-patient-records-from-3-hacked-healthcare-organizations.html.

31. *United States of America v. Nathan Wyatt*, November 8, 2017, p. 6, www.justice.gov/opa/press-release/file/1227441/download.

32. Charly Haley, "Police: Cyber Threats to Johnston Students Not Credible," *Des Moines Register*, October 3, 2017, www.desmoinesregister.com/story/news/crime-and-courts/2017/10/03/police-cyber-threats-johnston-students-not-credible/727547001/.

33. Haley, "Police: Cyber Threats to Johnston Students Not Credible."

34. Ms. Smith, "Dark Overlord Hacks Schools Across U.S., Texts Threats Against Kids to Parents," CSO, October 9, 2017, www.csoonline.com/article/3230975/dark-overlord-hacks-schools-across-us-texts-threats-against-kids-to-parents.html.

35. Linh Ta and Jason Clayworth, "'Dark Overlord' Hackers Posted Stolen Student Info, Johnston Officials Say," *Des Moines Register*, October 5, 2017, www.desmoinesregister.com/story/news/crime-and-courts/2017/10/05/dark-overlord-hacker-johnston-schools-threats/735950001/.

36. Ta and Clayworth, "'Dark Overlord' Hackers Posted Stolen Student Info."

Eventually, TDO was banned from Twitter, Reddit, and other social media platforms, disrupting the gang's public relations processes.[37] A member of the group, Nathan Wyatt, was extradited from the United Kingdom, charged in U.S. district court, and sentenced to five years in federal prison for his role.[38]

The TDO gang popularized exposure extortion and introduced tactics such as deliberate public relations efforts, which were later adopted by other cybercriminal gangs. However, their hacking and extortion efforts were largely a manual process, which limited their growth.

As we will see in the next sections, during the coming years cyber extortionists introduced scalable hacking and data exposure practices that took exposure extortion to the next level.

Case Study: Early Cyber Extortion

Cybercriminals launched exposure extortion attacks long before ransomware became rampant. For example, in 1999, a Kazakhstani hacker named Oleg Zezev broke into Bloomberg's systems and gained access to CEO Michael Bloomberg's personal account, as well as the accounts of other employees and customers. Zezev emailed Bloomberg with screenshots and threatened to notify customers, as well as the media, unless Bloomberg paid him $200,000.[39]

Michael Bloomberg, in collaboration with the FBI, agreed to the hacker's terms—on the condition that Zezev meet with him and his computer experts in London to explain how the attack was executed. Zezev agreed, and was promptly arrested by Scotland Yard detectives after the meeting.[40,41] Later, he and a co-conspirator were extradited to the United States, where he was tried and sentenced to more than four years in prison. According to the U.S. Department of Justice, at the time, this sentence was "amongst the longest ever imposed for a computer intrusion charge."[42]

---

37. "Banned from Twitter & Reddit, Dark Overlord Disappears from Steemit," *E-Crypto News*, https://e-cryptonews.com/banned-from-twitter-reddit-dark-overlord-disappears-from-steemit/.

38. "UK National Sentenced to Prison for Role in 'The Dark Overlord' Hacking Group," U.S. Department of Justice, September 21, 2020, www.justice.gov/opa/pr/uk-national-sentenced-prison-role-dark-overlord-hacking-group.

39. "U.S. Convicts Kazakhstan Hacker of Breaking into Bloomberg L.P.'s Computers and Attempting Extortion," U.S. Department of Justice, February 26, 2003, www.justice.gov/archive/criminal/cybercrime/press-releases/2003/zezevConvict.htm.

40. "U.S. Convicts Kazakhstan Hacker of Breaking into Bloomberg."

41. John Lehmann, "Jury Convicts Wacky Bloomberg Extortionist," *New York Post*, February 27, 2003, https://nypost.com/2003/02/27/jury-convicts-wacky-bloomberg-extortionist/.

42. "Kazakhstan Hacker Sentenced to Four Years Prison for Breaking into Bloomberg Systems and Attempting Extortion," U.S. Department of Justice, July 1, 2003, www.justice.gov/archive/criminal/cybercrime/press-releases/2003/zezevSent.htm.

2.8 Double Extortion

Why extort victims using one method when you can use two? By the end of 2019, ransomware was rampant—but many organizations had introduced effective backup practices and were able to restore their data without paying a ransom demand. This glaring weakness in the ransomware business model was a problem waiting for a solution, and in November 2019 that solution was unleashed with the emergence of the Maze ransomware cartel.[43]

The Maze gang took a two-pronged approach: They encrypted their victim's files, and they also stole the data and threatened to publish it if the victim did not pay up. For example, in December 2020, Maze attacked Southwire, a leading cable and wiring manufacturer, encrypting 878 devices and disrupting the organization's operations. The criminals demanded 850 Bitcoin (roughly $6 million at the time of the attack). Southwire refused to pay the ransom, and within a day had already started restoring critical systems.[44]

The criminals were prepared for this, however. "We have also downloaded a lot of data from your network," they wrote in the ransom note, "so in case of not paying this data will be released."[45]

Unlike other ransomware gangs, the Maze group launched a data leak website to support publication of their stolen goods. "Represented here companies don't wish to cooperate with us, and trying to hide our successful attack on their resources," read the headline on the Maze cartel's website. They encouraged the public to check back for updates. "Watch for their databases and private papers here. Follow the news!"[46] Much like TDO, Maze also regularly engaged with journalists, responding to questions, giving interviews, and releasing public statements.

When Southwire still did not pay, the Maze group published a subset of the data on their website. In an unusual twist, Southwire filed a lawsuit against the criminals and sought an injunction against their web hosting provider, which was based in Ireland.[47]

---

43. Pieter Arntz, "Maze: The Ransomware That Introduced an Extra Twist," Malwarebytes Labs (blog), updated July 16, 2021, https://blog.malwarebytes.com/threat-spotlight/2020/05/maze-the-ransomware-that-introduced-an-extra-twist/#:~:text=Maze%20ransomware%20was%20developed%20as,Segura%20in%20May%20of%202019.

44. Jessica Saunders, "Cybersecurity Incident at Metro Atlanta's 4th-Largest Private Company Disrupts Manufacturing, Shipping," *Atlanta Business Chronicle*, December 11, 2019, www.bizjournals.com/atlanta/news/2019/12/11/cybersecurity-incident-at-metro-atlantas-4th.html.

45. John E. Dunn, "'Maze' Ransomware Threatens Data Exposure Unless $6m Ransom Paid," Naked Security by Sophos, January 7, 2020, https://nakedsecurity.sophos.com/2020/01/07/maze-ransomware-threatens-data-exposure-unless-6m-ransom-paid/.

46. From a screenshot taken by LMG Security, December 2019. Also available from https://web.archive.org/web/20191218035420/https://mazenews.top/.

47. Lawrence Abrams, "Maze Ransomware Sued for Publishing Victim's Stolen Data," *Bleeping Computer*, January 2, 2020, www.bleepingcomputer.com/news/security/maze-ransomware-sued-for-publishing-victims-stolen-data/.

Southwire was successful in taking down the Maze website,[48] but the victory was short-lived. Soon afterward, Maze was back with a vengeance, this time using a different hosting provider. The gang leaked more than 14 GB of Southwire's stolen data, and threatened to publish another 10% each week until the ransom demand was paid.[49]

Suddenly, organizations that had been well prepared for a ransomware attack found themselves at risk of a different kind of cyber extortion. And just as suddenly, effective backups couldn't save the organization from an information disclosure threat.

It was the beginning of a new attack trend: exposure extortion, conducted using scalable techniques. Maze closed its operation in November 2020, but that did not mean that the individuals behind the extortion were truly gone.

Heads Up! Triple Extortion?

In 2021, news headlines began to blast the term "triple extortion." Some vendors and journalists used this term to refer to the situation in which an adversary directly threatens customers, patients, or other third parties as part of their extortion attempt.[50] This threat was not novel, as the media would have had readers believe: Adversaries such as TDO had been contacting third parties as a pressure tactic for years.

Confusingly, other journalists simply used the term to refer to the introduction of a third threat—such as a denial-of-service attack, in addition to ransomware and data exposure.[51] A new wave of articles combined the two concepts, as in an *Insurance Journal* article that defined "triple extortion" as incidents that "combine distributed denial-of-service (DDoS) attacks, file encryption and data theft—and don't just target one company, but potentially also its customers and business partners."[52]

In this book, we will refrain from using the term "triple extortion" due to the lack of consensus on definition. Undoubtedly, the use of this term will continue to evolve along with adversary threat models.

48. Matthew J. Schwartz, "Maze Ransomware Victim Sues Anonymous Attackers," Bank Info Security, January 3, 2020, www.bankinfosecurity.com/maze-ransomware-victim-sues-anonymous-attackers-a-13574.

49. "Data of Southwire Company Leaked by Maze Ransomware," Secure Reading, January 15, 2020, https://securereading.com/data-of-southwire-company-leaked-by-maze-ransomware/.

50. Becky Bracken, "Ransomware's New Swindle: Triple Extortion," Threat Post, May 14, 2021, https://threatpost.com/ransomwares-swindle-triple-extortion/166149/.

51. Jie Ji, "The New Trend of Ransomware: Triple Extortion," NSFocus, August 16, 2021, https://nsfocusglobal.com/the-new-trend-of-ransomware-triple-extortion/.

52. L. S. Howard, "Biz Interruption, Recovery Costs Drive Financial Losses from Cyber Attacks: Report," *Insurance Journal*, October 14, 2021, www.insurancejournal.com/news/international/2021/10/14/637049.htm.

2.9   An Industrial Revolution

Cyber extortionists had hit on an effective business model. Total ransom payments ballooned 344% between 2019 and 2020, with criminals raking in more than $406 million in 2020 alone, according to Chainalysis.[53] (Criminals almost certainly raked in more funds than that, since many cyber extortion wallet addresses remain unknown to this day.) In late February 2022, the massively successful Conti gang suffered a data leak that revealed they had made more than 65 million Bitcoin (equivalent to more than $2.7 billion at the time of the leak) in less than 5 years of operation.

This dramatic increase in revenue was driven by advancements in cybercriminal technologies, combined with maturing business processes. The Maze group's massive success paved the way for other cyber extortion gangs such as REvil, Conti, and others, which then launched their own data leak platforms and expanded their leverage using exposure extortion.

What did the adversaries do with their riches? They reinvested some of their profits into improving cyber extortion technology and operations, enabling them to conduct cyber extortion operations far more efficiently and on a massive scale. Here are specific areas in which cyber extortionists improved and expanded:

- Specialized roles
- Paid staff
- Automated extortion portals
- Franchising
- Public relations programs
- Standardized playbooks and tools

We will discuss each of these advancements in the following sections.

2.9.1   Specialized Roles

Extortion is hard work. In the early days, the process of extorting a victim was largely a manual task. The network had to be compromised, data stolen, ransomware deployed and detonated. Communications had to be established with the victim. Then, a ransom had to be negotiated, decryptors needed to be generated, and the transaction had to be finished. On top of that, there were language barriers and time zone differences, and adversaries were operating in a hostile environment in which responders were constantly trying to lock them out. It was, undoubtedly, exhausting.

---

53. Chainalysis, *Ransomware 2021: Critical Mid-Year Update*, May 2021, p. 6.

Practically speaking, accomplishing these tasks required a wide variety of skill sets and tools. For example, here are just a few of the tasks that adversaries must usually complete to execute a cyber extortion attack, and the skills needed to do so:

- **Initial entry:** Exploit development, deployment (typically through phishing or use of remote access credentials), hacking skills

- **Data exfiltration:** Basic IT skills, understanding of the victim's business (enough to identify which data to exfiltrate and how to blend with normal traffic)

- **Communications with the victim:** Language/translation capabilities, strong written and verbal communications skills, familiarity with incident response processes and key players such as insurance

- **Negotiation:** Understanding of the victim's business model and applicable regulations (often, adversaries refer to HIPAA/GDPR and other notification statutes), strong communication skills (as just mentioned), comfort with psychological scare tactics, ability to build/maintain trust with victim throughout the negotiation

- **Decryption:** Development and deployment of a decryption utility, technical support capabilities in the event that the victim experiences issues

- **Payment receipt:** Familiarity with cryptocurrency, ability to launder funds and convert them to cash if desired

Any business manager reviewing this list would quickly conclude that it's rare to find all of these skill sets in a single person. Even if you could, it wouldn't be an efficient use of human resources. Over time, cyber extortion gangs began defining separate roles to handle specific parts of the cyber extortion process. This led to efficiency gains and increased return on investment.

For example, "initial access brokers" emerged on dark web marketplaces and forums offering already-established access to victim networks for a fee, meaning ransomware operators didn't have to actively search out and compromise a victim on their own.[54]

Ransomware operators focused on developing and deploying software to launch attacks, such as new and improved ransomware strains, victim portals (as described in the next section), decryptor tools, and more. Other adversaries used this software to facilitate their cyber extortion attacks, often in exchange for a percentage of the revenue.

Money laundering services like "mixing" or "tumblr" services became popular methods of obscuring blockchain transactions. These services operate by transferring cryptocurrencies between multiple anonymous wallets, splitting the payments into smaller transactions, and redistributing the funds. In April 2021, the administrator of Bitcoin Fog,

---

54. Charlie Osbourne, "Ransomware Operators Love Them: Key Trends in the Initial Access Broker Space," *ZDNet*, August 2, 2021, www.zdnet.com/article/ransomware-operators-love-them-key-trends-in-the-initial-access-broker-space/.

which provided this exact service, was arrested after processing more than $360 million in Bitcoin over a decade of operations.[55]

A myriad of new criminal enterprise support services have emerged, such as the "Anti-analysis" dark web service, which enables cyber extortionists to evaluate the risk that their cryptocurrency wallets may be flagged as suspicious by law enforcement agencies and investigators. Each lookup costs approximately $3, although the service offers bulk plans.[56]

> ## Heads Up! The Insider Threat
>
> Why hack into a victim's network when you can convince an insider to install malware for you? Modern cyber extortion cartels actively court legitimate employees of high-value organizations, offering lucrative rewards to employees willing to assist with their attacks. In 2021, the Lockbit cartel posted the following advertisement on their blog:
>
> > Would you like to earn millions of dollars?
> >
> > Our company acquires access to networks of various companies, as well as insider information that can help you steal the most valuable data of any company. You can provide us accounting data for the access to any company, for example, login and password to RDP, VPN, corporate email, etc. Open our letter at your email. Launch the provided virus on any computer in your company.[57]
>
> In a ransomware attack, evidence of the point of entry is often destroyed—meaning the victim organization might never know that a trusted employee turned against it.

2.9.2 Paid Staff

As cyber extortion operations became increasingly sophisticated, adversaries began hiring employees and contractors to handle day-to-day tasks. Large cyber extortion groups regularly need IT support, system administrators, programmers, web developers, "penetration testers" (also known as "pen testers," and a euphemism for hackers), administrative support staff, public relations teams, human resources, customer support teams, and more.

---

55. Samuel Haig, "Alleged $366M Bitcoin Mixer Busted After Analysis of 10 Years of Blockchain Data," *Coin Telegraph*, April 29, 2021, https://cointelegraph.com/news/alleged-366m-bitcoin-mixer-busted-after-analysis-of-10-years-of-blockchain-data.

56. Brian Krebs, "New Anti Anti-Money Laundering Services for Crooks," Krebs on Security, August 13, 2018, https://krebsonsecurity.com/2021/08/new-anti-anti-money-laundering-services-for-crooks/.

57. Lawrence Abrams, "LockBit Ransomware Recruiting Insiders to Breach Corporate Networks," *Bleeping Computer*, August 4, 2021, www.bleepingcomputer.com/news/security/lockbit-ransomware-recruiting-insiders-to-breach-corporate-networks/.

"We can see the discipline they have, we can see that they are active during office hours, they take the weekends off, they work regular hours, they take holidays," said Caleb Barlow, head of IBM's Threat Intelligence team, describing how cybercriminal groups mirror legitimate enterprises during a 2019 interview with CNBC.[58]

Even small cybercriminal shops now employ staff. In an interview conducted by the authors' research team, one small cyber extortion group shared, "Yes we have employees … a full-time web developer and 2 pen testers."[59]

Why would skilled technical workers work for cybercriminal enterprises? One threat actor who called themselves a "contractor" explained in an interview with Flashpoint:

> On the one hand, you are afraid all the time. You wake up in fear, you go to bed in fear, you hide behind a mask and a hood in a store, you even hide from your wife or girlfriend. I'm younger than you, but I've already earned for the rest of my life. Not millions, but enough to live in peace and never work. Here is also a second factor: how to quit a job that brings such earnings in a country where you are not much sought after?[60]

Not all cyber extortion staff are fully aware that they work for a criminal enterprise—or at least, they maintain plausible deniability. In October 2021, news broke that the Fin7 cybercriminal gang had created a front company that it leveraged for recruitment purposes. Fin7, which has historically been linked to payment card theft and fraud (such as the Saks Fifth Avenue and Lord & Taylor hacks revealed in 2018), has reportedly been moving into ransomware.[61]

Instead of exclusively searching for new team members on dark web forums, which can be infiltrated by law enforcement, Fin7 created a company named Bastion Secure Ltd. and began advertising for salaried "IT" positions on the clear web and mainstream job sites in Russia and Ukraine.[62] The job descriptions sounded legitimate and included titles such as the following:

- Windows network administrator
- Python programmer
- System administrator
- C++ programmer

58. Kate Fazzini, "Cybercrime Organizations Work Just Like Any Other Business: Here's What They Do Each Day," CNBC, May 5, 2019, www.cnbc.com/2019/05/05/heres-what-cybercriminals-do-during-the-workday.html.

59. Derek Rowe, interview with Kajit/Orange from Groove Ransomware (RAMP forum), LMG Security, September 2021.

60. "Russian Hacker Q&A: An Interview with REvil-Affiliated Ransomware Contractor," Flashpoint (blog), September 29, 2021, www.flashpoint-intel.com/blog/interview-with-revil-affiliated-ransomware-contractor/.

61. Gemini Advisory, "FIN7 Recruits Talent for Push into Ransomware," Recorded Future (blog), October 21, 2021, www.recordedfuture.com/fin7-recruits-talent-push-ransomware/.

62. Robert McMillan, "Ransomware Gang Masquerades as Real Company to Recruit Tech Talent," *The Wall Street Journal*, October 21, 2021, www.wsj.com/articles/ransomware-gang-masquerades-as-real-company-to-recruit-tech-talent-11634819400.

- PHO programmer
- Reverse engineer

Work hours were advertised as Monday to Friday, nine-hour days (lunch break provided).

According to the fraud intelligence firm Gemini Advisory, an investigator posed as a job applicant and went through Bastion Secure's interview and hiring process. The first stage "proceeded similarly to a legitimate job hiring process and gave no indication that Bastion Secure was a fake company for a cybercriminal group." After "hiring," however, the recruit's first assignment involved accessing a "client" organization's network and gathering sensitive information, with several red flags indicating that the activity was a precursor to a ransomware attack.[63]

2.9.3 Automated Extortion Portals

Successful cyber extortion cartels quickly found that they had large numbers of victims to manage. Manual processes that worked sufficiently at a small scale quickly became unmanageable at larger volumes. Enter the automated extortion portal. This website is created for each victim and provides services such as the following:

- Basic information about the extortion attempt, such as the ransom demand and amount of time left to pay
- Proof-of-life decryption service, which enables victims to upload small sample files and demonstrate that they can be decrypted
- Standardized resources such as links to purchase cryptocurrency
- Decryptor delivery service
- Encrypted chat portal, which enables victims to communicate directly with the adversary (no need to track multiple email threads or accounts)

Typically, the victim portal is created by ransomware automatically during execution. GandCrab pioneered the technology during its run in 2018, but groups like REvil, Lockbit, and Darkside/Blackmatter really took it to another level during 2020.

Automated victim portals substantially reduced the amount of labor required for executing an extortion attack, and enabled criminals to stay organized while scaling up their volume.

2.9.4 Franchising

After GandCrab's success with a distributed RaaS model, many other players in the cyber extortion market began to mimic its strategy for their own gains. Prior to GandCrab, ransomware operations were usually single groups with a focus on carrying out their

---

63. Gemini Advisory, "FIN7 Recruits Talent for Push unto Ransomware," October 21, 2021, https://geminiadvisory.io/fin7-ransomware-bastion-secure.

own attacks. This "lone wolf" mentality came to an abrupt end when GandCrab "retired" and announced their $2 billion bounty—a figure high enough to inspire other would-be cyber extortionists to adopt the group's franchise model.

The REvil cartel quickly emerged and picked up where GandCrab left off. It wasn't long before additional groups like Maze, Conti, Darkside, Lockbit, and many others began adopting the franchise model, too. Terminology evolved: Victims were referred to as "clients," and distributers were now referred to as "affiliates."

2.9.4.1 Evolving Technology

Cyber extortionists adapted their technology to suit the needs of their new "affiliates," or franchisees. The automated portals used by GandCrab to streamline its operations became common among cyber extortion groups as a means of lowering the barriers to entry and supporting higher volumes of victims.

RaaS operators routinely touted their platforms' features in ads on the dark web. For example, the Lockbit cartel provided a full list of features in its affiliate marketing materials highlighting the benefits of its software. A few of the unique features included:[64]

- TOR-based administrative control panels

- Anonymous chat rooms for victims, with push notifications alerting the operator when a new message arrived

- Automatic exploit detection

- Automatic log deletion

- Automatic file exfiltration tools

The operators took their profits as a percentage of the revenue their affiliates generated. This gave them incentive to compete for skilled affiliates by investing time and capital into improving their technology products.

Case Study: The Kaseya Master Decryptor

The infamous Kaseya ransomware attacks illustrate how RaaS operators have adapted their technology to support franchise models. In July 2021, adversaries affiliated with the REvil ransomware cartel executed what was, at the time, the largest single ransomware deployment in cybersecurity history[65] when they exploited multiple zero-day vulnerabilities in the Kaseya VSA remote monitoring and management system. Thousands of organizations were hit with ransomware in one fell swoop.

---

64. Megan Roddie, "LockBit 2.0: Ransomware Attacks Surge After Successful Affiliate Recruitment," Security Intelligence, September 9, 2021, https://securityintelligence.com/posts/lockbit-ransomware-attacks-surge-affiliate-recruitment/.

65. Associated Press, "Scale, Details of Massive Kaseya Ransomware Attack Emerge," NPR, July 5, 2021, www.npr.org/2021/07/05/1013117515/scale-details-of-massive-kaseya-ransomware-attack-emerge.

Shortly thereafter, REvil's infrastructure mysteriously went dark, on July 13, 2021.[66] Its dark web site, command-and-control servers, social media presence, and more all went down. The situation became even more mysterious on July 21, when Kaseya released a decryptor capable of unlocking all systems encrypted in the attack.[67] Kaseya did not disclose exactly how it acquired the decryptor—only that it was delivered by a "trusted third party."[68] Later, it was revealed that the Federal Bureau of Investigation (FBI) had infiltrated REvil's servers and recovered the decryption key, but waited nearly three weeks to release the key to Kaseya—a decision that launched an outcry from victims later.[69]

Unfortunately, the REvil cartel did not stay gone for long. Its dark web sites quietly came back online on September 7, 2021, and the group resumed operations, actively encrypting victims' systems all over the world.

New hope emerged for victims on September 16, 2021, when the antivirus company Bitdefender released a universal decryptor.[70] Just like Kaseya, Bitdefender disclosed only that the decryptor was provided by a "trusted source."[71] The decryptor was reportedly effective on all REvil victims attacked prior to the group's sudden disappearance on July 13.

The existence of both the Kaseya master decryptor and a universal decryptor is telling, in and of itself. According to a REvil representative, the cartel's systems were capable of generating individual ransomware decryption keys for each individual victim computer (between 20 and 500 decryption keys for each Kaseya victim), or a single master decryptor key for all devices encrypted in the attack.[72] The fact that the REvil cartel operators were capable of universally unlocking all victim systems illustrates the extent to which they maintained centralized control and oversight, even while giving affiliates the power to use their software and turn a profit.

Not only do modern ransomware cartels leverage asymmetric encryption effectively, but they also use it to facilitate their sophisticated franchise-style business models, providing redundancy and supporting centralized oversight.

66. Lisa Vaas, "Ransomware Giant REvil's Sites Disappear," Threat Post, July 13, 2021, https://threatpost.com/ransomware-revil-sites-disappears/167745/.

67. "Important Notice August 4th, 2021," Kaseya, August 4, 2021, https://helpdesk.kaseya.com/hc/en-gb/articles/4403440684689-Important-Notice-August-4th-2021.

68. Lawrence Abrams, "Kaseya Obtains Universal Decryptor for REvil Ransomware Victims," *Bleeping Computer*, July 22, 2021, www.bleepingcomputer.com/news/security/kaseya-obtains-universal-decryptor-for-revil-ransomware-victims/.

69. Ellen Nakashima and Rachel Lerman, "FBI Held Back Ransomware Decryption Key from Businesses to Run Operation Targeting Hackers," *The Washington Post*, September 21, 2021, www.washingtonpost.com/national-security/ransomware-fbi-revil-decryption-key/2021/09/21/4a9417d0-f15f-11eb-a452-4da5fe48582d_story.html.

70. Lawrence Abrams, "Free REvil Ransomware Master Decrypter Released for Past Victims," *Bleeping Computer*, September 16, 2021, www.bleepingcomputer.com/news/security/free-revil-ransomware-master-decrypter-released-for-past-victims/.

71. Martin Zugec, "Bitdefender Threat Debrief," Bitdefender, August 25, 2021, https://businessinsights.bitdefender.com/bitdefender-threat-debrief-august-2021.

72. Lisa Vaas, "REvil's Back; Coder Fat-Fingered Away Its Decryptor Key?," Threat Post, September 13, 2021, https://threatpost.com/revil-back-coder-decryptor-key/169403/.

2.9.4.2 Affiliate Recruitment Methods

The pioneering GandCrab group recruited affiliates mainly through underground forums and tightly controlled messaging.[73] By keeping their recruitment efforts confined to these exclusive audiences, the GandCrab group was at a much lower risk of accidentally interacting with law enforcement or unwanted media contacts. Their recruitment specified that they would not work with native English speakers, they would not attack Commonwealth of Independent States (CIS) countries, and applicants had to navigate an extensive interview process to join the organization.

REvil, which is considered to be the successor to GandCrab, largely followed the same recruitment playbook, although the group took the extra step of depositing large amounts of Bitcoin in the forums they were advertising with as a sign that they could be trusted by potential affiliates.[74]

Despite the success of this strategy, the need for more affiliates led to increasingly public methods of attracting the attention of potential candidates. Lockbit 2.0, for example, published its affiliate program directly on its dark web extortion portal for all to see, even announcing proudly at the top of the page that "Lockbit 2.0 is an affiliate program." Key benefits of using the Lockbit platform were advertised prominently on the post, including encryption speed comparisons, key ransomware features, and the availability of a custom "StealBit" data theft utility designed to exfiltrate files and upload them directly to the Lockbit blog.[75]

2.9.4.3 Protections for Affiliates

Work as an affiliate is risky. To protect "affiliates," many RaaS operations choose to deposit large amounts of cryptocurrency into third-party controlled accounts, ensuring that the affiliates will still get paid for their work even if something goes wrong with the primary operation. This level of security is designed to provide a sense of confidence in the ransomware group and boost its reputation among potential new affiliates.

In May 2021, this "shadow" court system ended up on full display when the Darkside ransomware group went dark without paying its affiliates.[76] At that point in time, a sum of roughly 22 Bitcoin (roughly $1 million at the time) that had been deposited by the Darkside group was under the control of moderators for the infamous XSS.is hacker forum. Affiliates began to submit claims that they had not been paid for their work.

---

73. Brian Krebs, "Who's Behind the GandCrab Ransomware?," Krebs on Security, July 8, 2019, https://krebsonsecurity.com/2019/07/whos-behind-the-gandcrab-ransomware/.

74. Lawrence Abrams, "REvil Ransomware Deposits $1 Million in Hacker Recruitment Drive," *Bleeping Computer*, September 28, 2020, www.bleepingcomputer.com/news/security/revil-ransomware-deposits-1-million-in-hacker-recruitment-drive/.

75. "Ransomware Profile: LockBit," Emsisoft, July 21, 2021, https://blog.emsisoft.com/en/38915/ransomware-profile-lockbit/.

76. Becky Bracken, "DarkSide Getting Taken to 'Hackers' Court' for Not Paying Affiliates," Threat Post, May 21, 2021, https://threatpost.com/darkside-hackers-court-paying-affiliates/166393/.

What made this a truly unique event was the revelation that a "hacker court" existed on these underground forums for the purpose of resolving disputes exactly like this one. Affiliates would submit their claims of work, and an adjudicator from the forums moderator group would review the "evidence" and either award or deny the claim. In some cases, moderators even went as far as using the term "defendant" to describe the defunct Darkside group in their rulings.[77]

An underappreciated part of the story, which seemed to be pushed aside by the "hacker court" proceedings, was the revelation that underground forums like XSS.is had quietly created a full infrastructure that RaaS groups could leverage to market, recruit, and secure operations for their ransomware activities.[78]

2.9.4.4 A Reputation to Uphold

In this franchising model, RaaS operators were at risk if an affiliate "went rogue"—attracting too much attention from law enforcement or simply giving out too much information to the press. The franchise model used by many large cyber extortion groups provided major benefits in regard to the overall scope of attacks, but also took a lot of the control over who was being attacked and how those attacks were being carried out away from the developers.

It was inevitable that this type of freedom would eventually result in a ransomware affiliate going too far with an attack, drawing the eyes of mainstream media, international law enforcement, and even other ransomware groups concerned about one affiliate destroying their collective ability to continue operating. A prime example of this exact type of overreach is the attack on Colonial Pipeline carried out by an affiliate of the Darkside group in May 2021.[79]

Taking down a retail business or law firm is bad, but disrupting fuel supplies to the entire eastern seaboard of the United States is absolutely worse, and Darkside felt the heat pretty quickly. The unwanted attention to this organization for what some in the media called an "act of war"[80] prompted a quick response from Darkside:

> We are apolitical, we do not participate in geopolitics, do not need to tie us with a defined government and look for other motives.. Our goal is to make money, not create problems for society. From today we introduce moderation and check each company that our partners want to encrypt to avoid social consequences in the future.[81]

77. Dan Goodin, "Hear Ye, DarkSide! This Honorable Ransomware Court Is Now in Session," ARS Technica, May 22, 2021, https://arstechnica.com/gadgets/2021/05/darkside-ransomware-makers-accused-of-skipping-town-without-paying-affiliates/.

78. Kevin Lee and Austin Merritt, "Underground Markets: A Tour of the Dark Economy," Threat Post (webinar), https://threatpost.com/webinars/underground-markets-a-tour-of-the-dark-economy/.

79. Anthony M. Freed, "Inside the DarkSide Ransomware Attack on Colonial Pipeline," Cybereason: Malicious Life, May 10, 2021, www.cybereason.com/blog/inside-the-darkside-ransomware-attack-on-colonial-pipeline.

80. Fox Business Staff, "Varney: Colonial Pipeline Attack Could Be "Act of War," Fox Business, May 10, 2021, www.foxbusiness.com/politics/varney-colonial-pipeline-attack-shutdown-economy.

81. From screenshot of Darkside site, taken by Derek Rowe, LMG Security, 2021.

Even other ransomware groups spoke out against the attacks and their severity, leading many groups to publicly announce that they would no longer attack critical infrastructure, oil pipelines, hospitals, or other high-profile targets that could put a bull's eye on their backs.[82]

2.9.5 Public Relations Programs

Public shaming is a key weapon wielded by cyber extortionists. To effectively threaten the confidentiality of information, extortionists needed a way to dump it into public view. They also leveraged the potential embarrassment and shame associated with being hacked to further pressure their victims.

Today, extortion gangs often explicitly use regulations and laws as leverage, promising to keep quiet if the victims pay so that the victim can avoid triggering notification laws, regulatory investigations, and fines. For example, in 2019 the REvil ransomware gang hacked into the CyrusOne managed service provider, and subsequently attacked customer environments. After stealing the data, the gang laid out their rationale for payment in a public Russian forum:

> In case of refusal of payment—the data will either be sold to competitors or laid out in open sources. **GDPR**. Do not want to pay us—pay ×10 times more to the government. No problems.[83]

As detailed in the book *Data Breaches*, data exposure perpetrators learned to weaponize data by leveraging social media, posting data on dedicated data leak websites, and cultivating relationships with mainstream media.[84] Modern adversaries also have the option of leveraging third-party exposure extortion services, which handle all of the challenging public relations and extortion details for them.

2.9.5.1 Social Media

Social media are often used by both adversaries and victims in their efforts to advance their public narrative. As an example, the City of Baltimore was the victim of a ransomware attack in 2019 when the "RobbinHood" ransomware group encrypted the city's servers and effectively took the city offline.[85] When ransom negotiations broke down, the

---

82. Tonya Riley, "The Cybersecurity 202: Ransomware Groups Are Going Underground, Which Could Make Them Harder to Track," *The Washington Post*, May 17, 2021, www.washingtonpost.com/politics/2021/05/17/cybersecurity-202-ransomware-groups-are-going-underground-which-could-make-them-harder-track/.

83. Lawrence Abrams, "Another Ransomware Will Now Publish Victims' Data If Not Paid," *Bleeping Computer*, December 12, 2019, www.bleepingcomputer.com/news/security/another-ransomware-will-now-publish-victims-data-if-not-paid/.

84. Sherri Davidoff, *Data Breaches: Crisis and Opportunity* (Addison-Wesley Professional, 2019), pp. 307–310.

85. Emily Sullivan, "Ransomware Cyberattacks Knock Baltimore's City Services Offline," NPR, May 21, 2019, www.npr.org/2019/05/21/725118702/ransomware-cyberattacks-on-baltimore-put-city-services-offline.

individuals behind the attack moved to social media—Twitter specifically—to announce to the world that Baltimore had been hacked and was suffering because of it.[86] The attackers took steps to ensure the conversation was noticed by tagging major news organizations and other media outlets in their post. The spat between Baltimore's mayor and the attackers quickly became a national story.

Twitter was also used as a point of communication by the victim, too. Baltimore's mayor, Jack Young, used the platform to provide updates and distribute information about the attack as progress was made. Twitter also played a role when a *New York Times* article claimed that the infamous EternalBlue exploit, which was stolen from the National Security Agency (NSA) and leaked by The Shadow Brokers in 2017,[87] was used in the attack.[88] This was enough to prompt a rare public statement from U.S. government officials disputing the story.[89]

Twitter and other social media platforms have since developed and enforced policies to reduce the power that threat actors can wield via social media. In 2018, Twitter introduced a policy that prohibited posting of hacked materials.[90] The policy update caused a flurry of questions about how much control the platform would assert over the distribution of information on criminal activities. There was widespread concern over censorship and how legitimate media organizations might be impacted. Since then, Twitter and other social media platforms have continued to refine their policies, struggling to find a balance between protecting journalists and protecting privacy.

In the meantime, cyber extortionists adapted and found new avenues for developing relationships with the mainstream media.

2.9.5.2 Branded Data Leak Sites

Frequently banned from social media platforms, adversaries shifted to launching their own, branded web portals, which they used to "name and shame" victims. This tactic was popularized by the Maze group in late 2019 (as discussed in Section 2.8), and quickly copied by REvil, Conti, and other major ransomware players. Typically, these sites are hosted on the dark web, although in some cases (as with the Maze group) they are on the clear net.

---

86. "Baltimore Hackers Leak Data on Twitter After No Ransom Was Paid," *CISO Magazine*, June 7, 2019, https://cisomag.com/baltimore-hackers-leak-data-on-twitter-after-no-ransom-was-paid/.

87. Lily Hay Newman, "The Leaked NSA Spy Tool That Hacked the World," *Wired*, March 7, 2018, www.wired.com/story/eternalblue-leaked-nsa-spy-tool-hacked-world/.

88. Nicole Perlroth and Scott Shane, "In Baltimore and Beyond, a Stolen N.S.A. Tool Wreaks Havoc," *The New York Times*, May 25, 2019, www.nytimes.com/2019/05/25/us/nsa-hacking-tool-baltimore.html.

89. Shannon Vavra, "Ruppersberger: NSA Has No Evidence EternalBlue Was in Baltimore Attack," Cyberscoop, May 31, 2019, www.cyberscoop.com/dutch-ruppersberger-nsa-eternalblue-robbinhood-baltimore/.

90. Catalin Cimpanu, "Twitter Bans Distribution of Hacked Materials Ahead of US Midterm Elections," *ZDNet*, October 2, 2018, www.zdnet.com/article/twitter-bans-distribution-of-hacked-materials-ahead-of-us-midterm-elections/.

The criminals' public-facing websites evolved to include several common features:

- **Branded home page:** In some cases, these included eye-catching illustrations, such as the Cuba group's colorful portrait of Fidel Castro and the Karakut gang's whimsical cartoon of monkeys smoking and having tea. Other groups were more simplistic, such as REvil's "Happy Blog," which simply featured a listing of the group's latest victims.

- **Victim "name-and-shame" section:** An area where victims are publicly listed and threatened.

- **Auctions:** Criminals often auction victim data off to the highest bidder if the victim does not pay. Typically, there is a starting bid and a time limit. If the data is not purchased, the criminals release a link to the world.

- **News:** Updates from the criminals (also referred to as "press releases"). This may include statements on major cases, such as the Darkside gang's announcement in response to the Colonial Pipeline backlash.[91]

- **"About" section:** Information about the cyber extortionist gang (typically intended to be inspiring or flattering).

- **Contact method:** A contact form or chat feature enabling visitors to reach out to the cyber extortion cartel.

The tactic was so effective that data leak sites proliferated. REvil, the top ransomware strain at the time, spun up the "Happy Blog" for publishing and even auctioning off stolen data.[92] New ransomware strains emerged with their own blogs, such as the Cuba strain ("This site contains information about companies that did not want to cooperate with us. Part of the information is for sale, part is freely available.").[93] In early 2021, the NetWalker RaaS operators advertised that their software included "a fully automatic blog, into which the merged data of the victim goes, the data is published according to your settings."[94]

2.9.5.3 Press Programs

Attention from the mainstream media made cyber extortion cartels more powerful. The Maze group recognized the power of the press early on, encouraging their victims to

---

91. Viewed in screenshot of the Darkside site, taken by Derek Rowe, LMG Security, 2021.

92. "REvil Hackers Continue to Wrack up High-Profile Targets with Ransomware Attacks," Dark Owl, updated June 2, 2020, www.darkowl.com/blog-content/revil-hackers-continue-to-wrack-up-high-profile-targets-with-ransomware-attacks.

93. LMG Security case, February 2021.

94. Nathan Coppinger, "Netwalker Ransomware Guide: Everything You Need to Know," Varonis, November 17, 2020, www.varonis.com/blog/netwalker-ransomware/.

Google past victims' names so that they could see the nasty headlines for themselves. Since the early days of TDO, cyber extortion gangs have been giving interviews with the press, leveraging the mainstream media like a megaphone to increase pressure on their victims and spread their viewpoints.

Extortionists may reach out directly to known journalists. For example, in one case that the authors of this book handled, the Cuba ransomware gang stole data from a financial firm. The adversary deliberately emailed a reporter, sharing information about the ransom demand, the new current price (after the victim decided not to pay the ransom), and a full file list of all stolen items.[95]

Today, journalists routinely follow data leak sites, dutifully posting articles when sensational leaks are announced.[96] (The Maze gang, like other groups, published a "press release" when announcing their retirement, another indicator of their growing engagement with mainstream media.[97])

Once cyber extortion websites became popular, the cartels had a way to build a community and interact with the public. For example, the Darkside cartel had a "Press Center" where they encouraged journalists and recovery companies to register on their site, describing the following benefits:[98]

Why do I need to register?

- You can ask questions and get information from the primary source.
- Notifying you of data breaches before posting. The ability to receive non-public information.
- Fast replies within 24 hours.

Recovery
Why do I need to register?

- Automatic receiving of decryptors after payment.
- Get an additional discount. The discount increases depending on the number of payments.
- Communication with the support in a personal chat.

To register, journalists or recovery organization staff were required to provide an email address. If the email domain was a generic hosting provider such as gmail.com, they would be required to prove their affiliation before their registration was approved.

---

95. LMG Security case, February 2021.

96. Brian Krebs, "Ransomware Gangs Don't Need PR Help," Krebs on Security, July 1, 2020, https://krebsonsecurity.com/2020/07/ransomware-gangs-dont-need-pr-help/.

97. Pierluigi Paganini, "Maze Ransomware Gang Shuts down Operations, States Their Press Release," Security Affairs, November 2, 2020, https://securityaffairs.co/wordpress/110318/cyber-crime/maze-ransomware-teminates-operations.html.

98. Website of the DarkSide ransomware criminal gang, available on the dark web via Tor (since removed). From a screenshot obtained by LMG Security, June 2021.

2.9.5.4 Third-Party Exposure Extortion Services

The abundance of data being exfiltrated created a market for third-party data exposure services like the infamous Marketo[99] "leaked data marketplace,"[100,101] which provided cyber extortion groups with an easy way to host, market, and distribute data that had been stolen from a victim's network. The operators behind marketplaces like Marketo did not actively hack anyone or distribute any malicious software, but provided a service to advertise stolen data.

These services go far beyond common dark net e-commerce markets. Marketo actively engages with victims, competitors, and the larger community.[102] In Marketo's manifest, the group explains that stolen data is always first offered to the victim themselves.[103] If the victim chooses not to pay, then Marketo threatens to notify "every company affiliate." This includes competitors, who have received emails such as the following:

> Hello, we are Marketo and we know you have a competitor—[NAME REDACTED]. So we would like to inform you that we attacked them and downloaded quite a bit of data. We have confidential and personal data, info about their tax payments, clients and partners. That might be significantly lower than the NASDAQ price.[104]

Marketo also advertises a list of "partners" that receive a weekly report of victims, along with supporting documentation. These include regulatory agencies such as the Federal Deposit Insurance Corporation (FDIC), Consumer Financial Protection Bureau (CFPB), Office of the Comptroller of the Currency (OCC), the Financial Crimes Enforcement Network, and media entities such as Bleeping Computer and SC Media. It is not clear whether these entities are voluntarily receiving these reports, or whether they act upon them.[105]

By specializing in data leaks, centralized exposure extortion services such as Marketo can build strong relationships with the media, They can also invest in tools and templates, which can help their clients (the data thieves themselves) more effectively leverage their stolen goods.

---

99. Note that the cybercriminal enterprise Marketo is in no way affiliated with the legitimate Adobe Marketo software suite.

100. Photon Research Team, "Marketo: A Return to Simple Extortion," Digital Shadows (blog), July 8, 2021, www.digitalshadows.com/blog-and-research/marketo-a-return-to-simple-extortion/.

101. Lawrence Abrams, "Data Leak Marketplaces Aim to Take over the Extortion Economy," *Bleeping Computer*, May 7, 2021, www.bleepingcomputer.com/news/security/data-leak-marketplaces-aim-to-take-over-the-extortion-economy/.

102. Dmitry Smilyanets, "'Yes, We Are Breaking the Law:' An Interview with the Operator of a Marketplace for Stolen Data," *The Record*, September 17, 2021, https://therecord.media/yes-we-are-breaking-the-law-an-interview-with-the-operator-of-a-marketplace-for-stolen-data/.

103. Marketo.cloud, https://marketo.cloud/manifest.

104. Lawrence Abrams, "Data Leak Marketplace Pressures Victims by Emailing Competitors," *Bleeping Computer*, June 21, 2021, www.bleepingcomputer.com/news/security/data-leak-marketplace-pressures-victims-by-emailing-competitors/.

105. Smilyanets, "'Yes, We Are Breaking the Law'."

2.9.6 Standardized Playbooks and Toolkits

Cyber extortion gangs didn't just invest in technology—they also invested time and labor into developing standardized playbooks and tools for their employees and affiliates to use. This included the emergence of step-by-step instruction manuals, as well as distribution of hacking tools, exploits, and even common IT utilities useful for remote access and data exfiltration. These packages dramatically reduced the investment needed for affiliates to engage in cyber extortion and increased their chances of success.

As an example, in 2021, a disgruntled Conti affiliate leaked a full version of the playbook and tools that the Conti cartel used to execute their attack.[106] At the time the playbook was leaked, the authors of this book were handling a Conti ransomware case and personally verified that the tactics, techniques, and procedures (TTPs) observed in the case matched those documented in the leaked playbook.

In addition to providing scripts for the affiliates to use, the playbook outlined many other procedural steps to a successful ransomware infection:[107]

- **Attack playbook:** A full written manual, as well as a collection of notes, files, and scripts useful for various components of the attack. The documentation includes step-by-step instructions for leveraging exploits, establishing persistence, expanding access, gaining access to data repositories, and exfiltrating data. It also includes links to third-party sites where the user can obtain the latest exploits and supplemental tools.

- **Common IT utilities:** Helpful utilities such as the Atera remote access tool, netscan, rclone, routerscan, and more (along with instructions for their use). The tools are both useful for the adversary and commonly used in normal networks, meaning they are unlikely to trigger antivirus alerts by themselves. Adversaries using these tools can lurk inside of networks for weeks or even months without being detected, siphoning sensitive data the entire time.

- **Exfiltration guidance:** Tips for users on how to search for high-value information, and what types of data to target. This includes practical guidance for finding data that may be useful for setting a ransom demand, expanding the compromise, or putting pressure on their victim. For example, in one section, the Conti playbook instructs:[108]

---

106. Caitlin Huey, David Liebenberg, Azim Khodjibaev, and Dmytro Korzhevin, "Translated: Talos' Insights from the Recently Leaked Conti Ransomware Playbook," Talos (blog), September 2, 2021, https://blog.talosintelligence.com/2021/09/Conti-leak-translation.html.

107. Catalin Cimpanu, "Disgruntled Ransomware Affiliate Leaks the Conti Gang's Technical Manuals," *The Record*, August 5, 2021, https://therecord.media/disgruntled-ransomware-affiliate-leaks-the-conti-gangs-technical-manuals.

108. Leaked Conti playbook, September 2021, translated from Russian to English using Microsoft and author research. The list of search keywords was originally in English and was not translated.

```
need accounting reports. bank statements. for 20-21 years. all fresh.
especially important, cyber insurance, security policy documents.
Keywords for search:
cyber
policy
insurance
endorsement
supplementary
underwriting
terms
bank
2020
2021
Statement
and anything that can be juicy.
```

Using this type of data, the ransomware operators would be able to maximize the ransom being demanded from the victim and increase the chances of extracting a payment. The manual subsequently instructs the user to immediately upload any valuable information to a third-party file sharing site.

The distribution of a standardized playbook enabled the Conti cartel to ensure consistent adoption of successful tools and techniques. In turn, it helped affiliates achieve their own goals:

- Quickly leverage new vulnerabilities and exploits, since all the information they needed was distributed in the package

- Evade detection, by using normal IT tools and evasion tactics detailed in the playbook

- Expand farther, faster, and more effectively across victim networks

- Exfiltrate high-value data that would be useful for negotiations and gaining leverage over victims

Ultimately, by developing and distributing centralized playbooks and toolkits, cartels can leverage economies of scale and generate higher margins, leading to greater profits.

2.10 Conclusion

The cyber extortion business has undergone its own "Industrial Revolution." What started as a primarily manual attack gained efficiency and scale through automation, turning cyber extortion into the bustling criminal enterprise that it is today.

Tools like the dark web and cryptocurrency were fundamental to the growth of cyber extortion, facilitating anonymous communication and fast payments. Criminal cartels evolved into franchise models, in which centralized operators provided tools, templates, and support staff, lowering the barriers to entry for cyber extortion. Meanwhile, threat actors with specialized skill sets, such as malware development or public relations expertise, found that they could specialize and become RaaS programmers, operators, initial access brokers, data leak specialists, and more.

In the next chapter, we will step through the anatomy of a cyber extortion attack, dissecting the attack at each phase. Along the way, we will point out opportunities for detection, which can help facilitate an effective response.

2.11 Your Turn!

Every cyber extortion incident is unique. The response team's options and priorities will vary depending on the victim organization's industry, size, and location, as well as the details of the incident itself.

Based on what you learned in this chapter, let's dissect the technology and business model underlying a cyber extortion attack.

Step 1: Build Your Victim

Choose one characteristic from each of the three columns to describe your victim's organization:

Industry	Size	Location
Hospital	Large	Global
Financial institution	Midsized	United States
Manufacturer	Small	European Union
Law firm		Australia
University		India
Cloud service provider		Country/location of your choice
Organization of your choice		

Step 2: Choose Your Incident Scenario

Select from one of the following incident scenarios:

A	Ransomware strikes! All of the victim's files have been locked up, including central data repositories, servers, and workstations.
B	A well-known cyber extortion gang claims to have stolen all of the victim's most sensitive data and threatens to release it unless the victim pays a very large ransom demand. The gang posts the victim's name on their dark web leaks site, along with samples of supposedly stolen data.
C	Double extortion! Both A and B occur at the same time.
D	The victim is hit with a denial-of-service attack on its Internet-facing infrastructure that slows its access and services to a crawl. The adversary threatens to continue and even escalate the attack unless a ransom is paid.

Step 3: Discussion Time

Your victim is experiencing a cyber extortion incident. Given what you know about the victim and the scenario, answer the following questions:

1. The adversary left ransom notes behind on the infected systems directing the victim to visit a specific dark web site. What might your victim expect to see if they decide to visit the site?

2. What is the difference between an operator and an affiliate?

3. A journalist calls the victim organization, asking about the attack it is experiencing, but to the best of the victim's knowledge no information has been shared beyond the Incident Response team. What are some possible ways the journalist may have obtained the information?

4. Explain why modern ransomware typically leverages both asymmetric and symmetric key cryptography. What are the benefits of each?

5. Name two ways that the adversary might create pressure for the victim to pay a ransom demand.

Chapter 3

Anatomy of an Attack

If you know the enemy and know yourself, you need not fear the result of a hundred battles.

—Sun Tzu

Learning Objectives

- Identify the key activities associated with a cyber extortion incident
- Understand common technical methods that cyber extortion gangs use to gain access to victim networks
- Describe tools and tactics that adversaries use to gain entry, expand, appraise, prime the environment, and gain leverage over their victims
- Identify opportunities for detection at each phase

A cyber extortion attack is never *just* a cyber extortion attack. There is always an escalation in activities from the adversary's initial entry, expansion throughout the environment, and ultimately the extortion threat.

While every attack is different, there are common adversary activities associated with most, if not all, cyber extortion attacks. Understanding these common threads can help victims more effectively respond to cyber extortion attacks, minimize damage, and in some cases, prevent extortion from occurring in the first place.

In this chapter, we deconstruct a cyber extortion attack into key components and present these along with common indicators of compromise and effective response tactics.

3.1 Anatomy Overview

Cyber extortion attacks do not begin and end with the extortion demand itself, although this is often the most visible part. The authors of this book have analyzed hundreds of

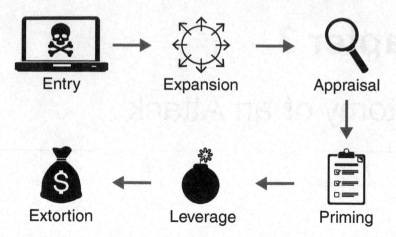

Figure 3.1 Anatomy of a cyber extortion attack

(Illustration courtesy of LMG Security. Graphics: computer, grmarc/Shutterstock; skull and crossbones, Sergey Siz`kov/123RF; circle with arrows, bloomua/123RF; magnifying glass, olesya k/Shutterstock; clipboard, HSDesain/Shutterstock; bomb, AcaG/ Shutterstock; money bag, Pensiri Saekoung/123RF)

extortion cases, many firsthand, and identified common adversary tactics observed throughout these attacks. A visual representation of this anatomy is shown in Figure 3.1.

Importantly, cyber extortion attacks are not a linear process. An adversary may cycle through various components multiple times, or even repeat the entire process as part of a single overarching attack.

The common components of cyber extortion attacks include:

- **Entry:** The adversary gains unauthorized access to the victim's information technology resources.

- **Expansion:** The adversary engages in a recursive process of expanding access. During this phase, the adversary typically gains persistence, conducts reconnaissance, increases the scope of their access, and transfers access to other adversaries.

- **Appraisal:** The adversary assesses the victim's strengths and weaknesses, including data repositories, financial posture, operational infrastructure, and more. This information is used to define and refine the adversary's ongoing attack strategy.

- **Priming:** The adversary modifies the environment to maximize leverage in the following phases. This may include destroying backups, dismantling security, monitoring systems, and more.

- **Leverage:** The adversary actively threatens the confidentiality, integrity, or availability of the victim's information resources. This is commonly accomplished by detonating ransomware, exfiltrating data to systems under the adversary's control, launching a denial-of-service attack, or all of these.

- **Extortion:** The adversary demands payment or services in exchange for restoring availability, integrity, or confidentiality of data or technology resources.

In the following sections, we discuss each of these components in detail, highlight opportunities for early detection, and discuss effective response strategies.

A Word About "Kill Chains" and "Attack Frameworks"

In general, a "kill chain" is a detailed breakdown of the phases and structure of an attack. Originally a military term, this concept was adapted for use in a cybersecurity response by Lockheed Martin[1] in 2011. Each step of the kill chain describes a specific activity or element of an attack and is used to develop defensive strategies that can potentially stop or prevent the attack at each point.

In 2013, MITRE developed the ATT&CK framework[2] and expanded the kill chain model to include detailed tactics and procedures for each of the portions of an attack. The MITRE framework is an excellent model for analyzing and communicating the latest adversary tactics, and understanding different types of cyber extortion attacks.

Since cyber extortion attacks constantly evolve, the authors of this book elected to present a general, high-level "anatomy" of cyber extortion attacks. This anatomy is intended to be used as a foundation for understanding all types of cyber extortion attacks. It can be used in conjunction with a more detailed kill chain model such as the MITRE ATT&CK framework when analyzing specific cases or attack trends.

3.2 Entry

In the entry phase, the adversary gains a foothold inside the victim's technology environment. While this may mean that the adversary gains access to a computer inside the victim's network, it could also be a cloud-based resource such as a virtual machine, a hosted application such as email, or a remote system such as an employee's personal computer. Whatever the point of entry, the adversary will leverage this initial access during the next phase (expansion) to spread throughout the environment.

Common methods of entry include:

- **Phishing:** The adversary sends an email, text, or other message designed to trick the victim into taking an action that gives the adversary information and/or access to the victim's environment.

---

1. "The Cyber Kill Chain," Lockheed Martin, www.lockheedmartin.com/en-us/capabilities/cyber/cyber-kill-chain.html.

2. "ATT&CK," Mitre, https://attack.mitre.org/.

- **Remote logon:** The adversary successfully gains access to an interactive session via a remote logon interface such as Remote Desktop Protocol (RDP), using credentials that have been guessed, stolen, purchased, or otherwise obtained.

- **Software vulnerability:** A vulnerability is found in the victim's Internet-facing applications, servers, or network equipment.

- **Technology supplier attack:** The adversary has access to a supplier's technology resources (such as a software provider or managed service provider [MSP]), whether legitimately or through compromise, and leverages this to gain access to the victim's environment.

Let's discuss how adversaries execute each entry method, and highlight the corresponding opportunities for detection and effective response techniques.

Definition: Indicators of Attack and Compromise

Throughout this book, we will refer to the terms "indicators of attack" and "indicators of compromise." Here are their definitions to set the stage:

- **Indicators of attack** (IoA): Evidence that an adversary is attempting to gain unauthorized access to devices or services. It can include detections of multiple failed login attempts, exploitation attempts, and more.

- **Indicators of compromise** (IoC): Evidence of successful unauthorized access, such as logs of successful authentication, IDS/IPS alerts, or other system behaviors indicative of suspicious activity.

Sources of evidence may include log alerts, forensic artifacts, or system behavior. See Chapter 6 for more detail regarding sources of evidence.

3.2.1 Phishing

Cyber extortion events often start with a phishing attack, in which the adversary sends a message designed to trick the intended victim into taking an action, such as clicking on a link or opening an infected attachment. Phishing kits, which automate the attack process, often sell for $5 to $15 on the dark web.

Phishing attacks can be conducted via any form of messaging, from email to SMS messages to social media. (Carrier pigeon, anyone?[3]) However, cyber extortionists typically aim to get a foothold within an organization's network, and email is the most widely

---

3. D. Waitzman, "A Standard for the Transmission of IP Datagrams on Avian Carrier," April 1, 1990, https://tools.ietf.org/html/rfc1149.

used method for transmitting messages from external to internal senders in these types of environments.

3.2.1.1 Remote Access Trojans

The payload of phishing messages is often a remote access Trojan (RAT), which is a software utility designed to enable an adversary to remotely control or access a computer system.

The features of RATs vary widely, but typically they enable an adversary to do the following:

- Establish a communication channel between the compromised endpoint and a controlling server

- View data about the infected computer

- Control the infected computer remotely

- Evade detection

Sophisticated RATs can include advanced capabilities, enabling the adversary to take the following steps:

- Automatically steal sensitive information from the victim's computer, such as credit/debit card numbers, stored passwords, computer system information, and more

- Interactively log on using Virtual Network Computing (VNC) or a similar program

- Produce reports of user activity, account balances, web history, and more

- Execute advanced privilege escalation attacks and facilitate the adversary's lateral movement

- Install addition malware (including ransomware)

- Leverage the victim's computer(s) to attack other organizations

Malicious Swiss Army knives such as Emotet and Trickbot rely on phishing campaigns to deliver their malware, which adversaries leverage to gain persistent access, steal information, and distribute other threats. The presence of a RAT is often a precursor of a cyber extortion attack.

Traditionally, RATs are delivered via social engineering attacks such as phishing emails, malicious websites, or compromised applications. The adversary who installs a RAT may conduct cyber extortion, or sell or rent access to other criminals, who in turn may choose to conduct cyber extortion themselves.

Opportunities for Detection

When an extortion attack starts with phishing, typically a user device is "patient zero," the first system entered by the adversary. From there, the adversary establishes persistence, which typically involves a reverse shell of some kind (since most devices are blocked by the firewall from direct inbound Internet access). The adversary then leverages stolen credentials or unpatched vulnerabilities to escalate their account privilege, move laterally, and spread throughout the environment.

Specific indicators include the following:

- **Warnings and alerts in email security software:** In some cases, the suspicious email may be automatically quarantined; in others, the email is sent along with a warning to the users, email administrator, or both. The user's email system may also insert a warning in the subject or body of an email if the email meets certain criteria that are in line with characteristics of a phishing attack.

- **User report:** A user may report the phishing message to the response team. When this happens, IT staff should quickly look for other users who received the same or similar phishing emails and remove those emails from other users' inboxes. If any user clicked on a link or attachment in the suspected email, this should activate the organization's incident response processes to ensure that any resulting infection is contained.

- **Malware sample:** By analyzing a malware sample, you can often match it to specific known phishing campaigns or hacker groups and obtain lists of additional indicators to search for in the affected environment.

- **Email application logs:** Application logs may contain warnings related to emails that have been processed, or alerts on blocked attempts, which can help you identify high-risk users, periods of unusual activity, changes in user risk profiles, and more.

- **Antivirus log entries:** When a user clicks on a link or attachment in a phishing email and downloads or runs malware, it may generate an antivirus software alert.

- **Event logs:** Similarly, when a user clicks on a link or attachment in a phishing email that results in code execution, it may generate records of unusual activity such as privileged command execution, scheduled task creation, or application and service starts or stops.

3.2.2   Remote Logon

Many cyber extortion attacks occur because the adversary gained access to a remote logon interface, such as an RDP platform. Quite often, cyber extortionists purchase stolen credentials on the dark web from an initial access broker rather than stealing or guessing them.[4] Then, the extortionists use these credentials to gain a foothold in the network and deploy their attack.

---

4. Victoria Kivilevich and Raveed Laeb, "The Secret Life of an Initial Access Broker," KELA, August 6, 2020, https://ke-la.com/the-secret-life-of-an-initial-access-broker/.

There are good reasons why "open" RDP services have traditionally been the root cause of a large percentage of extortion attacks:

- No special tools are needed to gain remote access to the service.

- RDP is a common protocol that often does not trigger alerts, particularly if it is actively used by employees or an IT administrator.

- The adversary can often pivot through the compromised computer to gain access to other systems using RDP inside the network.

Many organizations use RDP or other remote access tools so that employees can log in to their workstations from home or while traveling, or so IT administrators or vendors can access an internal network remotely at all hours. This is also—and unfortunately—convenient for adversaries, who frequently steal credentials or use password-spraying attacks to gain unauthorized access.

The vast supply of stolen passwords available for free or for sale on the dark web has fueled these attacks. By the summer of 2020, researchers had identified more than 15 billion stolen username and password combinations on the dark web.[5] At the time of this writing, stolen RDP credentials sell for $16 to $24 each.[6]

Many people reuse the same password for multiple accounts.[7] Adversaries leverage this tendency by conducting "credential stuffing" attacks, in which they take stolen credentials and attempt to use them on a wide variety of logon interfaces. When they successfully log in to another account, they can either leverage it themselves or sell access to the newly compromised account.

In 2020, the COVID-19 pandemic suddenly created a rush to remote work. In response, many organizations rapidly enabled remote access with little security oversight, and were compromised as a result.

Opportunities for Detection

Common signs of remote authentication attack or compromise include the following:

- **Failed logon attempts:** When an adversary conducts password spraying or credential stuffing attacks, there are often repeated failed logons (sometimes followed by a successful logon). This can occur at the perimeter, or it can occur within the network as the adversary attempts to move laterally. Unfortunately, many networks are not configured to record or report failed logon attempts on Microsoft Windows hosts within

5. Davey Winder, "New Dark Web Audit Reveals 15 Billion Stolen Logins from 100,000 Breaches," *Forbes*, July 8, 2020, www.forbes.com/sites/daveywinder/2020/07/08/new-dark-web-audit-reveals-15-billion-stolen-logins-from-100000-breaches-passwords-hackers-cybercrime/.

6. "The Price of Stolen Remote Login Passwords Is Dropping. That's a Bad Sign," Threats Hub (blog), July 8, 2022, www.threatshub.org/blog/the-price-of-stolen-remote-login-passwords-is-dropping-thats-a-bad-sign/.

7. "Online Security Survey: Google/Harris Poll," February 2019, https://services.google.com/fh/files/blogs/google_security_infographic.pdf.

their network, meaning that an adversary can automate attempts to authenticate within the network without being detected.

- **Unusual successful logon attempts:** These may include logins at odd times or places, distinct user-agent strings, and "impossible travel" alerts notifying of logons from geographically distant locations in a quick succession.

- **Creation of new accounts:** Such accounts may suddenly be used for remote access.

3.2.3   Software Vulnerability

Adversaries routinely search for exploitable vulnerabilities in widely used software and leverage these to launch cyber extortion attacks, as seen in the Kaseya attacks, as well as adversaries' response to the ProxyShell and Log4j vulnerabilities (among many others). In the case of Accellion, the Cl0p group was able to exploit a critical vulnerability in Accellion FTA devices and steal sensitive data affecting more than 9 million individuals, resulting in a $8.1 million class-action settlement in January 2022.[8]

The "Shodan.io" search engine, which indexes Internet-connected devices, can be used by adversaries and defenders alike to identify potentially vulnerable Internet-facing services.

Timely patch deployment can dramatically reduce the risk of a perimeter device compromise. However, IT administrators are often unaware that their specific firmware or software version is vulnerable, particularly in organizations that have limited resources for IT management. Furthermore, zero-day vulnerabilities exist for perimeter devices, and may be incorporated into high-end exploit kits before the manufacturer has time to identify the issue.

Opportunities for Detection

Common signs of attack via perimeter software vulnerability include the following:

- Alerts on port or vulnerability scans on perimeter devices (although this is a normal occurrence, so it's important to review such alerts carefully and resist the urge to be lulled into complacency)

- Strange error messages relating to that application or system, performance degradation (processes that overwhelm the processor or memory), or system/application crash

- Unexpected outbound connections from servers or even workstations

- Unusual and unrecognized processes or applications running on perimeter systems

---

8. Sara Merken, "Accellion Reaches $8.1 Mln Settlement to Resolve Data Breach Litigation," Reuters, January 13, 2022, www.reuters.com/legal/litigation/accellion-reaches-81-mln-settlement-resolve-data-breach-litigation-2022-01-13/.

Case Study: VPN Vulnerability

A school district in the Midwest was infected with the Dharma ransomware, circa 2021. All of its primary servers were down. While the district managed to hobble along and hold classes, all administrative functions were effectively halted: payroll, supply ordering, bill payment, and so on.

How did the hackers break in? Two things had gone wrong. First, the FortiGate VPN/firewall on which the school district relied had a terrible vulnerability. A patch had been released more than 8 months prior to the attack, but the school district had never applied it. Second, the local administrator accounts on the servers and workstations all shared the same passwords. Once the adversary hacked one system, they were able to log in to all the rest using standard remote access tools. RDP was available to the local administrator, which made the adversary's job even easier.

Once inside, the adversary worked very quickly to encrypt the systems. They logged in for only a few minutes at a time—just long enough to install the ransomware and log out. Once the VPN was compromised, it took only 15 to 20 minutes for the adversaries to detonate ransomware on the primary servers. They didn't bother touching the workstations at all.

Luckily, the school district had backups that were offline and off network, and that were not encrypted. Even so, it took 10 days to get its systems back up and running. Unfortunately, the servers held large volumes of private student information, including medical, mental health, and disciplinary data. The district was required to launch an investigation to determine the risk of a data breach.

Forensic investigators were able to determine that the attack was largely automated. The interactive logons were extremely short and not long enough to support any significant data acquisition or access. This was consistent with most Dharma attacks up to this point. A specialized team of data breach attorneys concluded that there was very low risk of data exposure, and the incident did not meet the definition of a data breach.

3.2.4 Technology Supplier Attack

Frighteningly, the entry point for a cyber extortion attack may be a supplier, such as an IT provider, MSP, equipment vendor, or cloud provider. In 2019, 22 towns in Texas were hit with a devastating REvil ransomware attack, which was traced back to their common MSP.[9] After infiltrating the MSP's network, the adversary leveraged the MSP's normal remote administration tool, ConnectWise Control, to deploy the ransomware throughout

---

9. "Texas Municipalities Hit by REvil/Sodinokibi Paid No Ransom, Over Half Resume Operations," Trend Micro, September 10, 2019, www.trendmicro.com/vinfo/us/security/news/cyber-attacks/texas-municipalities-hit-by-revil-sodinokibi-paid-no-ransom-over-half-resume-operations.

customer networks. Thanks to an effective backup and recovery strategy and strong response plan, the towns' operations were successfully restored within a week.[10]

Cloud providers, too, suffer ransomware attacks that can dramatically impact customers. In May 2020, Blackbaud, a leading provider of cloud-based fundraising software, was hit with a ransomware attack. Customers were notified in July and told that "the cybercriminal removed a copy of a subset of data from our self-hosted (private cloud) environment ... we paid the cybercriminal's demand with confirmation that the copy they removed had been destroyed."[11]

Blackbaud's ransom payment was little consolation to the thousands of customers who stored sensitive data in the cloud, many of whom were required to conduct their own investigations—often at their own expense. Without direct access to evidence, however, their response was hampered. Within just a few months, Blackbaud had been sued in 23 proposed class-action lawsuits, received approximately 160 claims from customers and their attorneys, and been hit with inquiries from a plethora of government agencies and regulators.[12]

Opportunities for Detection

Customers typically have little visibility into the operations and risk management practices of suppliers, even those that have a high level of access to their sensitive data or network resources. They also have no way to directly detect an intrusion into supplier networks and must rely on suppliers to implement effective detection capabilities to prevent the spread of ransomware.

Visible signs of a supplier compromise may include the following:

- Unusual logins or activity from supplier accounts

- Spam emails originating from a supplier's address

- Unusually slow service or full outages

- Notification or media reports of a cybersecurity compromise relating to the supplier

3.3   Expansion

Once an adversary gains access to the target's technology resources, typically they engage in a recursive process in which they establish persistence, conduct reconnaissance, update their attack strategy, and broaden their access. These activities build off each other and often occur at the same time, rather than in a clear linear progression, as illustrated in Figure 3.2.

---

10. O'Ryan Johnson, "MSP at Center of Texas Ransomware Hit: 'We Take Care of Our Customers'," *Channel Program News*, September 17, 2019, www.crn.com/news/channel-programs/msp-at-center-of-texas-ransomware-hit-we-take-care-of-our-customers-.

11. "Security," Blackbaud, www.blackbaud.com/securityincident.

12. Sergui Gatlan, "Blackbaud Sued in 23 Class Action Lawsuits After Ransomware Attack," *Bleeping Computer*, November 3, 2020, www.bleepingcomputer.com/news/security/blackbaud-sued-in-23-class-action-lawsuits-after-ransomware-attack/.

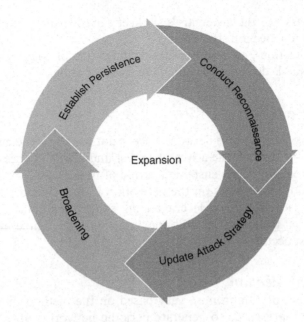

Figure 3.2 The "expansion" phase of a cyber extortion attack

Activities at this stage include the following steps:

- **Establish persistence:** The adversary works to establish sustained, reliable access over an extended period of time and evade detection. To accomplish this, the adversary may install remote access tools, neutralize antivirus software, add new accounts, and so on.

- **Conduct reconnaissance:** The adversary gathers information that will enable them to expand the scope of compromise. This may include network mapping, password cracking and interception, and more.

- **Update the attack strategy:** The adversary uses the information gleaned to refine their goals, plan, and processes.

- **Broadening:** The adversary increases their access to systems, accounts, or other network resources, by escalating privileges, moving laterally through the network, and gaining access to different applications and technology resources.

Along the way, all of the adversary's activities provide defenders with opportunities to detect and eradicate the threat. Each interaction generates unique and identifiable indicators that a security team can monitor to identify the threat.

In particular, during the early stages of an attack, the adversary is at their most vulnerable, since they are likely still unfamiliar with the network topography and may unwittingly create "noise" while engaging in network reconnaissance and other expansion activities.

The method of access and the adversary's skill set can also vary significantly, leading to variations in IoCs and detection strategy.

In the following sections, we describe specific indicators of compromise that can facilitate detection and enable defenders to break the chain of attack.

3.3.1 Persistence

Simply gaining access to a victim's network once is not usually sufficient to gain extensive leverage over a victim. Instead, the adversary must find a way to access resources on the victim's network repeatedly over a sustained period of time.

Frequently, the adversary lurks on the network for an extended period of time (even weeks or months) prior to gaining leverage (e.g., exfiltrating data, detonating ransomware). This means that the target has an opportunity to detect and eradicate the compromise before the worst occurs.

Opportunities for Detection

The specific indicators of compromise vary based on the method of access, but almost universally, the adversary needs to generate periodic network traffic. They often use a command-and-control server, otherwise known as a C2 server, in which an infected endpoint "phones home" to an adversary-controlled server. They may also use standard IT remote access tools such as RDP, Anydesk, or others.

Defenders should be on the lookout for telltale signs of suspicious network activity:

- Suspicious source/destination IP addresses and domains
- Network communication originating from unfamiliar or unexpected processes
- Malformed communications—for example, DNS requests with Base64 encoded content instead of normal URLs
- Unauthorized remote access attempts

3.3.2 Reconnaissance

Now that the adversary has established a consistent method of entering the environment, they will often perform information gathering tasks to better understand the network, its connected devices, and potential targets for further exploitation. The adversary can perform these activities using built-in system tools, third-party software, or both. The adversary will often look for the following items:

- Local IP address range information
- Available subnets
- Domain information

- Available network services

- DNS information

Using information gathered from the network, the adversary can effectively map the environment they now have access to and determine their best options for additional actions after the initial compromise. Additionally, because system administrators often include function descriptions in network computer names (i.e., Fileserver-01 or DC-01), the adversary can specifically target anything that they identify as a potentially high-impact target.

Often, indicators of network reconnaissance are observed during the early stages of an incident. This provides an opportunity to greatly reduce an adversary's ability to spread through the network or possibly stop it entirely.

Opportunities for Detection

The following indicators can signal potentially malicious network reconnaissance:

- Indicators of port scanning (NMAP)

- Increased network resource usage from suspicious computers

- Outbound network traffic spikes at irregular hours

- Increased outbound network traffic

3.3.3 Broadening

Once the initial foothold is secured, the adversary works to expand access to additional network resources, including high-value systems that hold confidential information or can be used to control resources. Along the way, the adversary will attempt to gain additional privileges, specifically targeting domain administrator privileges and administrative access to cloud tenants/applications. Typically, the adversary's activities include at least the following:

- **Privilege escalation:** The adversary attempts to gain a higher level of user privileges. In the early stages, this is often accomplished by scraping credentials from system memory using a tool such as Mimikatz, extracting saved passwords from web browsers, capturing Kerberos tokens, or simply searching the infected host for documented credentials. Once the adversary has moved laterally throughout the network, they may engage in more sophisticated privilege escalation attacks involving theft of private keys, Security Assertion Markup Language (SAML) token forgery, and more.

- **Lateral movement:** The adversary attempts to gain access to other hosts on the network by using stolen passwords, exploiting vulnerabilities, or applying other tactics. Commonly, this process is facilitated by the widespread practice of configuring a static local administrator password shared by all endpoints.

- **Application/cloud access:** The adversary accesses applications and cloud tenants, typically by using stolen passwords or leveraging trust relationships between local systems and services.

If an adversary is able to establish a significant breadth of access, it becomes much more difficult to fully eradicate the threat.

Opportunities for Detection

Common indicators of broadening or expanding access by adversaries include the following:

- Unusual Local Administrator account activities, including network authentications or shared folder access

- Connections to core assets from unusual or unauthorized workstations

- Suspicious application access

- Impossible travel alerts

3.4   Appraisal

Once inside a victim's environment, adversaries often explore and identify any valuable data. This can include information that is useful for the following purposes:

- **Applying pressure in extortion:** The adversary can use regulated data such as electronic protected health information (ePHI) or Social Security numbers to remind the victim of the potential for fines, regulatory investigation, or other government actions. In some cases, victims may store direct contact information for data subjects, whom adversaries can contact and attempt to intimidate.

- **Setting a ransom demand:** Financial details and cyber insurance coverage can inform the amount of the adversary's ransom demand.

- **Sale:** Intellectual property and personally identifiable information (PII) are valuable information that can be sold to third parties.

The adversary may update their attack strategy based on these findings. This may include determining whether to install ransomware, identifying information to exfiltrate, setting a ransom demand, and more.

Opportunities for Detection

Look for the following indicators that an adversary may be appraising your infrastructure (among others):

- Unexpected or unauthorized access to files. Typically this is identified using third-party security software or security information and event management (SIEM) conditional alerting.

- Last read/modified dates on files that are more recent than expected.

- Forwarded or copied emails containing information about insurance coverage, finances, and so on.

3.5 Priming

Prior to gaining leverage, the adversary will typically "prime" the environment to maximize the potential damage and impact. For example, before detonating ransomware, the adversary may modify key network configuration settings and disable antivirus software. These steps are intended to remove roadblocks and improve the chances of a successful detonation during the next stage of the attack.

Adversaries commonly modify and/or disable the following network components:

- Antivirus/security software

- Processes and applications

- Logging/monitoring systems

- Filesystem permissions and configuration

In the remainder of this section, we discuss each of these in turn.

3.5.1 Antivirus and Security Software

Security and antivirus software present hurdles for adversaries and can issue alerts during any phase in the compromise. Signature-based antivirus software may detect and delete the malicious files used by the adversary, or heuristic security software may detect the actions associated with file encryption and stop the process before it completes. As a result, neutralizing security software is often a top priority for the adversary. Typically, this will take the form of one or more of the following actions:

- **Disabling security software:** If the adversary is not worried about making too much noise on the network, a common tactic is to simply disable the active security software currently in use by the victim by killing the active process. This can prevent the software itself from alerting, but it can also set off alerts within the victim's network notifying IT security personnel that something is wrong.

- **Modifying configuration:** In some cases, an adversary may gain access to the centralized console used to manage a security application. If the software allows for global changes, the adversary may modify the configuration so as to neutralize the software across the entire domain. For example, often the adversary will put the security software into a "monitor-only" mode, allowing the adversary to freely distribute malware without interference.

- **Allowlisting signatures:** An adversary with sufficient access may simply allowlist signatures associated with their specific malware in the victim's security software. Like service alteration, this type of change requires access to a central administration platform but will rarely generate an alert from the software itself. While not the most common method of evasion, signature exceptions can often be nearly invisible to the victim.

Opportunities for Detection

The following indicators suggest that security software on your network may be under attack:

- Alerts for nonresponsive antivirus software on endpoints
- State-change alerts from security software

3.5.2   Running Processes and Applications

Many software applications are designed to prevent other services from modifying open files or databases while they are in use, thereby minimizing the risk of corruption. This is especially common in software that maintains a database, such as a SQL server application or a financial application like QuickBooks. One unexpected silver lining is that these applications may inherently block ransomware from encrypting important databases and files if they are actively in use.

Opportunities for Detection

How can you recognize that an adversary may be actively compromising services and applications on your network? Look for the following indicators:

- System health indicators, which you can use to flag modifications of this type
- Signature identification of tools such as ProcessHacker

3.5.3 Logging and Monitoring Software

Event logging and monitoring software can enable victims to:

- Detect anomalous activity quickly and thwart the adversary
- Trace the adversary's activities through the network and close any security gaps
- Quickly eradicate the adversary from the network
- Gain information that could be leveraged in a negotiation

As a result, adversaries often take steps to undermine event logging and monitoring capabilities. Without accurate logging, activities including access times, filesystem exploration, indicators of exfiltration, and other valuable information may no longer be available. Many small and midsized organizations rely on local log files on the affected host, and do not have a central SIEM, which makes the adversary's job easier.

Often, adversaries will undermine event logging and monitoring using the following tactics:

- **Log deletion:** The adversary may delete key elements of the available log data to completely obscure local system activities. These sources of data commonly include Windows Event Log data, Link files, Jump lists, Windows Explorer history, web browser history, and more.

- **Stop services**: If a log collection service like Winlogbeat or Rsyslog is in use to centralize log collection, the adversary may simply kill the export service on the local system, effectively stopping the collection of data.

- **Time-stomping:** The adversary may alter timestamps on log data to make investigating the attack and correlating logs between multiple systems difficult, if not impossible. This may also be done to obscure the identification of files or programs used in the attack.

Opportunities for Detection

The following evidence suggests that logging and monitoring solutions have been tampered with:

- Event log data indicating that logs have been cleared (i.e., Event ID 1102 on a Windows host)

- Use of a specialized utility such as the Sysinternals SDelete tool to make deleted log recovery impossible

- Alerts for data stoppage from monitored hosts

3.5.4   Accounts and Permissions

To ensure an effective rollout of ransomware encryption software, the adversary typically adds at least one account and carefully modifies access permissions to ensure that the ransomware spreads as quickly and effectively as possible. Here are some specific, commonly used tactics:

- **Create new administrative user accounts:** By the time the adversary is in the "priming" phase, they usually already have domain administrator access. However, the adversary will typically create a different account to use for the ransomware deployment. This will make it more difficult for the victim to trace the attack back to the actual accounts that the adversary used prior to detonation.

- **Add the account to the "remote users" groups:** This gives the newly created user access to all endpoints that have remote access enabled.

- **Gain unauthorized network share access:** This enables the ransomware to encrypt shared drives and connected devices (including, much of the time, backups).

- **Perform unauthorized software installations:** The adversary uses common administrative tools (such as PsExec) to automate deployment of the ransomware.

Opportunities for Detection
Set up logging and automated alerts for the following indicators:

- New or unknown administrative user accounts

- Increases in remote connection activity or unusual accounts accessing remote services

- Unauthorized access to network shares

- Installation of unauthorized software

3.6   Leverage

To actually launch an extortion attack, the adversary first needs to gain leverage by actively threatening the confidentiality, integrity, and/or availability of information resources. Most commonly, adversaries accomplish this by encrypting files with ransomware, or stealing sensitive data so they can later threaten to publish it if they do not receive payment.

In this section, we discuss the two most common scenarios: ransomware detonation and data exfiltration. Keep in mind that these are only selected examples—there are many other ways for adversaries to gain leverage over a victim. Ultimately, adversaries are limited only by their imaginations.

3.6.1 Ransomware Detonation

The detonation phase represents the last piece of "hands-on" access that an adversary will normally execute. Once the adversary has mapped their targets, obtained sufficient access, and potentially exfiltrated everything they want, the final fireworks show at the end of the incident is the detonation of a ransomware executable. This phase of the attack is often the first indicator of compromise a victim sees directly and, unfortunately, at this point it is usually too late to prevent the attack.

An adversary can distribute and detonate their encryption software in many different ways. Here are three common methods:

- **Group policy:** An adversary with access to a domain controller and domain administrator credentials can use the software distribution system built into most Windows networks as a springboard to distribute their malicious software. This activity is typically accompanied by the creation of a scheduled task that can simultaneously detonate the ransomware payload on all computers within the victim's environment. This shortens the overall period in which a defender could stop the attack, and also makes investigating the attack more difficult because it can effectively obfuscate the origin of the malware execution.

- **System administration toolkit:** Adversaries are frequently observed using the PsExec toolkit or similar utilities to distribute their malicious payload. Configuring a network to accept this type of software push is trivial, and the previous expansion steps taken by the adversary usually provide them with exactly what they need to initiate this form of detonation. The PsExec utility is part of the Microsoft SysInternals toolkit and automates the process of distributing executable programs to domain-connected hosts.

- **Manual distribution and detonation:** In some cases, the adversary may choose to avoid automated distribution and simply install and execute the encryption software manually on selected targets within the overall network. This tactic is observed in both small networks with a minimal number of overall targets and large organizations. In the latter case, an adversary is more concerned with encrypting the "crown jewels" of the network than with encrypting every individual host.

Once the ransomware payload is detonated, the exact sequence of events varies depending on the strain. However, there are some common actions that the software typically executes:

- Adds malicious software to startup sequences, which facilitates persistence between reboots.

- Creates ransom notes.

- Deletes shadow volume copies, to prevent file restoration.

- Enumerates drives, often starting with drive A:\ and moving alphabetically through the hosts' mapped drives.

- Encrypts files. Most ransomware strains encrypt a targeted list of files, often based on a preloaded list of file extensions.
- Encrypts backup files once found on the network.

Opportunities for Detection

While some might seem obvious, here are the signs indicating that ransomware has been detonated on a network:

- Unauthorized software installations
- Unauthorized or unusual scheduled task creation
- Registry modification
- Visible ransom notes
- Encrypted files

3.6.2 Exfiltration

The adversary may deliberately exfiltrate data to use it as leverage in extortion, commit fraud, or sell it. This type of exfiltration is distinct from the network reconnaissance discussed in Section 3.2.3, in that the purpose is to gain some benefit beyond simply increasing access.

For example, the Conti playbook that was leaked in 2021 (discussed in Section 2.9.6) illustrated how adversaries now purposefully search for financial documents, accounting information, client data, and more.[13] The adversaries also seek out details that are specifically useful for negotiating extortion payments, such as cyber insurance policies. Today, this has become standard practice, and the exfiltration often occurs quickly and in bulk.

Adversaries could exfiltrate data from any repository, including systems on a local network, mobile device, or cloud repository. In today's cloud-driven technology landscape, sensitive data is often stored via Amazon S3, Dropbox, SharePoint, and other cloud-based storage systems. Adversaries often access the data held within the cloud using credentials and access keys obtained during their takeover of their victims' local network, and vice versa.

Because the adversary might transfer or sell access to the victim's technology environment at any point, it is entirely possible for a victim's data to be stolen multiple times by different adversaries.

Adversaries commonly use the following tools for exfiltrating data:

- **Mainstream cloud services:** The advantage of these services—which include Dropbox, Google, OneDrive, and others—is that they are often already supported by the local environment and can blend with normal usage.

---

13. Leaked Conti playbook, September 2021, translated from Russian to English using Microsoft and author research.

- **File transfer programs:** The adversary can use common Windows utilities such as WinSCOP or Powershell to send data to a server under their control. Typically the data is encrypted or encoded in transit.[14]

- **Anonymous file sharing services:** MEGA, FreeFileSync, and similar services are very convenient aids for adversaries, since they require little effort to set up and are free up to a certain volume of data. MEGA has become particularly popular. It includes built-in end-to-end encryption, making it difficult for data loss prevention systems to detect, and the user can transfer files using a web browser or desktop app. Since these services are not normally used in a standard enterprise environment, it can be easy to detect and block applications of this type.

Three data exfiltration patterns are commonly seen in cyber extortion cases:

- Automated RAT exfiltration

- Mass repository theft

- Curated theft

Each of these exfiltration patterns leaves a different footprint in the network and may require different response tactics. In the following subsections, we discuss each in turn.

3.6.2.1 Automated RAT Exfiltration

Quite often, a RAT installed on the victim's network is configured to automatically steal files and upload them to a system controlled by the adversary. When this occurs, the RAT typically has a configuration file that allows the operator to select files based on an extension and/or keywords in the filename. For example, the authors of this book studied one widely used RAT, Atmos, which shipped with a default configuration that exfiltrated all files with .pdf and .docx extensions, plus any documents containing the keywords "bank" or "payroll" in the filename. In this case, as in many others, the adversary's goal was likely to facilitate financial fraud.

Modern RATs are sophisticated and typically include built-in techniques to help the user avoid detection. When files are automatically exfiltrated, typically the data transfer is slowly metered so that it doesn't set off network monitoring alerts.

RATs typically transfer data over the built-in command-and-control channel, which is often encrypted, again for evasion purposes. Although the functionality of RATs varies, the data normally winds up on a server under the adversary's control—often another hacked server that is part of a botnet. Depending on the RAT's level of sophistication, the adversary may even have point-and-click access to view and sort stolen files through the RAT's interface.

---

14. Jeremy Kennelly, Kimberly Goody, and Joshua Shilko, "Navigating the MAZE: Tactics, Techniques and Procedures Associated with MAZE Ransomware Incidents," Mandiant (blog), May 7, 2020, www.fireeye.com/blog/threat-research/2020/05/tactics-techniques-procedures-associated-with-maze-ransomware-incidents.html.

3.6.2.2 Mass Repository Theft

Today, "smash-and-grab" data exfiltration is a popular technique. Many adversaries enter the network with the goal of stealing data, and invest little time in curation before theft. Why bother sorting through the data while on the victim's network, when the adversary can steal it en masse and analyze it on their own systems?

In cyber extortion cases, typically there is no need to pick through data extensively to accomplish the adversary's objectives. Once the adversary has access to the victim's network, they seek out large data repositories and transfer them out in bulk. Then, during the negotiation phase, they can share screenshots of the stolen data or provide file lists. No matter if the bulk of the stolen files is unimportant; the presence of even a few documents containing PII can spell reputational disaster for the victim.

In some cases, bulk file transfer can cause significant headaches for the victim. Once the victim is aware that data may have been stolen, typically the next step is to take an inventory of the potentially exposed data and create a notification list. Firms that conduct e-discovery normally charge by the gigabyte, so even if the majority of the stolen files contain no sensitive data, the cost for verifying this fact may be large.

In some cases, the adversary "stages" data on a single system prior to exfiltration. This process gives the adversary time to organize files, ensure everything is compressed and encrypted, and then exfiltrate it all at once, giving the victim limited time to respond before all the data flies out the door. The Lockbit extortion gang was observed staging data and organizing files based on the system from which they were stolen, and then copying the directories to a single MEGA console before uploading them. However, quite often adversaries do not bother "staging" data at all, but simply copy it directly from the hacked systems.

As RaaS kits become more automated, adversaries are curating less and automatically exfiltrating data more. The Netwalker RaaS platform advertised "[a] fully automatic blog, into which the merged data of the victim goes, the data is published according to your settings."[15] The RaaS automatically exfiltrated the victim's data to MEGA, and then created a blog where the MEGA links would appear at the proper time.[16]

3.6.2.3 Curated Theft

In some cases, an adversary may steal only specific files of value, such as source code, databases of PII, or other material. To accomplish this, the adversary needs to first identify these files on the network, typically through manual examination. Often, content of this type is curated due to the size of the repository, or because the attack is targeted and the adversary has a predetermined goal in mind.

---

15. Jim Walter, "NetWalker Ransomware: No Respite, No English Required," Sentinel Labs, June 4, 2020, https://labs.sentinelone.com/netwalker-ransomware-no-respite-no-english-required/.

16. Lawrence Abrams, "Ransomware Recruits Affiliates with Huge Payouts, Automated Leaks," *Bleeping Computer*, May 15, 2020, www.bleepingcomputer.com/news/security/ransomware-recruits-affiliates-with-huge-payouts-automated-leaks/.

For example, the gaming company CD Projekt Red was hit with a ransomware attack in 2021, when adversaries specifically leveraged stolen source code in their ransom note. "We have dumped FULL copies of the source codes from your Perforce server for Cyberpunk 2077, Witcher 3, Gwent and the unreleased version of Witcher 3!!!"[17]

Due to the size of the source code repositories, and the fact that these were stored in the dedicated Perforce software, exfiltration of this material was undoubtedly purposeful and curated. The adversary also explained that they had stolen materials relating to accounting, human resources, and more, but specifically leveraged the intellectual property in their extortion efforts. "If we will not come to an agreement," they threatened, "then your source code will be sold or leaked online, and your documents will be sent to our contacts in gaming journalism."[18]

Opportunities for Detection

Signs of data exfiltration may include the following unexplained or unusual activities:

- Increases in network traffic, particularly outbound direction
- Connections to cloud file sharing services
- Use of MEGA and other third-party file sharing websites that are not typically used
- File movement and staging activities
- Connected sessions with unknown or suspicious destinations

3.7 Extortion

The final phase of a cyber extortion incident is often the loudest and most aggressive. The adversary has already taken the time to infect the network, compromise assets, exfiltrate data, and/or encrypt the filesystem, and now the adversary is looking to monetize the attack.

With the need for stealth gone, the adversary begins the process of extortion. The primary extortion notification methods typically include:

- Passive notification (i.e., the ransom note)
- Active notification (e.g., phone calls, voicemails)
- Third-party outreach (e.g., direct communications with customers, data subjects)
- Publication (e.g., dark web blogs, Telegram channels, Twitter feeds)

We discuss each of these tactics in turn in the following subsections.

---

17. Catalin Cimpanu, "CD Projekt Red Game Studio Discloses Ransomware Attack, Extortion Attempt," *ZDNet*, February 9, 2021, www.zdnet.com/article/cd-projekt-red-game-studio-discloses-ransomware-attack-extortion-attempt/.

18. Lily Hay Newman, "*Cyberpunk 2077* Maker Was Hit with a Ransomware Attack—and Won't Pay Up," *Wired*, February 9, 2021, www.wired.com/story/cd-projekt-red-ransomware-hack-cyberpunk-2077-source-code/.

3.7.1   Passive Notification

The adversary typically makes it obvious to the victim that they are being extorted. This can be, and often is, as simple as a ransom note left on the desktop. However, many adversaries have leveled up, and now include multimedia such as audio versions of the ransom demand.

The ransom note commonly includes the following information:

- An announcement of what happened

- Instructions for how to recover files

- A clear deadline (this may be a countdown timer or a simple deadline)

- Contact information for the adversary (typically an email address or link to a portal)

- Advice for obtaining cryptocurrency

- Psychological pressure, such as threats (e.g., "Your business is at serious risk."[19]) as well as reassurances (e.g., "But do not worry. You have a chance! It is easy to recover in a few steps."[20])

Figure 3.3 shows an example of a ransom note left by the Maze hacking group in 2020.[21]

```
Attention!

-----------------------------
| What happened?
-----------------------------

All your files, documents, photos, databases, and other important data are safely encrypted with reliable algorithms.
You cannot access the files right now. But do not worry. You have a chance! It is easy to recover in a few steps.

-----------------------------
| How to get my files back?
-----------------------------

The only method to restore your files is to purchase a unique for you private key which is securely stored on our servers.
To contact us and purchase the key you have to visit our website in a hidden TOR network.

There are general 2 ways to reach us:

1) [Recommended] Using hidden TOR network.

   a) Download a special TOR browser: https://www.torproject.org/
   b) Install the TOR Browser.
   c) Open the TOR Browser.
```

Figure 3.3 A sample Maze ransom note from the LMG Security malware lab

(Illustration courtesy of LMG Security)

---

19. Ryuk ransom note, https://blog.malwarebytes.com/wp-content/uploads/2019/12/ryuk-ransom-note-versions-600x415.png.

20. Alexandre Mundo, "Ransomware Maze," McAfee (blog), March 26, 2020, www.mcafee.com/blogs/other-blogs/mcafee-labs/ransomware-maze/.

21. Maze ransom note, LMG Laboratory, 2020.

3.7.2 Active Notification

The adversary might actively engage in communicating with the victim throughout the extortion phase. This commonly includes sending emails, but can also involve phone calls, text messages, voicemails, Telegram messages, and other methods. Typically, the aim is to intimidate the victim and demonstrate the adversary's level of access. In many cases, adversaries monitor the victim's emails and may even make snide comments on current response activities.

3.7.3 Third-Party Outreach

Adversaries have been known to reach out directly to third parties affected by the compromise, including customers, patients, data subjects, and business associates, to encourage them to pressure the victim organization into paying a ransom. In some cases, they may also reach out to competitors or others in an effort to sell stolen data.

As discussed in Section 2.7, The Dark Overlord (TDO) cyber extortion group hacked the Johnston Community School District Iowa in 2017 and texted threatening messages to parents. More recently, cyber extortion gangs have taken to leveraging scalable communications methods such as email so as to connect directly with data subjects and affiliates. For example, one convenience store chain that was extorted by the Clop ransomware gang discovered that its customers had received the following email notifying them of the compromise:[22]

> Good day!
>
> If you received this letter, you are a customer, buyer, partner or employee of [VICTIM-REDACTED]. The company has been hacked, data has been stolen and will soon be released as the company refuses to protect its peoples' data.
>
> We inform you that information about you will be published on the darknet (http://█████████████████████████████) if the company does not contact us.
>
> Call or write to this store and ask to protect your privacy!!!!

3.7.4 Publication

Adversaries may publish extortion notification on dark web sites, Telegram channels,[23] social media platforms, and more, anticipating that victims will view their posts and receive pressure from third parties. In addition, adversaries routinely leverage the mainstream media, particularly when threatening to publish data, as discussed in Section 2.8.

---

22. Brian Krebs, "Ransom Gangs Emailing Victim Customers for Leverage," Krebs on Security, April 5, 2020, https://krebsonsecurity.com/2021/04/ransom-gangs-emailing-victim-customers-for-leverage/.

23. Lily Hay Newman, "The Lapsus$ Hacking Group Is Off to a Chaotic Start," Wired, March 15, 2022, www.wired.com/story/lapsus-hacking-group-extortion-nvidia-samsung/.

3.8   Conclusion

In this chapter, we stepped through the anatomy of a cyber extortion attack, including each of its components: entry, expansion, appraisal, priming, leverage, and extortion. Along the way, we described the adversary's activities in depth, and provided indicators of compromise that can help responders identify these activities.

In the next chapter, we will discuss the initial response once an intrusion has metastasized into a cyber extortion attack.

3.9   Your Turn!

Every cyber extortion incident is unique. The response team's options and priorities will vary depending on the victim organization's industry, size, and location, as well as the details of the incident itself.

Based on what you learned in this chapter, let's think through key elements of a cyber extortion attack.

Step 1: Build Your Victim

Choose one characteristic from each of the three columns to describe your victim's organization:

Industry	Size	Location
Hospital	Large	Global
Financial institution	Midsized	United States
Manufacturer	Small	European Union
Law firm		Australia
University		India
Cloud service provider		Country/location of your choice
Organization of your choice		

Step 2: Choose Your Incident Scenario

Select from one of the following incident scenarios:

A	Ransomware strikes! All of the victim's files have been locked up, including central data repositories, servers, and workstations.
B	A well-known cyber extortion gang claims to have stolen all of the victim's most sensitive data and threatens to release it unless the victim pays a very large ransom demand. The gang posts the victim's name on their dark web leaks site, along with samples of supposedly stolen data.
C	Double extortion! Both A and B occur at the same time.
D	The victim is hit with a denial-of-service attack on their Internet-facing infrastructure that slows their access and services to a crawl. The adversary threatens to continue and even escalate the attack unless a ransom is paid.

Step 3: Discussion Time

Your victim organization has experienced a cyber extortion event. Given what you know about the victim and the scenario, answer the following questions:

1. Should the victim organization assume that the extortion demand was the adversaries' only activity relating to their environment? Why or why not?

2. Name the steps that adversaries often take in the leadup to cyber extortion.

3. Describe at least one way that the victim can often detect early signs of this type of attack prior to the extortion phase.

4. What are the most common methods of entry that the victim organization should check for?

5. Which means might the adversary use to try to notify the victim of the extortion demand?

Chapter 4

The Crisis Begins!

Don't panic when the crisis is happening or you won't enjoy it.

—Fiachra Murphy, age 9

Learning Objectives

- Understand that cyber extortion is a crisis
- Recognize common signs of a cyber extortion attack, even at the earliest stages
- Identify who should be involved during a cyber extortion response
- Understand how to triage events to effectively prioritize response efforts
- Learn how to develop an effective response strategy and keep it updated

---

When you're hit with a cyber extortion attack, every second counts. You need to immediately work to triage your response and develop your initial strategy.

Crises never play out exactly as responders expect. Adversaries routinely subject their victims to new and ever-changing tactics. Don't expect anyone to whip out the manual when your network is down and cybercriminals are leaving voicemails at 3 a.m. threatening to leak your data on the dark web.

Instead, think of your response processes as muscles in the body. Your muscles are designed to work together to achieve a wide spectrum of goals, directed by your brain. Similarly, your response processes should enable you to react to a wide variety of situations.

Adversaries' tactics constantly change, and every victim's environment is unique. In turn, no two cyber extortion crises are the same. When preparing for such an open-ended situation, it's important to build a response function that is flexible and enables you to adapt to the situation.

In this chapter, we step through the critical activities that occur when a cyber extortion incident is detected. We discuss techniques for recognizing the signs of a cyber extortion attack (ideally before it metastasizes into a full-blown acute crisis). Next, we present a model for conducting triage and prioritizing response efforts and discuss how to craft an effective response strategy. Along the way, we point out ways that you can operate efficiently during this critical stage.

4.1   Cyber Extortion Is a Crisis

Cyber extortion creates a crisis for the victim—an "unstable condition involving an impending abrupt or significant change that requires urgent attention and action to protect life, assets, property or the environment."[1] Crisis management expert Steven Fink further defines a crisis as a situation that carries the following risks:[2]

- Escalating in intensity

- Falling under close media or government scrutiny

- Interfering with the normal operations of the business

- Jeopardizing the positive public image presently enjoyed by the organization or its officers

- Damaging the organization's bottom line in any way

Clearly, cyber extortion crises create risks in all of these categories and should be managed as part of the organization's crisis response program.

Often, swift and skilled action is needed to avert disaster or mitigate damages. On the one hand, a cyber extortion crisis can easily devolve into a chaotic downward spiral, if not carefully controlled. On the other hand, an effective response can facilitate resolution and enable the organization to learn and improve in the long run. As Merriam-Webster says, a crisis is a "turning point for better or worse."[3]

Definition: Phases of a Crisis

According to expert Steven Fink, every crisis moves through four phases:[4]

- **Prodromal:** The "pre-crisis" phase, in which there are warnings or precursors that, if acted upon, can enable responders to minimize the impact of the crisis.

- **Acute:** The "time when chaos reigns supreme," according to Fink. At this stage, the crisis has become visible outside the organization, and leadership must address it.

---

1. ISO 22300:2021, www.iso.org/obp/ui/#iso:std:iso:22300:ed-3:v1:en.

2. Steven Fink, *Crisis Management: Planning for the Inevitable* (Bloomington, IN: IUniverse, 2000).

3. "Crisis," Merriam-Webster, www.merriam-webster.com/dictionary/crisis.

4. Steven Fink, *Crisis Communications* (New York, NY: McGraw-Hill, 2013), p. 46.

> • **Chronic:** During this stage, "litigation occurs, media exposes are aired, internal investigations are launched, government oversight investigations commence . . . ." As the name implies, the "chronic" stage can last for years.
>
> • **Resolution:** The crisis is settled, and normal activities resume.

Ideally, responders will recognize the signs of a prodromal event, and move directly from there to resolution, skipping the acute and chronic phases. For example, IT staff may quickly identify signs of a remote access Trojan (RAT) in the network and eradicate it before an adversary ever has an opportunity to infiltrate, steal data, or install ransomware. When cyber extortion events hit the headlines, however, you've reached the acute stage of the crisis, and there's no turning back.

4.2   Detection

Before the victim can respond to a cyber extortion attack, they need to realize that one is occurring. A cyber extortion event can be detected either early (in the prodromal phase) or later (in the acute phase). Once it has metastasized into a full-blown acute crisis, the risks are high. Ideally, victim organizations should routinely conduct threat hunting to detect the prodromal signs of a cyber extortion event, when the attack is still in the entry or expansion phase. See Section 5.8 for more information about threat hunting.

Let's take a moment to discuss key signs of a cyber extortion attack before we dive into triage and first response.

Most cyber extortion attacks are detected in the acute phase, after the attack has been fully launched. However, it's also possible (and ideal) to detect the attack in the prodromal (symptomatic) phase when the pieces have been put in place but the attack itself has not been launched.

Recall from Chapter 3 that typically the adversary lurks in the environment for days, weeks, or even months before launching a cyber extortion threat. As a result, early signs of a cyber extortion attack are often the same as a general internal compromise, and may include the following:

• **Alerts:** Monitoring systems such as antivirus, anti-malware, and endpoint monitoring solutions may detect some activity or file signatures related to extortion-related malware and send alerts. Threat hunting, or actively searching for malware, can also identify abnormal or suspicious files. See Chapter 5 for more information about threat hunting.

• **Unusual authentication activity:** Keep an eye out for suspicious authentication activity, such as an increase in the number of failed authentication attempts, locked accounts, or logins from unusual or unexpected IP addresses.

- **New, unauthorized accounts:** Once an adversary gains access, they may attempt to create a new privileged account. Review your Active Directory or authentication structure for accounts that have been created recently or that are not recognized as a legitimate administrator of the domain.

- **Unexplained applications:** Applications such as Mimikatz and Cobalt Strike have valid uses as penetration testing tools, but adversaries have also been known to use them in cyberattacks. If the organization is not actively undergoing penetration testing, the presence of such tools may be considered suspect. The presence of any kind of malware should immediately raise red flags, and especially signs of a RAT (discussed in Chapter 3).

After an attack, signs of a cyber extortion attack are usually very obvious and may include the following:

- **Ransom note:** Ransom notes might be found in a variety of places, including on the desktops of servers or workstations, in directories with encrypted files, printed on printers, or in email.

- **Direct communications:** If the adversary has studied your organization, they may target individuals within the organization, and perhaps place a direct call and attempt to pressure the organization into paying a ransom. Some adversarial groups also use social media accounts to taunt or try to pressure the organization. For example, they may use a Twitter account to direct message the organization or post publicly and tag the organization in an attempt to shame it into paying.

- **Inaccessible resources:** Many victims detect a ransomware cyber extortion event when their help desk receives calls from users who can't open any of their files.

Once an attack has been detected, it's time to respond.

Tip: Understanding Normal

One of the best tools in an incident responder's arsenal is understanding what "normal" looks like in an environment. When you review logs, alerts, and traffic patterns regularly, you are much more likely to quickly catch abnormal traffic or behavior.

4.3   Who Should Be Involved?

People are your most important asset during a cyber extortion crisis. Make sure each incident has a clearly assigned incident manager who will maintain responsibility for oversight of the response, communication, and status. The incident manager, in turn, can ensure that other people are looped in as appropriate. Note that the assigned incident manager can (and often does) change as a cyber extortion evolves, particularly if the impact increases.

Key players in a cyber extortion response typically include the following people:

- **IT:** Responding to a cyber extortion event requires a huge investment of time and energy from all members of the incident response team, especially the IT staff. Your existing IT staff is probably sized to support business as usual. Consider bringing in supplemental IT contractors to assist with imaging new computers, moving files, or assisting users as the rebuilt systems come online. If you already leverage a managed service provider (MSP) or outside IT consultants in your day-to-day operations, make sure to involve them in your response planning.

- **Leadership:** Your leadership team may be called upon to make fast and difficult decisions in a cyber extortion crisis. It is best if they are familiar with core concepts and tradeoffs ahead of time. What's more, during a cyber extortion crisis, your leadership may need to procure emergency sources of funding, deal with the media, and provide updates and explanations to a board of directors or shareholders. This is quite a tightrope act, and it is wise to review and discuss it ahead of time.

- **Finance:** Key members of the finance team may be called upon to move funds quickly, apply for emergency funding, review cash flows, or engage in other tasks to support the organization.

- **Human resources:** A crisis is unnerving for all staff, and cyber extortion can be particularly frightening and embarrassing. In some cases, sensitive employee information is exposed. The human resources team should be prepared to proactively engage employees and field (often very difficult) questions.

- **Other internal staff:** Cyber extortion cases can involve a myriad of people, depending on the size and unique structure of your organization. This may include risk management, legal counsel, marketing, communications, public relations (PR), physical security, and many others.

- **Insurance:** If your organization has cyber extortion insurance or related coverage such as breach response support or a business interruption endorsement, you may choose to involve the insurer. Make sure to contact the insurer within the specified notification window, so as to increase the likelihood that response activities will be covered. In many cases, the insurer must approve the response strategy prior to execution. Once you've filed a claim, your insurance provider may have preestablished relationships with individuals or organizations that specialize in assisting organizations with cyber extortion events. It can connect you with legal counsel, ransom negotiators, ransom payment processors, and even companies to support call center and notification efforts.

Tip: Cyber Insurance and Vendor Selection

To receive coverage for expenses or losses, you may be required to select vendors from your insurer's panel, such as your external legal counsel or incident response firm. In addition, you may need to get approval from your insurer before making key decisions, such as whether to pay a ransom.

It's wise to identify your chosen vendors in advance and get preapproval from your insurer to use your preferred vendor. Depending on the insurer, this process may be as simple as sending over a rate sheet and receiving email confirmation, or it may be more complex, involving a more in-depth vendor vetting/approval process.

Whatever your situation, you want to make sure that you will have the opportunity to get to know your chosen vendors in advance, and ideally include them in tabletop exercises and other training exercises. This will help to ensure a smooth response and reduce delays when a crisis occurs, which will improve your outcomes.

- **External legal counsel:** Although you might already have inside counsel or an external attorney, strongly consider contacting an attorney who has specialized experience with cyber extortion, including familiarity with laws and regulations regarding ransom payments and data breaches. In some cases, your cyber insurer may require you to involve external legal counsel to be eligible for coverage down the road.

- **Incident response/forensics firm:** An experienced incident response firm can help you navigate the dicey waters of a cyber extortion case in order to recovery quickly, reduce the risk of reinfection, and ensure the threat is fully eradicated. It is especially helpful if the team you engage has experience in cyber extortion. If there is a potential data breach, the firm can assist you in quickly gathering evidence and conducting a forensic investigation.

- **Ransom negotiator:** An experienced ransom negotiator helps to manage your relationship with the adversary if you need to interact with them. These discussions can be delicate, and a wrong move can have long-lasting consequences.

- **Public relations:** Control the messaging regarding your incident from the beginning. Beyond public messaging, a good PR team can provide templated language for help desk staff who are receiving employee calls or front desk personnel; they can also handle tasks such as speaking to the public, coaching executives, and fielding media calls.

- **Key technology suppliers:** Consider involving key suppliers such as MSPs, software providers, cloud vendors, or others in your response planning. Adversaries are increasingly leveraging access to suppliers in an effort to gain a foothold within the victim organization. You may need to coordinate with suppliers to preserve evidence or contain threats that stem from their environments.

- **Law enforcement and/or regulators:** Your relationship with law enforcement can prove invaluable in a cyber extortion event. In some cases, law enforcement may have access to special decryptors that are not publicly available. Notifying law enforcement can also work to your advantage after the fact. For example, the U.S. Department of Treasury has said that the Office of Foreign Assets Control (OFAC) "will also consider a company's full and timely cooperation with law enforcement both during and after a ransomware attack to be a significant mitigating factor when evaluating a possible enforcement outcome."[5]

Case Study: FBI Decryptor

A financial services organization in northern California was hit with a ransomware attack carried out by the BitPaymer ransomware group. The authors were called in to respond. This was the second attack in the same month that the organization had suffered. During the first attack, prior to the authors' involvement, the organization fortunately had backups that the adversary had not encrypted, and it was able to restore the data.

Unfortunately, the organization chose to move on with business without performing a full investigation. Unbeknownst to the organization, it had restored its data using backups that contained the Dridex RAT. This was the adversary's original backdoor into the network, and it was reinstalled during the restoration process.

Days after resuming business, the victim got a call from the FBI. The agent delivered an ominous warning: The adversary was still in the network, and was actively communicating with a server that the FBI was monitoring. Based on the malicious activity, another ransomware attack was likely imminent.

The CIO went home for the night, planning on investigating in the morning. But it would be too late. The next day, employees arrived at work to find their workstations and files completely locked. Ransomware had been detonated overnight. Workstations, servers, databases, and more were all encrypted. This time, even the backups were locked up. The criminals had doubled the ransom demand, angry that they had to repeat their work. The organization had no good options for recovery—or so executives thought.

---

5. U.S. Department of the Treasury, "Advisory on Potential Sanctions Risks for Facilitating Ransomware Payments," October 1, 2020, https://home.treasury.gov/system/files/126/ofac_ransomware_advisory_10012020_1.pdf.

Luckily for them, the FBI had been working on an experimental decryptor of its own, which was specifically designed to decrypt files locked up by the BitPaymer ransomware strain. Since the victim had no other good options, the authors obtained a copy of the FBI's decryptor and ran it on the encrypted files.

Happily, the decryption (mostly) succeeded. It effectively recovered about 80% of the victim's data, and the remaining data consisted of archived client files with paper backups. The victim did not need to pay a ransom, thanks to the FBI's experimental decryptor.

4.4   Conduct Triage

Imagine a 32-car pileup on the freeway. People are injured, and some are trapped in their cars. Others have successfully exited, but now stand in the midst of the wreckage with the potential to be hit by oncoming traffic or cars unable to stop before joining the pileup. Emergency first responders arrive on scene. They can't be everywhere at once. So what do they do in the face of such chaos? They triage. They prioritize and coordinate their rescue efforts according to criticality of injuries and the immediate risk.

When a cyber extortion event occurs, a similar process must take place. There is far too much to be done to tackle everything at once. First responders need to evaluate the risk and come up with a plan. In this section, we discuss the "triage" process.

Definition: Triage

Historically, the term *triage* has been used medically to describe actions taken to sort and prioritize people who need emergency treatment. Merriam-Webster defines triage[6] as follows:

1: a: the sorting of and allocation of treatment to patients and especially battle and disaster victims according to a system of priorities designed to maximize the number of survivors
   b: the sorting of patients (as in an emergency room) according to the urgency of their need for care
2: the assigning of priority order to projects on the basis of where funds and other resources can be best used, are most needed, or are most likely to achieve success

---

6. "Triage," Merriam-Webster, www.merriam-webster.com/dictionary/triage.

In a cyber extortion attack, triage should occur immediately following the victim's recognition of the attack. The response team needs to evaluate the impact of the attack quickly and then cooperatively create a plan. Decisions made during the triage phase will have a powerful effect on the outcome; the results will affect the subsequent response strategy and the ultimate outcome.

4.4.1 Why Is Triage Important?

Just like emergency responders on the scene of the large accident, your incident response team cannot respond to every outage, impact, or risk at once. Therefore, the team must work together to assess the current state of the attack and determine which actions and activities will provide the biggest immediate relief. If an organization has not created and practiced an incident response plan ahead of a real attack, they are likely to skip triage altogether. Their response becomes chaotic, with responders tripping over each other, duplicating efforts, overwriting changes, and losing valuable evidence. Worst of all, their efforts are likely to increase the damage by failing to stop the attack quickly and eject the adversary from the network.

An effective triage process can ensure that the response team appropriately prioritizes efforts and maximizes the value of the resources at their disposal.

4.4.2 Example Triage Framework

Although triage is an important step, keep in mind that it will happen quickly and often while the steps of first response are being pulled together—picture the emergency department of a hospital after the crash victims are brought in. Responders need simple, clear guidelines for prioritizing and taking action. A *triage framework* is a reference chart that provides responders with easy-to-understand diagnostic guidelines and next steps for response.

Keep your triage framework straightforward and simple, so that the first responders can make decisions quickly and confidently. Table 4.1 shows an example of a simple cybersecurity triage framework:

Table 4.1 A Simple Cybersecurity Triage Framework

Triage Scale Category	Response Time	Description	Indicators
Immediate	ASAP (<1 hour)	Business operation outage, credible cyber extortion threat, data exposure, current unauthorized access	Operational outage, extortion, data publication on the Internet/dark web, indicators of current unauthorized access, compromised email accounts, alert from law enforcement

Triage Scale Category	Response Time	Description	Indicators
Urgent	< 4 hours	Threat requiring time-sensitive response to avoid an outage and/or data exposure	Signs of malware infection, failed command-and-control communication, general industry-wide alerts, potentially compromised account
Standard	1–2 business days	Potentially threatening, situational urgency	Phishing emails, intermittent alerts of malicious software, HR policy violations
Scheduled	2 weeks+	Less urgent or administrative/policy issues	Minor technical glitches in security software, logging configuration issues, forensics in support of litigation, policy updates, process reviews, etc.

4.4.3   Assess the Current State

The first people to detect signs of a cyber extortion attack need to quickly evaluate the current state to properly assess the impact and risk and to determine the appropriate next steps. However, these individuals may not be subject-matter experts. Depending on the type of organization, staffing levels, time of day, and other factors, they may be entry-level IT workers, managers, or PR staff. Make sure to define a few simple questions ahead of time that your first responders can use to assess the situation. Here are some examples:

4.4.3.1   Operational Impact

- Which processes have been impacted, and what is their criticality to the organization? Most likely, some systems are required for the organization to function, while others may tolerate a longer outage.

- Is the organization able to operate at some level? If not, are there quick workarounds that could enable the organization to reach a minimum level of functionality quickly?

- What are the financial impacts of downtime over time?

- Does the organization have business interruption insurance or other coverage that can help to offset losses caused by outages?

- What third-party pressures exist? If the organization is part of a supply chain, the unavailability of some systems or data may impact parties outside of the organization.

- Which systems are at further risk? If immediate action is not taken, some systems may be more likely to sustain further damage or loss.

4.4.3.2 Data Sensitivity

- Which kinds of sensitive data does the organization hold?

- What is the risk that sensitive information may have been accessed or acquired by an unauthorized party?

- What legal, regulatory, and contractual obligations may apply? For example, is the organization required to be HIPAA compliant? Which state data breach notification laws may apply?

Keep in mind that data breach notification laws are often based on the current residence of the individual whose record was accessed or lost lives, not the organization's geographic area of service. For example, if your organization is operating in New Jersey, but it loses records of individuals living in New York, you will likely need to follow New York's data breach law notification requirements for those individuals. Consult a qualified attorney for more details.

4.4.4 Consider Recovery Objectives

During the triage process, responders should take into account two very important metrics used to guide operational recovery efforts and measure the success of the response. As defined in NIST 800-34, "Contingency Planning Guide for Federal Information Systems":[7]

- **Recovery Point Objective (RPO)** is "the point in time to which data must be recovered after an outage."

- **Recovery Time Objective (RTO)** is "the overall length of time an information system's components can be in the recovery phase before negatively impacting the organization's mission or mission/business processes."

---

7. Marianne Swanson, Pauline Bowen, Amy Wohl Phillips, Dean Gallup, and David Lynes, *Contingency Planning Guide for Federal Information Systems*, NIST Special Publication 800-34 Rev. 1 (National Institute of Standards and Technology, May 2010), p. G-2, https://nvlpubs.nist.gov/nistpubs/Legacy/SP/nistspecialpublication800-34r1.pdf.

Ideally, these objectives should be defined in advance of a cyber incident. In a cyber extortion event—particularly a ransomware attack or similarly disruptive attack—it's critical for responders and leadership to have a clear understanding regarding the victim's RPO and RTO.

Recovery is never instantaneous, and there are many decision points at which responders may choose to sacrifice activities that support long-term objectives (such as forensic evidence preservation) in favor of short-term restoration efforts so as to achieve the recovery objectives. Ensure that everyone understands the victim's RPO and RTO upfront to lay a foundation for alignment throughout the recovery process.

4.4.5   Determine Next Steps

First responders need to obtain the results of the initial assessment, consult the organization's cybersecurity triage framework, and use this information to assign a triage status and determine next steps. Often this happens informally, but the outcomes are far better when first responders have clear guidelines, training, and support.

It is imperative that first responders have enough training to understand how to determine the appropriate triage status. A seemingly small event, such as a single encrypted workstation, can be the tip of an iceberg that belies a major data breach. Make sure first responders have resources to understand which systems contain sensitive data or are critical to operations, and know how to accurately determine the correct triage category.

Equally important are the next steps: Who does the first responder contact, and with what urgency? A ransomware attack detected at 6 p.m. can spread to the entire organization, but may affect only a small portion of the network if a first responder takes immediate action. It's critical that first responders are empowered to act when appropriate and have clear escalation procedures and contact lists that are applicable at all hours.

Tabletop exercises are extremely valuable tools for ensuring that first responders are trained and have the resources they need. While it is not possible to enumerate every possible scenario, running a tabletop exercise can guide all participants to think through the logistics of a crisis, strengthen communications procedures, and understand their roles.

At the conclusion of the triage stage, the first responder should hand off responsibility for managing the incident on a longer-term basis, and communicate in an appropriate time frame based on the triage category.

4.5   Assess Your Resources

Resources include the money, people, and other tools that are necessary for your response. Before a crisis occurs, make sure you have a good understanding of your available resources and how to tap into them. This is critical for ensuring that your response plans are realistic and that you have plans to supplement your resources when needed and possible. For example, you may not have enough internal IT staff to handle all the necessary response tasks, but during the planning phase you can identify supplemental staff and make arrangements to bring them in quickly if needed.

When a crisis strikes, review and fine-tune your assessment of resources to gain an accurate and up-to-date picture. In this section, we walk through a list of key resources that are important for cyber extortion response.

4.5.1 Financial

Many responders assume that the budget for cyber extortion response is unlimited. Nothing could be further from the truth. Victims are financially at their most vulnerable during a crisis, and careful attention needs to be paid to cash flow throughout a cyber extortion response. Financial staff and/or executives may need to apply for emergency lines of credit, tap into disaster funds, or find other ways to weather what can be a full operational outage. In addition, the victim may need to notify creditors, lenders, shareholders, or other key stakeholders, and keep them apprised of the organization's financial status.

4.5.2 Insurance

Cyber insurance has evolved to play a critical role in ransomware and cyber extortion attacks. Insurers have a vested interest in supporting effective response practices and minimizing damage, since they foot a portion of the bill in the event of a claim. Unlike with car accidents, in cyber extortion cases, the insurer has time to affect the outcome of the incident by providing support and guidance in the response process.

The majority of victims do not have the resources to have their own trained and experienced response staff in-house (particularly small and midsize businesses [SMBs], nonprofit organizations, and public entities). To fill this gap, cyber insurers have put together cyber incident response teams and can provide valuable services during the response process.

Response services provided by cyber insurers include (but are not limited to):

- A hotline for reporting cyberattacks
- A panel of vendors (often vetted) that provide:
    - Incident response services
    - Ransom negotiation
    - Legal guidance (especially important for breach investigations)
    - Public relations
    - Crisis management support

- Funding for response/recovery services and ransom payment
- Business interruption coverage
- Dependent business interruption coverage

Every cyber insurer is different, of course, and some are more effective in providing services than others. Make sure your responders are familiar with your insurer's services and requirements when preparing for cyber extortion incidents.

4.5.3   Evidence

When a cyber extortion crisis strikes, your response team needs to understand how the adversary got in, which systems and data they accessed, whether they still have access to the environment, and more. The answers to these questions will enable the recovery team to effectively contain the damage, lock out the hackers, reduce risk, and support legal or regulatory investigations.

Unfortunately, in many cases the evidence needed to piece together a picture of events is simply not available, or it might be difficult to obtain. With every minute that ticks by, the potential for damage increases.

Before a crisis hits, consider which evidence exists in your environment that would be useful in a cyber extortion response. (See Chapter 5 for a detailed list of sources of evidence.) Then, make sure this evidence will be readily available when you need it.

4.5.4   Staff

There's a lot of extra work to do in a cyber extortion crisis—but only for certain staff members. On the one hand, your IT staff will likely be overwhelmed. On the other hand, many other employees may be twiddling their thumbs, waiting for the network to come back online.

Carefully consider the additional workload needed during a crisis, and plan on repurposing underloaded employees (when possible), contracting extra support staff as needed, and engaging vendors to assist. It's always best to establish relationships ahead of time and know who you will call to lend a hand in a crisis.

4.5.5   Technology Resources

The process of restoring normal operations requires access to hardware, software, backups, and other technology resources. For example, after a ransomware attack, responders must typically build a multi-segment network environment to support the recovery, restore data from backups, and carefully monitor "cleaned" systems to ensure the threat has been eradicated. If you are conducting evidence preservation on top of these steps, you will also need extra storage to hold images and workstations or forensic equipment to preserve the evidence.

Check the status of backups to determine if they are viable and available for recovery if needed. See Chapters 6 and 9 for more details.

4.5.6 Documentation

In a cyber extortion crisis, often responders hit early roadblocks because they don't have access to critical information, such as a network diagram of the full environment, documentation of application dependencies, domain configuration details, data inventories, and more. The more time responders spend hunting for data and spinning their wheels, the less time they can spend eradicating the threat and restoring the environment. While this is happening, the adversary could be actively siphoning data off of a server or encrypting key data repositories.

Having complete documentation that is readily available saves time and money and is key to an efficient cyber extortion response. Ideally, you should have copies of documentation available offline or in printed form, so that it can be available if the environment is encrypted by ransomware or otherwise inaccessible. See the checklists at the end of this book for a list of documentation that is useful in a cyber extortion crisis.

4.6 Develop the Initial Response Strategy

Every crisis is unique. Based on the results of the initial assessment and triage, responders need to quickly develop a response strategy. The response strategy is a living document that will guide your evolving response process, including evidence preservation, containment, investigation, recovery, and other activities. The strategy needs to be reassessed and updated throughout the response.

In this section, we discuss key steps in developing and maintaining a successful response strategy.

4.6.1 Establish Goals

Make sure to clearly define and communicate the goals of your response efforts. Your goals should be realistic and aligned with the organization's priorities. For example, consider a hospital that has been hit with a ransomware attack and discovers that patient data has been encrypted. Here are some possible goals:

- During the operational outage, successfully activate crisis management plans, which specify that the hospital will treat a subset of existing patients using backup procedures and reroute specific groups of patients to other local hospitals.

- Resume normal access to the electronic medical records (EMR) system within 10 business days.

- Ultimately, restore all patient data without any permanent destruction.

- Minimize the risk of patient data exposure.

- Comply with all relevant security and breach notification laws.

Quite often, responders find that they are forced to choose between competing priorities. For example, a breach coach may direct the response team to preserve evidence from a key server, while the CIO may direct the same team to rebuild the server right away. It is important to have a clear decision-making process and ensure that decision makers take input from all key players so that they can appropriately prioritize response activities.

4.6.2   Create an Action Plan

The response team leader should enumerate key milestones and tasks that must be accomplished to achieve the objectives, with input from fellow team members. This task list should then be available in a location where all members of the team can see it, and personnel should be encouraged to update it (or report to the response team leader with updates) throughout the response. The list should be considered a living document, since tasks and priorities may shift as the full scope of the cyber extortion incident is determined.

4.6.3   Assign Responsibilities

The next step is to assign tasks to appropriate staff or outside parties—including IT, legal counsel, insurers, incident responders, PR, and others. In addition, the leadership team needs to understand the investment required, and be actively involved in making key decisions that will impact the budget and time frame of the response.

It's important to be realistic when assigning responsibilities. Do not expect individual responders to work around the clock. A cyber extortion response is a marathon, not a sprint. Make sure to establish a staffing rotation and get extra support from contractors or vendors to handle tasks beyond what your in-house staff can realistically handle. Along these lines, it's a good idea to encourage your responders to speak up when they are overloaded. Otherwise, team members may silently drop the ball when they are overloaded, and critical tasks will be delayed or go without completion.

Tip: Take Care of Your Responders

In the chaos of a crisis, responders can end up working long hours with few breaks. Make sure to define clear work periods for your staff, including breaks, and call in outside support if needed. Consider ordering food for staff and implementing staggered work shifts early on.

A crisis response is stressful enough without interruptions and unnecessary prodding. Designate a single point of contact for inquiries and updates, and ensure your responders can work without constantly being asked, "Are you done yet?" This will smooth out the response process and lead to a faster overall remediation.

4.6.4 Estimate Timing, Work Effort, and Costs

As the response strategy is developed, it is critical for the response team to clearly communicate options and provide funding estimates to the leadership team. This can enable the leadership team to make informed decisions and take early action to secure funding that can help the victim organization weather the crisis.

> **Tip: Document as You Go**
>
> As part of the response strategy, leave room for documentation, and ask each member of the incident response team to take careful notes every step of the way. In the heat of a response, changes are often made quickly, steps may be taken in isolation, and systems may be reconfigured. If those items are not documented, they will be lost or forgotten, and recovery will be impacted. Don't assume that team members will "remember" or "document later"— the team is running on pure adrenaline (and pizza!). When all is said and done, exhaustion will set in, and the activities of the response will be a blur. Document as you go.
>
> At the beginning of the response strategy plan, include a section in which to document quick status updates and changes. Make it easy for every team member to track their progress.
>
> Documentation should include dates and timestamps, along with the initials or name of the responder. Acceptable formats for documentation should be agreed upon before ever experiencing an incident. For example, should notes be kept in Word or text files? Can they be handwritten? Should photos be included where helpful?

4.7 Communicate

Throughout the entire response process, effective communication is critical. Financial and operational impacts need to be explained to affected parties. Key stakeholders need information so that they can make sound decisions. Decisions need to be clearly communicated to those who will implement them. Regulators may require updates. The media may come knocking. Rumors will fly.

Effective communication is important for ensuring that the response team stays coordinated and makes decisions that are in line with the organization's available resources and risk appetite. In addition, good communication is critical for maintaining trust with key stakeholders, including shareholders, customers, regulators, and even the general public.

Here is a quick list of people who should be included in cyber extortion communication plans:

- The response team
- Affected parties
- The public

We will delve into more detail on each of these in the following sections.

> ### Tip: Remember to Listen!
>
> Communication is a two-way street. As important as it is to share updates and information, it is equally important to provide opportunities for input and feedback from your response team, as well from as those impacted by the cyber extortion incident. Make sure to invest time and effort in receiving communication. If the organization can't staff a call center, insurance carriers or breach coaches can recommend third parties that can handle this duty.

4.7.1   Response Team

Naturally, you need to communicate effectively within the response team, which typically includes IT, legal, insurance, executives, and others. In a fast-paced and stressful crisis, wires may get crossed and balls may get dropped. This is especially true when coordinating on a cross-departmental basis since team members may not routinely work together. Remember to overcommunicate and establish regular opportunities for the team to share information such as progress, pain points, and plans (we like to call these the "3 Ps"). Establishing regular touch points will also help to reduce stress by introducing structure and a form of routine to the response process.

At the start of a cyber extortion crisis, make sure the entire response team knows:

- Who is in charge
- Where to find the latest documented response strategy
- Where to document their work and observations
- Which communication methods are acceptable
- How often to provide updates

- The timing and format of regular meetings

- Any other key metadata

Response team members should be encouraged to share information internally within the team and to communicate openly. At the same time, communications outside the response team should be limited to specific, clearly defined spokespersons.

Tip: Pulse Check!

In the midst of a crisis, it is all too easy to get swept up in fast-moving events and forget to take a breath. As you plan your response, it is a good idea to establish a routine time and method for a "pulse check," in which you:

- **Reassess state:** Digest updates from responders, review feedback, observe the organization's current operational posture, evaluate current risks, and assess available resources.

- **Update documentation:** Ensure that response activities and key information are consistently documented in a central repository, such as ticketing software.

- **Revise the response strategy:** Revise your response strategy, including goals, tasks, responsibilities, estimates for timing, work effort, financial cost, etc. Adjust your ongoing response processes as needed.

- **Communicate:** Ensure that key information is relayed to responders, stakeholders, and third parties as appropriate. This may include updated response plans, results from investigations, and more. Relay information as needed to inform the response. Effectively control public messages. Listen to feedback.

Essentially, the pulse check is a quick, routine check-in that informs your response. Conducting regular "pulse checks" will help ensure that:

- Response activities remain aligned with current needs and risks.

- Documentation is accurate, complete, and up-to-date.

- Relationships are maintained to the best of your ability.

Your team effectively synthesizes information and uses it to make intelligent, informed decisions. This activity runs through the entire response from beginning to end.

4.7.2   Affected Parties

When a victim's operations are impacted or sensitive data is threatened, the effects may quickly be felt by third parties. Depending on the victim, this may include customers, patients, students, community members, affiliates, and others. This is especially true for cases where the adversary reaches out directly out to customers or other affected parties.

Victims commonly suffer a loss of trust with both the affected parties and their communities as a whole following a cyber extortion event. Rebuilding trust takes time and effort. Whenever possible, it's wise to proactively communicate with key stakeholders to establish and maintain trust. When doing so, focus on making communications timely, reliable, honest, and transparent.

Here are some tips for keeping affected parties informed:

- **Establish an effective method of communication.** Choose a method of communication that can be maintained and is easily accessible. A regular public release or a frequently updated web page can deliver updates to a wide audience without causing frustrating roadblocks. Consider your options for managing communications when the victim's technology infrastructure is offline or impacted.

- **Designate a spokesperson.** Clearly assign responsibility for acting as the primary public spokesperson in a cyber extortion crisis. It is often best to assign a single person to this role, so as to maintain consistent tone and content. Involving multiple spokespersons can muddy the waters and result in confusing differences in messaging. Pick an executive or PR representative and stick with them.

- **Create templates in advance.** Whenever possible, create and approve communication templates in advance, so that leadership teams, PR staff, and legal counsel have the opportunity to review and approve them while not in the throes of an actual emergency.

- **Have a formal public relations strategy.** Decide in advance who will create and approve content for different types of communication. For example, you may want to involve an outside PR team for public communication—or even updates to regulators and other third parties.

- **Consider timing and audience.** A quick update to the general public needs to be formatted for broad consumption, while an update to an executive team will need to be more business focused and provide realistic remediation timelines.

- **Maintain a consistent frequency.** Keep the flow of information consistent, even if the update is that there is no update. Set clear expectations (i.e., "Our next update will come at . . ."). Long periods of silence with no updates inevitably lead to speculation and fear—two of the worst responses from stakeholders in a ransomware or extortion incident.

- **Avoid radio silence.** Don't disappear. A lack of timely communication can be considered a sign of bad news and lead to unnecessary scrutiny or speculation about the current state or severity of an incident.

Case Study: Out of Office

A small law firm was hit with a ransomware attack. As they worked to respond, the firm's personnel began to receive concerned calls and messages from clients. A media inquiry quickly followed, even though the firm had not announced that the outage was due to ransomware.

It turned out that one overachieving attorney at the firm had set up an out-of-office message on his email when the ransomware attack hit. The email read:

> Our computers were infected with a ransom ware [sic] virus yesterday. We re [sic] doing everything possible to correct the problem and restore our systems. In the meantime please accept our apology for any inconvenience. If you need to please call us at [redacted].

This message was sent to every single contact that included him on an email, including external third parties.

While executives and incident responders might expect that employees will know that they should keep information about cyber extortion cases confidential, this is not always obvious to laypersons. Make sure to clearly communicate your expectations regarding confidentiality ahead of time, and reinforce those expectations when a cyber extortion incident occurs.

4.7.3 The Public

Don't expect information about a cyber extortion attack to remain confidential. At any time, the adversary may choose to publish anything they have accessed, including details about your negotiations, internal communications, stolen data, or other materials. Nothing is off-limits. Quite often, cyber extortionists make a point of notifying journalists, the original owners or subjects of the data, or the public. The victim will have little control over the timing.

The victim's PR team should be in the loop as early as possible. This includes both internal and external PR staff members. Ideally, the PR team should have preprepared statements to issue in response to inquiries, as well as a press release that has been preapproved for use.

For cases that hit the news, it is wise to hire an experienced PR team to support the effort, preferably one with experience in repairing organizations' image following cyber extortion attacks specifically.

4.8   Conclusion

Cyber extortion crises are unpredictable and potentially catastrophic. An effective response can dramatically reduce the impact and facilitate a speedy recovery.

In this chapter, we discussed how cyber extortion incidents are detected, provided a framework for triage, and offered guidance for developing your response strategy. The beginning of a cyber extortion response is a critical phase, in which responders work to quickly assess and prioritize activities. The outcomes of the triage phase lay the groundwork for the rest of the response process.

In the next chapter, we will present effective techniques for rapidly containing damage, including halting ransomware encryption, stopping data exfiltration, locking out the adversary, and threat hunting.

4.9   Your Turn!

Every cyber extortion incident is unique. The response team's options and priorities will vary depending on the victim organization's industry, size, and location, as well as the details of the incident itself.

Based on what you learned in this chapter, let's think through key elements of the triage process and response strategy.

Step 1: Build Your Victim

Choose one characteristic from each of the three columns to describe your victim's organization:

Industry	Size	Location
Hospital	Large	Global
Financial institution	Midsized	United States
Manufacturer	Small	European Union
Law firm		Australia
University		India
Cloud service provider		Country/location of your choice
Organization of your choice		

Step 2: Choose Your Incident Scenario

Select from one of the following incident scenarios:

A	Ransomware strikes! All of the victim's files have been locked up, including central data repositories, servers, and workstations.
B	A well-known cyber extortion gang claims to have stolen all of the victim's most sensitive data and threatens to release it unless the victim pays a very large ransom demand. The gang posts the victim's name on their dark web leaks site, along with samples of supposedly stolen data.
C	Double extortion! Both A and B occur at the same time.
D	The victim is hit with a denial-of-service attack on its Internet-facing infrastructure that slows its access and services to a crawl. The adversary threatens to continue and even escalate the attack unless a ransom is paid.

Step 3: Discussion Time

Your victim has just discovered signs of a cyber extortion event. Given what you know of the victim and the scenario, answer the following questions:

1. How might the victim's normal operations be impacted by the incident? Which processes are likely the top priorities for recovery?

2. Why is it important for the team to have ready access to documentation during the incident? Name two types of documentation that responders might need in this incident.

3. Who may be impacted by the effects of the incident? Consider not just the organization's staff, but any outsiders that may be affected.

4. What third-party pressures may exist that could affect your response? Consider any third parties that rely on the victim's organization, the legal landscape, whether the organization is likely to be regulated, etc.

5. Curveball: An employee posts about the incident publicly on social media. How do you handle this?

Chapter 5

Containment

Doing the best at this moment puts you in the best place for the next moment.
                                                                    —Oprah Winfrey

---

Learning Objectives

- Understand the goals of containment, and recognize why containment is important
- Know strategies for making effective decisions in the containment phase
- Learn tactics for reducing the risk of data exfiltration, halting file encryption/deletion, and resolving denial-of-service attacks
- Gain familiarity with techniques for rapidly locking the adversary out of the victim's environment

---

When a cyber extortion attack hits, you need to act quickly and contain the damage by halting any malicious activities such as encryption, unauthorized access, lateral movement, data exfiltration, denial-of-service attacks, command-and-control communications, and more. At the same time, responders must ensure that the adversary is locked out of the environment as quickly as possible.

All of this must occur as soon as possible—often before responders clearly understand the scope of the compromise or have actionable intelligence about the adversary. Actions taken (or not taken) during the containment process can have a major impact on the speed at which operations can be resumed, as well as the risk of a data breach or other damaging consequences.

In this chapter, we review common containment strategies, including methods for halting ransomware encryption/file destruction, stopping data exfiltration, resolving denial-of-service attacks, and locking out the adversary. Along the way, we discuss mistakes to avoid and provide tips for successfully containing damage.

5.1   The Need for Speed

The goals of containment depend on the specifics of each cyber extortion situation. Common containment activities include the following:

- Halt ransomware encryption/data destruction if it is still ongoing.

- Disable persistence mechanisms that can automatically relaunch ransomware or other malicious processes.

- Halt data exfiltration if it is in progress.

- Resolve denial-of-service attacks, restoring normal access to data and resources.

- Lock out the adversary: Ensure that all remote access mechanisms employed by the adversary have been blocked, so that they can no longer gain unauthorized access to network resources.

- Hunt for threats: Identify and eradicate lingering signs of malicious activity within the network, such as persistent backdoors or signs of malware.

During containment, a seemingly small mistake can have dire consequences. If one of the steps is performed incorrectly, all the work performed during the other steps can quickly become irrelevant. Often, an error at this point will result in the following potential outcomes:

- The adversary reenters the network.

- More data is exfiltrated.

- Encryption software re-detonates.

- Data is lost or destroyed.

- Critical evidence is overwritten.

In contrast, effective containment can save the organization from disaster, and even make the entire event seem relatively inconsequential. Quick and wise action can result in the following outcomes:

- Expedient resumption of normal operations

- Reduced risk of future damage or reinfection

- Minimal need for legal or regulatory response

- Limited media attention, which is aligned with the organization's chosen message

> ### Tip: Don't Stomp on the Crime Scene
>
> When a cyber extortion event is discovered, responders usually want to jump into action to contain the incident and get the organization back to business as usual as quickly as possible. However, to protect the organization, responders need to take care not to unwittingly destroy valuable evidence. See Chapter 6 for more details on evidence preservation.

5.2 Gain Access to the Environment

Before responders can secure the victim's environment, they first need to gain access—not always an easy task when an adversary has taken over! During the lead-up to a cyber extortion event, an adversary will often take advantage of established remote access methods to expand their own foothold into the environment.

Responders need to ensure that authorized parties have the access they need to remediate the incident, while simultaneously removing the adversary's ability to derail recovery efforts. Typically, responders use a combination of physical and remote access to accomplish these goals.

When possible, it is simplest for responders to begin with physical access only. With this approach, all remote administrative access can be blocked until responders are finished locking out the adversary (see Section 5.7).

If immediate remote access is necessary for responders, be sure to prioritize the steps in Section 5.7 right away, and restrict remote access as much as possible while still enabling responders to work. This can include allowlisting only known "good" IP address ranges for remote responders, increasing password strength requirements, setting a strong account lockout policy, enforcing multifactor authentication on all accounts, and taking similar actions to lock down remote access as much as possible in the early phases of the response.

> ### Heads Up! Endpoint Detection and Response Software
>
> During the initial containment of a cyber extortion attack, endpoint detection and response (EDR) software can be extremely useful for accessing the victim's environment and containing the compromise. EDR functions by combining features from multiple types of security software, including antivirus, intrusion detection/prevention systems, vulnerability scanners, and more. It also provides responders with a centralized system that can monitor and respond to potential threats to the network quickly and efficiently.

In general, EDR tools can be used to accomplish multiple tasks, such as the following:

- Root out malicious behavior

- Identify and block malicious software

- Quickly isolate and quarantine critical hosts

- Trace and eliminate suspicious system processes

If EDR tools are not already available in the victim's environment, responders may want to deploy them? (i.e., tools) as a first step, which then facilitates the remainder of the response. See Chapter 10 for more details about EDR software deployment.

5.3   Halting Encryption/Deletion

In "denial" cyber extortion attacks, the adversary typically encrypts or deletes data to limit the availability of the information. Possession of a decryption key or a copy of the deleted files gives the adversary leverage over the victim.

In attacks of this type, the most time-sensitive priority is to stop any active file encryption or deletion processes. Quick action in either case can enable defenders to save some of the victim's files or, at the very least, reduce the risk of repeat encryption during the recovery process.

Even if the malicious activity appears to be complete, it is best to treat any affected system as if the ransomware was still alive, well, and running—because it just might be.

Here are four strategies for halting malicious activity and preventing it from reoccurring:

- Change permissions

- Remove power

- Kill the program that's encrypting the files

- Disable persistence mechanisms

In this section, we discuss the tactics, benefits, and potential pitfalls of each of these approaches in turn. Any method may result in some data loss, so be prepared for that risk.

Tip: Free Decryption Utilities

At the onset of an incident, first responders such as IT staff may panic and attempt to decrypt files using any public decryption utility they can find. *This practice can have serious consequences!*

Unless the decryptor is specifically meant for the exact variant and version of ransomware on a system, it will fail to decrypt anything, and it may corrupt the data that has already been encrypted. Moreover, many public "decryptors" have been discovered to actually be ransomware, leading to a double-encryption scenario.

In 2020, the criminal organization behind the Zorab ransomware strain began launching and distributing fake decryption software that was advertised as being able to decrypt STOP ransomware, a popular variant at the time. However, instead of decrypting files, the fake decryptor would add a second layer of encryption to files on already encrypted systems, making victims purchase two individual decryptors instead of one.[1]

5.3.1 Change File Access Permissions

A quick approach to stop encryption can be to change file permissions. It may not be realistic to recursively change permissions on every file in a large filesystem, but large assets such as database files can be quickly modified to prevent encryption. This is also very effective on shared drives when it may take some time to track down the source of encryption. As a first step, simply restrict share access to only a small set of trusted users and change files to read-only (and also to immutable on Linux/UNIX). If you determine that an admin-level account is being used, adjust the account so that it cannot be used to reset or override the filesystem permissions.

Tip: Plan for Cleanup

When attempting to halt file encryption, thoroughly document any file permission changes. These changes will likely need to be reverted after containment to restore normal operations within the environment, and a failure to document these changes can lead to wasted time and effort during recovery when it's time to restore full operations.

---

1. Lawrence Abrams, "Fake Ransomware Decryptor Double-Encrypts Desperate Victims' Files," *Bleeping Computer*, June 6, 2020, www.bleepingcomputer.com/news/security/fake-ransomware-decryptor-double-encrypts-desperate-victims-files/.

5.3.2   Remove Power

In this approach, the responder removes power from impacted hosts by pulling the power cord. Removing power suddenly will halt any activity on the system immediately. The benefit of this action is that any files that are not encrypted or deleted will remain that way.

> ### Tip: Shut Down Computers Cautiously
>
> It is unwise to shut down an infected computer using a software or hardware shutdown button. A soft shutdown of this type can be undermined by the ransomware software itself or trigger additional destructive activities.

The downside is that a sudden power shutdown could potentially corrupt the entire filesystem. This is always a risk when suddenly shutting down power, but the risk is heightened due to the ransomware software's behavior. For example, some variants of ransomware encrypt files in place. If power is removed while a file is being encrypted, then the files will likely be corrupted and may not be recoverable even with the help of a decryption tool.

Knowing the variant of ransomware involved can help you gauge the risk of corruption. For example, certain variants create an encrypted copy of files and then subsequently delete the original. In these cases, the risk of corruption is lower, because the original file still exists until the encryption process is complete.

Coming up in Section 5.7.3.2, we'll discuss the order of volatility of evidence. For now, know that valuable information can be recovered from volatile evidence sources on affected hosts (e.g., the CPU cache, RAM, active network connections). This volatile evidence will be lost if power is removed from the system. It is often wise to quickly capture RAM from a system prior to shutting off the power, depending on the speed of the encryption process and the risk that the attack poses to the organization.

5.3.3   Kill the Malicious Processes

In any ransomware attack, some processes running on some computer in the environment are actively encrypting and/or deleting files. If responders choose not to cut the power, identifying the encryption process is key to halting the ongoing denial attack.

Identifying the ransomware encryption process can be tricky. For example, the Maze group was known to hollow out the legitimate svchost.exe process and inject encrypting software into it, so that the malware would appear to be a legitimate Windows process. The Dharma malware created a look-alike executable that would appear to be a Windows system utility, such as winhost.exe.

Encryption is a resource-intensive process. Responders can look for indicators of this activity such as high CPU usage or suspicious parent processes. In the case of Dharma, for example, if you examined a process tree, you could see that the process was spawned by a service that was not a Windows system utility. You can also identify these suspicious processes using a forensic memory analysis tool such as Volatility.

Responders can also track down the source of ransomware encryption by identifying the user associated with the encrypted files, analyzing the timeline, and in some cases leveraging this information to trace the attack back to a specific workstation or server.

Once you identify the process (or processes) that are encrypting data, kill them using a command prompt or Task Manager. Keep in mind that ransomware is often implemented using multiple processes, which can potentially run on different systems. Note also that killing processes that are hollowed-out Windows services can lead to system instability.

> ### Tip: Use Trusted Tools
>
> Often, the adversary modifies system tools such as Task Manager or command-line tools so that responders can't see or effectively kill suspicious processes. You can prevent this by running your process analysis tools from an attached drive rather than relying on potentially suspect system tools. The Windows Sysinternals utilities are a useful toolkit for response purposes.

5.4 Disable Persistence Mechanisms

Adversaries often modify the victim's systems to ensure that the malicious activities can continue, even if a process is killed or the system reboots. For example, depending on the specific variant used in the attack, ransomware may install additional malicious binaries throughout compromised hosts to create a persistent environment that will re-encrypt or destroy data periodically. In cases where ransomware is set to run automatically, the specific mechanisms need to be identified so malicious activities do not begin again during the recovery phase.

Identifying the adversary or ransomware strain can give responders a leg up when determining the best process response, as well as when evaluating the risk of ongoing encryption and persistence mechanisms. Although adversary tactics are constantly evolving, some behavioral characteristics are known to be associated with certain groups.

Adversaries typically create persistence using one or more of the following methods:

- Secondary monitoring process
- Scheduled tasks
- Automatic startup

Many adversaries will establish local system persistence using methods like these. If a defender does not identify these persistent processes early, there is a chance that the entire network could fall victim again.

> ### Heads Up! Evasion Tactics
>
> Highly successful ransomware strains and RaaS products such as Maze or Ryuk may purposefully minimize system changes and/or purge their software from the system upon completion. This reduces the risk of persistence, but also inhibits forensic analysis of the malware and impedes an investigation. In addition, these adversaries often have privileged access to network administration tools and core servers, enabling the reinstallation of ransomware even if defenders clean a specific system.

5.4.1 Monitoring Process

Often, the adversary will include a secondary program alongside a malicious executable designed to monitor the status of the process. If a primary malicious process stops, the monitoring program can detect this fact and restart it. The monitoring process (also referred to as a watchdog timer) can be more difficult to identify, since it does not require extensive use of the CPU or other system resources and can be made to resemble a legitimate system service.

5.4.2 Scheduled Tasks

The adversary may set up scheduled tasks in the operating system to relaunch ransomware-related executables periodically. For example, on Windows systems, look for Auto-Run keys in the registry.

First, responders should delete any scheduled tasks that invoke ransomware or another malicious process. If you need to take quick action, consider removing all scheduled tasks. While this may impact normal system performance depending on the victim's custom configuration, typically Windows can operate without scheduled tasks. Make sure to preserve evidence (such as registry keys) before modifying system configuration.

5.4.3 Automatic Startup

Many adversaries modify the system configuration so that if an infected computer is rebooted, the malicious process will relaunch. This is especially damaging with ransomware strains such as Dharma, as the new process will utilize a new encryption key following the reboot. As a result, an infected system may end up having files encrypted with two or more keys, depending on the number of times the infected host was rebooted.

> ## *Case Study: Double (and Triple, and Quadruple) Encryption*
>
> A midsized health care organization was infected with the GandCrab ransomware in 2018. Several workstations were infected, and all of them had access to the organization's central file-sharing repository.
>
> Unfortunately, this meant that the GandCrab encryption software ran multiple times on the same files. The first infected workstation encrypted all files in the shared repository and dropped the ransom note containing the link to the custom portal required to purchase the matching decryptor. Without this link, it was impossible to get the decryptor. The second infected computer subsequently encrypted all of the files again, including the ransom note. Then it dropped a new ransom note of its own. In consequence, to fully decrypt the files, the victim had to purchase the decryptor using the note left by the second infected computer, so that it could recover the first ransom note and gain access to purchase the original decryptor. Whew!
>
> By the end of the incident, four separate infected computers had encrypted the files, and responders had to go through the process of purchasing and decrypting four nested layers of encryption.

5.5 Halting Data Exfiltration

Stopping any current data exfiltration activity is also a top priority. If you are investigating a cyber extortion case and you are not sure whether data is being actively exfiltrated, assume that it is. At the time of this writing, approximately 84% of all ransomware attacks involve a threat to leak stolen data.[2]

The adversary may steal data from a local network, cloud repository, mobile device, or any other repository. As a result, responders must consider all data repository locations when attempting to halt exfiltration.

Immediately check alerts, logs, and outbound network traffic for any signs of suspicious outbound communication. If any are identified, stop data exfiltration as quickly as possible while balancing operational needs. Here are some tactics commonly used to stop data exfiltration:

- Block suspicious outbound network traffic at the perimeter firewall, or an intermediary internal firewall if available.

---

2. "Law Enforcement Pressure Forces Ransomware Groups to Refine Tactics in Q4 2021," Coveware (blog), February 2, 2022, www.coveware.com/blog/2022/2/2/law-enforcement-pressure-forces-ransomware-groups-to-refine-tactics-in-q4-2021#:~:text=84%25%20of%20Ransomware%20Attacks%20Included%20Data%20Exfiltration&text=RaaS%20affiliates%20expect%20exfiltrated%20data,pay%20a%20cyber%20extortion%20demand.

- Block access to any cloud services or file-sharing sites used by the adversary to transfer data, such as Dropbox or MEGA.

- Disallow the use of utilities such as FTP applications, PowerShell, or Win-SCP if they're not necessary.

- Restrict data repository access by modifying permissions, roles, and application configurations as appropriate.

- Remove any email forwarding rules that were created by an adversary.

- Take other steps to block data exfiltration as appropriate.

Victims might consider cutting off *all* network traffic as a temporary measure. This decision needs to be made on a case-by-case basis and consider the victim's business model, as well as weigh the potential damage of network cutoff against the potential benefits. Cutting off all network access is the "nuclear option" for most organizations, but nothing is really off the table after a cyber extortion attack is discovered.

5.6   Resolve Denial-of-Service Attacks

File encryption and exfiltration are not the only types of "denial" cyberattacks. Access to network resources and functionality can also be severely impacted by a distributed denial-of-service (DDoS) attack. In a DDoS attack, an adversary intentionally overloads the online infrastructure with network traffic and stops the services from operating normally. These types of attacks can be crippling to network infrastructure and require immediate attention.

Over the years, cybercriminals have attempted to leverage DDoS attacks in a variety of cyber extortion cases. For example, in August 2020, a group known as "Lazarus Bear Armada" launched a series of carefully planned DDoS attacks against targets in the financial and travel industries.[3] Depending on the resilience of the specific target and its position in the technology supply chain, a DDoS attack can either impact a single organization or cause widespread ripple effects.

In a DDoS extortion attack, criminals launch a DDoS campaign against a victim, and then offer to end the attack in exchange for a ransom payment. For example, in January 2021, security company Radware warned that customers had been receiving extortion emails threatening damaging DDoS attacks unless they paid the adversaries 5 to 10 Bitcoins (worth approximately $150,000 to $300,000 at the time).[4]

---

3. Arbor Networks, "Lazarus Bear Armada DDoS Extortion Campaign—December 2020," NetScout, www.netscout.com/blog/asert/lazarus-bear-armada-ddos-extortion-campaign-december-2020.

4. Catalin Cimpanu, "As Bitcoin Price Surges, DDoS Extortion Gangs Return in Force," *ZDNet*, January 22, 2021, www.zdnet.com/article/as-bitcoin-price-surges-ddos-extortion-gangs-return-in-force/.

Akamai, an Internet security company, warned shortly thereafter that DDoS attacks in 2021 had become "more targeted and much more persistent." In some cases, adversaries leveraged sophisticated attack strategies, "rotat[ing] through multiple DDoS attack vectors trying to increase the likelihood of disrupting the back-end environments."[5]

To defend against a DDoS attack, consider leveraging a DDoS mitigation service. Third-party providers such as CloudFlare, Akamai, and others specifically offer DDoS mitigation options, which include artificial intelligence (AI)–driven threat identification and response, distributed caching proxies, and more.

5.7 Lock Out the Hackers

Adversaries often remain in the compromised environment indefinitely, monitoring communications and potentially sharing access with others, unless responders deliberately and completely eradicate them.

During the initial steps to contain an incident, responders typically do not have a complete understanding of the adversary's method of entry, or even the current access mechanisms employed. This is normal. Despite this obvious challenge, it is absolutely critical to lock out the adversary from the system, so as to ensure that the damage is contained and additional malware is not installed during the course of the investigation.

Tactics for locking out the hackers include the following:

- Kill remote connection services

- Implement password resets

- Roll out multifactor authentication

- Restrict perimeter communications

- Review and minimize third-party access

- Mitigate risks of compromised software

We discuss each of these methods in the following subsections.

5.7.1 Remote Connection Services

Many enterprise environments allow employees, contractors, vendors, IT staff, and many others to have remote access to their networks, often in the form of Remote Desktop Protocol (RDP), virtual private networks (VPNs), and Secure Shell (SSH) logins. It should come as no surprise that remote access systems are also a prime target for would-be

5. Ionut Ilascu, "800Gbps DDoS Extortion Attack Hits Gambling Company," *Bleeping Computer*, March 31, 2021, www.bleepingcomputer.com/news/security/800gbps-ddos-extortion-attack-hits-gambling-company/.

attackers. The access is already configured, and in many cases the only thing an adversary needs to exploit these systems is a username and a password.

During the initial response to a cyber extortion incident, responders should consider taking the following actions to lock down remote connection services:

- Disable any port forwarding that allows RDP from the public Internet.

- Shut down any VPN access points.

- Disable SSH services from the public Internet.

- Kill any and all active remote sessions for RDP, VPN, SSH, and other remote connection tools, unless they are absolutely necessary and have been vetted by the response team.

5.7.2   Reset Passwords for Local and Cloud Accounts

Password resets are an essential tactic for quickly reducing the risk of ongoing damage, and should be implemented even before the scope of a compromise is fully understood.

5.7.2.1   Which Passwords Should You Reset?

During the first response, it is usually advisable to conduct a mass password reset for all domain-connected accounts, as well as cloud services such as Microsoft 365 and Quick-Books. This will prevent the adversary from accessing services using stolen passwords, and it often reduces the risk that the adversary will reenter the organization using sanctioned remote access tools.

Every environment is unique. When determining whether to reset passwords, or establishing a timeline for doing so, responders should weigh the potential benefits of a password reset with the difficulty and cost.

5.7.2.2   When and How to Reset Passwords

Simply changing passwords without preparation can be both ineffective and potentially disruptive. If an adversary has already established a persistent foothold in your network that does not rely on privileged access (such as a RAT), then changing passwords may just result in the new passwords being quickly exfiltrated as well.

Local system password resets should be performed as soon as possible after a host is determined to be no longer compromised. It is safest to perform this operation on an isolated network segment, separate from the compromised environment. Responders should be prepared to repeat this process as needed if an infected computer is connected to the network of "clean" computers.

Additionally, responders should make sure to reset Kerberos access tokens, as a means to prevent exploitation using token-based attacks against the domain. Refer to vendor documentation for the full reset process.

Cloud services are also a prime target for exploitation and need to be addressed quickly. Responders should revoke all active sessions to their cloud environments and then reset the passwords for all accounts. Passwords for cloud services should be reset only using a computer that is not infected by malicious software and is not part of the infected network.

5.7.2.3 New Password Selection

In all cases, new passwords should be secure, strong, and unique for each account.

It is not uncommon to encounter a shared local administrator password within an enterprise network that IT staff use for initial setup and continued maintenance. In such a case, responders should consider configuring a local administrator password tracking solution like Local Administrator Password Solution (LAPS) to avoid sharing passwords between multiple devices.

5.7.3 Audit Accounts

Many adversaries routinely alter account permissions or create new user accounts. Such changes can involve modifying file share access, software installation permissions, remote access, and more. If responders fail to identify and correct these changes, it can leave the door open for the adversary to regain entry to the environment and disrupt or negate recovery efforts.

Responders should audit and evaluate user accounts while looking for suspicious signs such as the following:

- Recently created accounts
- Newly enabled remote access permissions
- Administrative permission assignments
- New file share access
- Password changes

Make sure to immediately disable or restrict any accounts found to have been altered or created by an adversary. Access can be reestablished for authorized users once their accounts have been verified and properly secured.

5.7.4 Multifactor Authentication

Determine whether multifactor authentication (MFA) is set up for all remote access to the victim's technology environment. If it is not, or if it is only partially set up, identify gaps. Strongly consider rolling out multifactor authentication for all remote access, including VPN, webmail, and cloud environments.

While lack of MFA might not seem to be directly related to the cause of a cyber extortion attack, a speedy rollout of MFA can often dramatically reduce the risk of an ongoing compromise or reinfection due to password theft.

Many organizations spend months planning for a potential rollout of MFA, then miraculously implement it completely over the span of a weekend after a cyber extortion incident takes place. Although this accelerated time frame is not ideal, it is often a wise step for reducing risk.

5.7.5   Restrict Perimeter Communications

Restricting communication, both incoming and outgoing, may be the quickest route to locking out any ongoing unauthorized access. However, be careful: Perimeter network restrictions can also become a roadblock if responders need to access critical portions of the organization's infrastructure remotely. If possible, restrict the following services:

- RDP services, even if they're running through alternative ports
- VPN access, unless the access is from a specifically allowlisted IP address
- SMB, FTP, or any other file-sharing traffic
- SSH access
- Any nonessential services

5.7.6   Minimize Third-Party Access

Third parties, including managed service providers (MSPs), technology vendors, software providers, and others, can unintentionally act as a vector for unauthorized remote access to customer network. That outcome is particularly likely if their own technology ecosystem is compromised first.

For example, it is common to see cyber extortionists compromise MSP accounts with administrative privileges and leverage these to launch extortion attacks against the MSP's customers. In the event of a cyber extortion attack, it's typically a good idea to immediately notify the victim's MSP. This way, the MSP can provide support, and also adapt in response to any remote access or network configuration changes. In addition, any administrative accounts that an MSP uses to administer an environment should be quickly restricted or disabled, along with remote access software. This way, the adversary cannot easily leverage the MSP's privileged access if it has been compromised.

Technology vendors pose similar risks, particularly if they have ongoing remote access to the victim's environment. While specific vendors may not have full administrative accounts across the entire technology ecosystem, they may have access to more than a standard user, making them a target for exploitation.

To reduce the risk of an attack:

- Third-party remote access to the network should be minimized during the early phases of the response.
- All vendor accounts should be disabled unless absolutely necessary.
- Consider disconnecting any hardware or software managed by a potentially compromised vendor.

5.7.7 Mitigate Risks of Compromised Software

Unfortunately, software products may be vectors for injection of malicious backdoors or other malware into the victim's environment, as discussed in Section 1.6. These situations can be particularly knotty and difficult to resolve, especially in cases like the SolarWinds and Kaseya incidents, in which the affected software was integral to the victims' technology environment.

In the early phases of the response, it is wise to minimize software running in the environment until the source and scope of the compromise are fully understood. If evidence suggests that the adversary exploited existing software or leveraged an implanted backdoor:

- Contact the vendor right away to notify and obtain guidance.
- If possible, remove the affected software from the network.

Otherwise:

- Take steps to eradicate the adversary.
- Install software patches that address the issue as soon as practical.
- If patches are not yet available to fully address the issue, refer to government and vendor advisories for risk mitigation steps.

5.8 Hunt for Threats

Threat hunting refers to the process of proactively and manually searching a technology environment for indications of threats. Threat hunting often begins immediately upon detection and is used to identify suspicious activity within the environment so that the adversary can be fully eradicated.

Today, threat hunting is an integral part of an effective response to cyber extortion. To be effective, this activity is typically conducted by an experienced professional using specialized tools, and aims to detect subtle threats that automated software such as antivirus suites may miss. An experienced threat hunter can cut the period of active network compromise by days, if not weeks, if they are provided with quick access to a compromised network and responders are prepared to actively leverage their results. Threat hunting typically continues long after containment to reduce the risk of reinfection and prevent future incidents.

A comprehensive approach to threat identification is essential for effective eradication. In this section, we provide a high-level overview of threat hunting methodology, techniques, sources of evidence, tools, and staffing.

5.8.1   Methodology

Threat hunting is a cyclical, loosely defined process involving the following phases:

- Collect information
- Create and refine the hypothesis
- Hunt
- Identify threats

In each phase, the threat hunter leverages the results from the previous phase to hone in on suspicious activity and identify novel or advanced persistent threats.

Threat hunting is an ongoing process that needs to be included in each phase of the response, and will likely continue after recovery is complete. Organizations should strongly consider adding proactive threat hunting as a part of their cybersecurity testing routine, since adversaries are constantly innovating and finding new ways to gain persistence.

Case Study: Hunting Trip

A private charter school in the U.S. Northwest was hit with the Conti ransomware and completely locked up. The ransomware gang had stolen hundreds of student records, as well as other files, and threatened the school with double extortion. Local IT staff used Windows Defender to scan the network after it was encrypted with ransomware. Windows Defender did not identify any signs of additional malware.

The authors of this book were hired to conduct triage and ensure that the threat was fully eradicated. Knowing that the Conti ransomware is typically deployed using a remote access tool (RAT), we deployed an EDR threat hunting tool. It didn't take long to find the Trojan (QBot), a powerful threat distributor and information stealer, still lurking on the network. Once we identified the RAT, we worked with the local IT staff to fully eradicate the underlying threat and verify that the network was free of malware.

Had the school not invested the time and resources to carefully monitor the network and conduct threat hunting, a dangerous RAT would have remained in the network, and would likely have led to reinfection.

5.8.2   Sources of Evidence for Threat Hunting

Here are the minimum sources of evidence needed to conduct effective threat hunting on an infected network:

- Network flow records and/or firewall logs (both internal and external)
- Event log data
- Process activity
- User activity
- Authentication events (successful and failed)

Other information streams can supplement this data and can inform the threat hunting process.

5.8.3   Tools and Techniques

Threat hunting is not dependent on one single piece of software. Instead, a trained responder needs to understand how a network functions normally, then leverage tools as appropriate to identify behavior that is outside of the normal parameters.

During the entry and expansion phases of the attack, the adversary may have deployed tools to establish persistence, or to cause reinfection if the malware is eradicated using normal methods. These artifacts need to be rooted out to minimize the risk of future compromise.

Commonly, EDR software is used as the primary threat hunting tool. Possible tools include CrowdStrike,[6] Carbon Black,[7] SentinelOne,[8] and other EDR toolkits. Responders can also leverage the free and open-source ELK stack, which is composed of Elasticsearch, Logstash, and Kibana. Often, the best threat hunting software is the tool that is already installed in the victim's environment; every moment is precious during a cyber extortion response, and "living off the land" can be the fastest means of eradicating the threat if the existing tools are sufficient.

5.8.4   Staffing

Human involvement is of the utmost importance during threat hunting because threats evolve far more quickly than defenders can develop and deploy programmatic software.

---

6. CrowdStrike, www.crowdstrike.com/.

7. VMware Carbon Black, www.carbonblack.com/.

8. SentinelOne, www.sentinelone.com/.

For example, consider an adversary who has gained remote access to an IT administrator workstation within a network. The adversary uses stored passwords on the workstation to log in to a central database server, while pivoting through the workstation. This all-too-common scenario may not trigger an alert from the database server because the login characteristics are effectively "normal." Moreover, adversaries may use a variety of tactics to blend in with normal remote access tools or network behavior and evade detection.

This is where a manual hunt becomes central to the response strategy. A professional threat hunter may well detect unusual activity based on context and experience, while automated tools remain blind to the threat.

Most organizations do not have a full-time threat hunting specialist on staff, ready to be deployed at a moment's notice when a cyber incident occurs. Even for those that do, there is a benefit to hiring a threat hunting consultant who routinely works with many organizations. During a cyber extortion crisis, outsourcing can lighten the load of a victim's already taxed internal staff, and enable the victim to tap into specialized expertise.

5.8.5 Results

Since threat hunting is a cyclical process, it's important to analyze and communicate results at regular intervals. Along the way, the hunt may turn up anomalous activities that are not normal for the environment, such as the following outliers:

- Unusual external network connections
- Increases in inbound or outbound network traffic
- Abnormal file or device access
- Suspicious process invocations
- Multiple consecutive failed authentication events
- Activity at odd hours

Once such anomalous behaviors are identified, they need to be documented, vetted, and used to further refine the hypothesis.

Ultimately, when a verified threat is discovered, information about it needs to be quickly and clearly communicated to responders, who in turn can quickly eradicate it. Eradication can take many forms, but often includes the following steps:

- Removing suspicious hosts or virtual machines (VMs) from the environment
- Deactivating unexplained or malicious user accounts

- Disabling newly installed or suspicious software applications
- Eradicating any other sources of potential threats

As threats are identified and verified, make sure to generate signature data and update security solutions to leverage new information.

> ## Heads Up! No-Malware Attacks
>
> According to Crowdstrike's 2022 Global Threat Report, 62% of malicious activity detections in Q4 of 2021 were malware-free. Increasingly, hackers are co-opting normal IT administration tools and using them to push out malware or move laterally throughout an environment. As a result, antivirus tools flag legitimate pieces of software as potentially malicious with increasing regularity. This includes file transfer software such as FTP applications, penetration testing tools such as Cobalt Strike, and commonly used utilities such as PSExec. Exercise caution and verify that programs are actually malicious before terminating them.

5.9 Taking Stock

As the emergency activities slow, responders should conduct a "pulse check" (see Chapter 4) to assess the outcome of the triage activities and the victim's operational state. This assessment should include the following items:

- Effectiveness of the containment activities:
    - Was file encryption halted?
    - Was data exposure halted?
    - Has the denial-of-service attack been contained?
- Risk of continued adversary access to the victim's environment
- Volume and criticality of data that is currently unavailable or at risk of exposure
- Services or systems that are currently unavailable
- Current status of business operations
- Any additional resources that are needed

Based on the results, review and update your response strategy, which will continue to evolve over time.

5.10   Conclusion

Containment is a critical part of the early response process. In this chapter, we presented methods frequently employed in containment activities, including tactics for quickly stopping file encryption/deletion, halting data exfiltration, resolving denial-of-service attacks, and locking out the adversary.

During containment, response teams face special challenges due to their lack of information in this phase, combined with the high potential impact of their decisions. It is critical for responders to maintain good communications and have clear decision-making processes in place to achieve the best possible outcomes.

In the next chapter, we will discuss methods for investigating a cyber extortion crisis that will provide the organization with actionable intelligence and inform further response efforts.

5.11   Your Turn!

Every cyber extortion incident is unique. The response team's options and priorities will vary depending on the victim organization's industry, size, and location, as well as the details of the incident itself.

Based on what you learned in this chapter, let's think through key elements of containment.

Step 1: Build Your Victim

Choose one characteristic from each of the three columns to describe your victim's organization:

Industry	Size	Location
Hospital	Large	Global
Financial institution	Midsized	United States
Manufacturer	Small	European Union
Law firm		Australia
University		India
Cloud service provider		Country/location of your choice
Organization of your choice		

Step 2: Choose Your Incident Scenario

Select from one of the following incident scenarios:

A	Ransomware strikes! All of the victim's files have been locked up, including central data repositories, servers, and workstations.
B	A well-known cyber extortion gang claims to have stolen all of the victim's most sensitive data and threatens to release it unless the victim pays a very large ransom demand. The gang posts the victim's name on their dark web leaks site, along with samples of supposedly stolen data.
C	Double extortion! Both A and B occur at the same time.
D	The victim is hit with a denial-of-service attack on its Internet-facing infrastructure that slows its access and services to a crawl. The adversary threatens to continue and even escalate the attack unless a ransom is paid.

Step 3: Discussion Time

Your victim must contain their cybersecurity incident. Given what you know of the victim and the scenario, answer the following questions:

1. Based on the scenario you chose for your victim, list three appropriate goals for containment.

2. What is the worst-case scenario if the incident is not contained?

3. What are some strategies that the incident response team can use to stay in communication during containment? Consider how normal communications may be impacted by the incident.

4. There is evidence that the adversary had access to the infrastructure, and the incident response team is not sure if the adversary is still actively accessing it. Name three steps that responders can take to lock out the adversary.

5. Given the type of attack, would you recommend resetting passwords network-wide? Why or why not?

Chapter 6

Investigation

Knowledge itself is power.

—Sir Francis Bacon

> ### *Learning Objectives*
>
> - Understand the purpose of investigating a cyber extortion attack
> - Gain strategies for identifying an adversary and using this knowledge to inform the response
> - Articulate techniques for scoping an attack, including identifying indicators of compromise, tracking down "patient zero," and developing a timeline
> - Understand how and why to preserve evidence in cyber extortion cases
> - Learn the fundamentals of data breach investigations and how they relate to cyber extortion attacks

As soon as a cyber extortion attack is discovered, the investigation begins—at least informally, if not formally. *Investigation* refers to the process of systematically uncovering facts about the cyber extortion attack to inform response processes, reduce risk, and meet obligations. The results of an investigation can help the victim:

- Determine the root cause of the compromise or intrusion
- Ensure that the threat is fully eradicated
- Effectively contain damage and reduce risk to affected stakeholders
- Correct security weaknesses and minimize risk of a reoccurrence
- Fulfill ethical, regulatory, contractual, and legal obligations (e.g., data breach risk assessments and notifications)

Investigation is an iterative process that runs throughout the course of the response process. In a cyber extortion attack, three major types of investigative actions are typically used to support the response:

- **Adversary research:** Assessing the threat actor's communications and attack patterns to identify any association with known groups. This, in turn, can help responders understand the risk of data exfiltration, craft an effective negotiation strategy, and inform the response process.

- **Scoping:** Gaining a complete picture of the adversary's activities, including which systems were accessed, how the adversary entered and moved through the technology environment, which data might have been compromised, and more. Understanding the full scope of the compromise is critical for addressing security vulnerabilities and completing a breach investigation.

- **Breach investigation:** A formal inquiry used to determine the risk that data was improperly accessed or acquired. The definition of a "breach" varies from state to state, and from country to country. A qualified breach attorney should determine which laws and regulations apply, how the investigation should be conducted, and whether any follow-on actions need to be taken.

In the following sections, we discuss each of these investigative techniques, and provide tips for leveraging their results effectively. Throughout the investigation, responders should coordinate and communicate with public relations, leadership, and other teammates to inform the response strategy.

A Word About "Investigations"

Formal investigations are often carried out by digital forensic investigators, who are experts skilled in the art and science of finding and analyzing digital footprints left behind by the adversary. If the victim does not have an existing relationship with an individual or organization capable of performing a forensic investigation, most cybersecurity insurance providers or legal counsel can make recommendations or introductions.

6.1   Research the Adversary

The more you know about your cyber extortion adversary, the more effectively you can respond and minimize damage from the adversary's attack. Information about the adversary can help responders use resources efficiently and minimize unnecessary activities, as well as predict the adversary's reactions and understand key negotiation points.

For example, if you are dealing with a nation-state attacker, you might need to invest in very intensive threat hunting. Conversely, if the adversary is an amateur who leverages less sophisticated toolkits, your response may require only simple eradication tactics.

In this section, we review the goals of adversary research, and discuss tactics for identifying cyber extortion adversaries.

6.1.2 Actionable Intelligence

Understanding your adversary is more than just an intellectual exercise. It can produce valuable insights that responders can leverage immediately, such as the following information:

- **The average cost of the final negotiated ransom payment:** Ransom demands vary from a few thousand dollars to millions. In some cases, criminals base their final number on the victim's financial reports or insurance coverage, which is helpful information for the negotiator.

- **Prospects for receiving a discount:** Some adversaries are known to give 50% to 60% discounts, while others are offended by pressure to cut a deal. Understanding the adversary's likely response can help to ensure the best possible outcome.

- **Whether the adversary reliably sends the decryptor after payment:** Receiving the decryptor is not a guarantee, but some groups are more consistent than others.

- **Whether the decryptor works when received:** Some decryptors work flawlessly, while others require a lot of manual work and troubleshooting.

- **Whether you will need a decryptor for each device encrypted or if one key works for all:** Knowing that information while negotiating saves the pain of having to go back to the adversary for a second round of negotiations, if the decryptor works for only one device.

- **The risk that the decryptor contains additional malware:** A large percentage of decryptors contain malware that silently installs backdoors to your network, gathers information, or detonates more ransomware on a timer.

- **The likelihood that other malware such as information stealing Trojans is present on the victim's network:** As discussed in Chapter 3, many adversaries install remote access software designed to evade detection and maintain persistence prior to detonating ransomware. This malware must be discovered and eradicated, or the victim may suffer a reinfection.

- **Whether the adversary typically exfiltrates files:** Knowing typical behavior provides insights that will be useful for the forensic investigation.

- **Whether the adversary notifies the media proactively and/or maintains a data leak site:** Understanding the adversary's level of sophistication when it comes to the media can help to inform the victim's public relations strategy.

Heads Up! An Evolving Ecosystem

Adversary affiliations and tactics are constantly evolving. In recent years, the emergence of ransomware-as-a-service (RaaS) opened the door for franchise models, enabling a wide range of adversaries to leverage sophisticated attack platforms while RaaS operators extended their reach and opportunities for profit. Criminal contractors may serve multiple groups, often specializing in a particular task, such as gaining initial access. The result is that adversary identification is an ever-changing area of research, and it is wise to engage a subject-matter specialist when the stakes are high.

There is no guarantee that the way a particular cybercriminal gang behaved yesterday is the way they will act tomorrow—but knowledge of your adversary does increase your odds of achieving a better outcome.

6.1.3   Identification Techniques

So how do you identify your adversary? The following areas tend to be fruitful avenues for analysis:

- Ransom note

- Communications content analysis, including statements, format, subject matter, and styles

- Malware samples, including ransomware encryption software and other tools employed on the network

- Tactics, techniques, and procedures (TTPs)

6.1.3.1 The Ransom Note

As discussed in Chapter 3, most cyber extortionists leave behind a note that includes instructions and contact information. The note is most commonly a file on the desktop or in each encrypted directory of an infected computer, although it can also be an email, voicemail, audio file, fax, paper that comes out of printers, or any number of other message types.

Ransom notes are often templatized and might—or might not—explicitly name the threat actors. Fortunately, responders can analyze the format and style of the ransom note and match them to known adversary groups. Online services such as IDRansomware[1] and the No More Ransom Project[2] can enable responders to quickly identify an adversary based on the ransom note left behind and the specific type of encryption used.

To preserve the victim's privacy, it is important to remove identifying information from the ransom note prior to pasting it into a ransomware search engine. This can include the organization's name, email addresses, domains, IP addresses, and so on.

The same is true if you conduct searches via Google or leverage third-party software to assist in the investigation. Search engines may track searches, link them to identifying characteristics, and associate these with specific organizations. Make sure to remove identifying characteristics prior to searching for phrases in a note.

Case Study: Ransomware Masquerade

Adversaries may masquerade as known groups when they are actually not. For example, in 2017 a strain of ransomware that claimed to be part of the Globe ransomware group, originally identified in 2011, began encrypting networks around the world.

However, investigators soon realized that this new ransomware strain was not the original Globe ransomware, but was instead mimicking nearly every identifier from the original. This included the malware executable name and ransom note. The adversary behind this new strain, which was renamed GlobeImposter, was attempting to capitalize on the notoriety of the original Globe ransomware to make their demands seem more intimidating.

Another, more sinister example was NotPetya. In 2016, a strain of ransomware called Petya spread around the world, encrypting hard drives and demanding a Bitcoin payment to unlock files. In 2017, a new variant of the malware began spreading rapidly, primarily in Ukraine. However, the new variant was not ransomware at all. Files were encrypted just as with the earlier strains of Petya, but the new variant was modified so that files could never actually be decrypted. The victim computers were effectively destroyed.

Based on the level of sophistication employed by NotPetya, it is widely believed that the malware was, in reality, a nation-state attack executed by the Russian military against Ukraine.[3] It was designed to look like a common ransomware attack, when the actual intent was to destroy networks entirely.

---

1. ID Ransomware, https://id-ransomware.malwarehunterteam.com/.

2. No More Ransom, www.nomoreransom.org/.

3. Liam Tung, "'Russian Military Behind NotPetya Attacks': UK Officially Names and Shames Kremlin," *ZDNet*, February 15, 2018, www.zdnet.com/article/russian-military-behind-notpetya-attacks-uk-officially-names-and-shames-kremlin/.

6.1.3.2 Communications Content Analysis

Victims may exchange direct communications with the adversary, through custom portals, emails, voicemails, faxes, text messages, Telegram, social media platforms, or other methods. In addition, victims may be the subject of a post on an adversary's data leak site, exchanges with reporters, or adversary messages to customers, patients, and other stakeholders. Some adversaries also brag on separate dark web forums, which are often monitored by law enforcement and the media.

How can you gain actionable intelligence about the adversary from the content of their communications?

- Look for branded ransom notes, data leak portals, and messages that advertise the adversaries' affiliation.

- The adversary may come straight out and tell you who they work for during interactive communications. In some cases, adversaries even provide links to news articles about themselves as a demonstration of their previous success, in an effort to further intimidate the victim. Extortion groups such as REvil and Maze often employed this strategy.

- Analyze the grammar and content of messages to identify the native language of the writer (although if the adversary is using a RaaS platform or commercial software, the messages may be generated from templates provided by the software developer).

- Pay attention to the adversary's speech patterns. Look for odd phrasing or colloquialisms that may point to a specific geographic area.

- Identify images or styles used routinely by specific criminal gangs and their affiliates.

- Observe whether the adversary appears to be technically savvy.

- Look for references to adversary job roles or group members, to identify the size and type of the adversary's organization.

- Track the times of communications and attempt to establish the adversary's time zone by paying attention to the time of day when messages are sent or read.

Often, there are clear differences in communications of amateurs versus organized crime groups. Understanding the category to which your adversary belongs can guide your negotiations, as well as give you an indication of the likelihood of a successful outcome.

An amateur adversary will often:

- Respond to messages in a delayed or erratic manner

- Respond to messages only during certain hours

- Struggle with basics, such as decrypting sample files

An organized crime group is more likely to:

- Engage multiple staff members in providing "customer support" to the victim

- Respond to all messages within minutes or 1–2 hours at most

- Communicate through a portal or provide multiple email addresses

- Use templates for communications

- Offer to decrypt sample files or provide proof of exfiltration without being asked

When analyzing more subtle clues, it is best to involve a cyber extortion specialist, as the indicators that connect these with specific adversaries evolve rapidly.

Case Study: The Amateur

A midsized U.S. law firm lost access to its files due to a ransomware attack on a Wednesday afternoon. It contacted the authors of this book for help. After determining that the backups were not salvageable, negotiations began on Thursday, and almost immediately it was apparent that we were working with an amateur criminal.

The first indicator was that the adversary's response times were slow, but predictable. Email responses would always arrive around 8 a.m. PST, 12 p.m. PST, and 5 p.m. PST, and only on weekdays. The patterns were consistent with break times for a standard U.S. organization located in the Pacific Time Zone. The messages arrived only before, after, or at the lunch break of a typical workday. Messages never arrived outside of those times, and never on weekends. The response team hypothesized that the adversary might be using a work computer for their communications.

The initial messages included what appeared to be forced errors, likely in an attempt to lead the recipient to believe that English was the adversary's second language. However, most of the messages were well written using accurate spelling and grammar, and dollar signs and commas were all written in the American standardized way. As time went on, the pretense was dropped.

The final indicator that this was likely an amateur working alone came when the adversary was initially unable to decrypt the sample files. Initially, they accused the responders of altering the files in some way (though what the perceived gain would be remains a mystery). In the end, the adversary railed that they spent the "entire weekend" troubleshooting their own decryptor to provide the sample files, and demanded a higher ransom for their trouble, using a popular American expression as justification for the increase: "Time = $$."

After extensive negotiation and technical support from the response team, the adversary eventually relented and dropped the price back to the original demand, which was covered by insurance.

6.1.4   Malware Strains

Knowing the specific type of malware strains used in an attack can be extremely helpful in navigating your response. Quite often, specific adversary groups are associated with particular strains of malware. Accurate identification of a ransomware strain can help you predict indicators of compromise (IoCs), pinpoint affected systems, effectively eradicate the malware, and gauge the risk of reinfection.

Identification can be accomplished in several ways, but the quickest and most common are as follows:

- The malware has a distinct file extension (e.g., one of the common ransomware variants, such as .RYK or .Cerber).

- Encrypted files match a specific encryption algorithm used by a well-known adversary. For example, the GandCrab ransomware employed the SALSA20 algorithm, which left a file header in a specific format on encrypted files.

- The hash value for the ransomware executable matches previously identified malware, as per malware identification services or antivirus software.

- Behavioral analysis of the malware reveals IoCs associated with known extortion groups, such as IP addresses, domains, or TTPs (discussed in Section 6.1.5).

Responders can use a public malware analysis service such as VirusTotal[4] or Any.Run[5] to match specific malicious software to previously identified samples. However, remember that data submitted to online services may not remain private and can lead to the exposure of a security incident to the public. It's crucial for responders to exercise caution when submitting information to these services. Before uploading anything to a third-party service, consider taking the following precautions:

- Never submit files that contain sensitive or identifying data to a third-party service unless you are absolutely certain it will not be shared with researchers or other affiliates.

- Submit a cryptographic hash instead of the full piece of suspicious software. That way, if criminals have customized the software to suit the local environment, you won't accidentally reveal hard-coded IP addresses or other identifying information.

- Upload a generic file type encrypted by the malware, such as an image icon or a generic application file that is unlikely to contain sensitive or customized data.

- If you must submit a malware sample, redact sensitive data such as the organization's name or IP address range if you are able to reliably edit the sample before it is submitted.

---

4. VirusTotal, www.virustotal.com/gui/home/upload/.

5. Any.Run, https://any.run/.

Case Study: Honda

On June 8, 2020, Honda Motor Company disclosed via social media that customer and financial services were offline due to technical difficulties due to a cyberattack against the corporate network.[6] Details were scarce, but it became clear that Honda had been the victim of a ransomware attack.

While Honda did not initially provide a confirmation of the exact variant or adversary involved, clues were unearthed that gave security researchers and reporters what they needed to identify exactly who had taken Honda offline. Researchers identified a recently uploaded sample of the SNAKE ransomware on Virustotal.com, which provided key details that strongly suggested the sample was the very same piece of software that caused Honda's service outage.

Upon reviewing the ransomware binary in detail, two very curious pieces of information were discovered:

- A kill-switch built into the software that would terminate any activity if the domain MDS.HONDA.COM was not resolvable

- A secondary network identifier referencing the IP address 170[.]108[.]71[.]15, which resolved to UNSPEC179198.AMERHONDA.COM at the time of discovery

The domain MDS.HONDA.COM was not a public domain name and was specific to the internal Honda network, meaning that if the ransomware was executed anywhere else, it would terminate and fail to encrypt any data. After creating a customized network to mimic this internal configuration, researchers were able to successfully execute the ransomware and obtain details of the infection, including the ransom note and contact instructions left behind by the adversary.

BleepingComputer.com, a cybersecurity news organization, reached out to the adversary directly and attempted to confirm the attack. The adversary declined to do so, stating:

> At this time we will not share details about the attack in order to allow the target some deniability. This will change as time passes.[7]

---

6. Honda Automobile Customer Service (tweet), June 8, 2020, https://twitter.com/HondaCustSvc/status/1270048801307234304.

7. Ionut Ilascu, "Honda Investigates Possible Ransomware Attack, Networks Impacted," *Bleeping Computer*, June 8, 2020, www.bleepingcomputer.com/news/security/honda-investigates-possible-ransomware-attack-networks-impacted/.

6.1.5   Tactics, Techniques, and Procedures

It's always a good idea to take a step back and review the tactics, techniques, and procedures (TTPs) leveraged by an adversary to identify known groups or assess the accuracy of intelligence gathered to date. Analysis of the TTPs is traditionally broken down into three sections, each characterized by its level of detail:

- **Tactic:** A general high-level description of the behavior used by an adversary. Example: The adversary enters the network via RDP.

- **Technique:** A more detailed description of *how* the adversary employs the specific tactic. Example: The adversary enters the network by attacking RDP with a brute-force password attack.

- **Procedure:** A highly detailed description of the technique as it is commonly employed by the adversary. Example: The adversary utilizes a time-based password spraying attack against exposed RDP using curated password lists and probable usernames gathered through open-source intelligence gathering (OSINT).

The combination of TTPs used by an adversary can function as a fingerprint, enabling responders to trace the attack back to specific likely adversaries. For example, the authors handled a case in which the initial vector was a phishing email, and the adversary went on to deploy the Advanced IP Scanner and Cobalt Strike before detonating ransomware. This specific combination was associated with the Egregor ransomware group at the time of discovery, and it was rare to find another group using the same TTPs during that time frame.

Security vendors such as CrowdStrike, Sophos, and others publish detailed analyses of threat actors, which can be valuable resources.[8] However, few responders have time to pore over detailed whitepapers in the midst of a cyber extortion crisis. Incident response consultants who specialize in cyber extortion routinely track the latest TTPs associated with different groups and can typically identify the adversary based on experience and specialized industry knowledge.

6.2   Scoping

Scoping is the process of discovering and documenting precisely what occurred in a cybersecurity incident, as well as the known extent and impact of the incident. The results of the investigation will be used by:

- **Responders:** Contain the damage, eradicate the threat, close security gaps, and reduce risk.

---

8. CrowdStrike, https://adversary.crowdstrike.com/.

- **Legal teams:** Determine whether a breach investigation is necessary, and if so, inform the results.

- **Leadership:** Inform decision-making.

In addition, other external parties such as regulators and public relations teams may leverage the results of the investigation for their specific purposes. In this section, we discuss the goals of the scoping process, present an investigative model, and provide an overview of common deliverables.

6.2.1 Questions to Answer

Common scoping questions that support investigative goals may include (but are certainly not limited to):

Entry:

- How did the adversary get into the environment in the first place?

- Which system and/or account was "patient zero," the initial point of compromise?

Expansion:

- Which systems were accessed? This includes workstations, servers, network devices, cloud applications, and more.

- Which data repositories were accessed? Review an inventory of data, if possible, and determine whether any potentially sensitive or regulated data may have been affected.

- Which account(s) were compromised? Was it an entire Active Directory, or a smaller number of accounts?

- Did the compromise include unauthorized access to cloud repositories?

- Which tools, techniques, and procedures did the adversary use to move laterally and escalate privileges?

- Which actions did the adversary take after gaining unauthorized access?

Priming:

- Which malware or tools did the adversary install?

- Did the adversary make significant changes to the host or network configuration that need to be undone?

Leverage:

- If data was exfiltrated:

    - Did the adversary remove any data from the environment? Once again, review an inventory of data and determine whether any potentially sensitive or regulated data may have been affected.

    - What is the risk of harm if the affected data were published or sold?

- If ransomware was deployed:

    - How was the ransomware distributed and executed?

    - Which ransomware strain was deployed? Is it associated with any specific threat actors or activities?

6.2.2 Process

Using a standard digital forensic investigative model, responders can methodically uncover the scope of a cyber extortion incident. As defined by the Digital Forensics Research Workshop (DFRWS) in 2001, the general phases of a forensic investigation include:[9]

- **Preservation:** Ensure that relevant evidence is stored in a manner that maintains the integrity and availability of the data.

- **Collection:** Copy or move the evidence and store it in a format that facilitates access and analysis by investigators.

- **Examination:** Conduct a systematic review of the evidence designed to identify important artifacts and support investigative goals.

- **Analysis:** Interpret results and refine the theory of the case based on the findings.

- **Presentation:** Document and share the investigative process and findings with key stakeholders.

Although this process appears linear, it is typically iterative. Responders may choose to preserve and collect additional evidence at any point if it is available and engage in a cyclical process of examination and analysis, as needed.

---

9. "A Road Map for Digital Forensic Research," *Proceedings of Digital Forensic Research Conference*, Utica, NY, August 7–8, 2001, https://dfrws.org/wp-content/uploads/2019/06/2001_USA_a_road_map_for_digital_forensic_research.pdf.

> ### A Word About "Patient Zero"
>
> The term "patient zero" refers to the first compromised computer or account in a cybersecurity incident. Identifying this point early in the response is immensely helpful in effectively clearing out residual infections and potential secondary access vectors.
>
> Pinpointing patient zero informs both the investigation and recovery efforts. Often entry by an adversary on a network occurred much earlier than the organization initially believed. If the earlier access is not discovered, the organization risks restoring from a backup that is already infected, leading to a repeat incident.
>
> Once patient zero is identified, responders have a starting point from which to trace the adversary's activities. Often, when an attack is traced back to patient zero, responders are then able to analyze the initial point of compromise and trace the attack forward throughout the environment, effectively uncovering the full scope. This, in turn, enables responders to fully eradicate the threat and lock the adversary out of the environment.

6.2.3 Timing and Results

A full forensic investigation takes time. Most incidents involve large amounts of evidence—that is, data to parse through for answers. The search can happen only as quickly as hard drive and CPU speeds allow. Answers may take a few weeks to find.

Depending on the evidence available for analysis, the investigators may be unable to find concrete answers. For example, they may be able to determine that an adversary accessed a particular system, but unable to determine if files were accessed due to a lack of logging of file access.

One last note: A forensic investigation is unlikely to point to or bring about the arrest of a specific culprit. The information can be shared with law enforcement at the organization's discretion. Law enforcement will, in turn, combine it with evidence from similar cases, which may eventually lead to the apprehension of the responsible party. A single forensic investigation, however, is unlikely to do that.

6.2.4 Deliverables

To support responders, legal teams, leadership, and others in their efforts, investigators need to deliver the results of the investigation in a form that is useful and digestible. Key results to document and deliver include the following:

- Indicators of attack/compromise
- A list of known impacted hosts

- Evidence and details that may help identify the adversary

- Timeline of the incident, including initial entry, expansion, exfiltration, priming, detonation, and any other relevant facts

- Specific samples and descriptions of malware and tools deployed by the adversary

- Security tools that were disabled by the adversary or ineffective at detection

- Any alerts that were successfully generated but went overlooked

- Misconfigurations, vulnerabilities, or other weaknesses that were exploited by the adversary to gain or expand access

- Recommendations for eradicating the threat and reducing the risk of future compromise

In addition, responders should produce any evidence needed to support further investigation, such as hard drive images, network logs, mailbox exports, filesystem metadata, activity logs, and more. For more information on this topic, check out Dr. Darren Hayes's book, *A Practical Guide to Digital Forensics Investigations*.[10]

6.3 Breach Investigation or Not?

As early as possible, carefully consider whether to move forward with a breach investigation. Since "breach" is a legal term, the decision regarding whether to investigate an incident as a potential breach should be made by qualified and experienced legal counsel. There is no single universal definition of a breach; instead, federal, state, and local jurisdictions have varying definitions, in addition to any contractual obligations that may apply to the victim organization.

6.3.1 Determine Legal, Regulatory, and Contractual Obligations

If there is a possibility that the data is regulated, then counsel will need to identify relevant breach notification statutes and laws and determine appropriate next steps. Typically, counsel will determine that either:

- There is no risk of a reportable data breach, in which case there is no need for an investigation; *or*

- There is a risk of a reportable data breach, in which case counsel will open a breach investigation.

---

10. Darren Hayes, *A Practical Guide to Digital Forensics Investigations,* 2nd ed. (Boston, MA: Pearson, 2020).

Victims might be required to notify third parties. This often occurs when the adversary accessed sensitive data, triggering data breach notification laws. In other cases, operational impacts may trigger notification obligations to downstream customers, regulators, or other third parties. For example, in the United States, federal agencies require financial institutions to notify their regulator within 36 hours in the event that they experience a cybersecurity incident that is reasonably likely to disrupt the bank's operations.[11]

Tip: Take an Inventory

Take an inventory of your data and identify relevant breach notification statutes, regulations, and contractual obligations in advance. Make sure to document and update this assessment periodically, with input from a qualified external attorney. This can save you a huge amount of time and stress during a cyber extortion response, and also help you effectively develop risk mitigation strategies ahead of time.

6.3.2   Decide Whether to Investigate Further

The victim must weigh many factors when determining how deeply to investigate a potential breach. Investigations can help the victim meet regulatory and ethical obligations, facilitate an accurate understanding of risk, and support harm reduction; however, they can also be expensive and time-consuming. Cyber insurance coverage can help cover the costs in many cases.

If the victim chooses to skip the investigation, and a data breach later comes to light, the victim maybe subject to fines and may be at greater legal risk.

Tip: Criminals Lie

In incidents where the adversary does not claim to have stolen data, or if they show "proof" that they deleted it after a payment was made, the victim may hesitate to investigate the incident in depth. It is important to remember that you are dealing with criminals, and they may not be truthful in their claims.

The claims of the adversary do not take the place of a proper investigation. Skipping a full investigation also increases the likelihood of future incidents; without a full understanding of the compromise, it is difficult to effectively manage the risks that affect all parties.

---

11. U.S. Department of the Treasury, Federal Reserve System, and Federal Deposit Insurance Corporation, "Computer-Security Incident Notification Requirements for Banking Organizations and Their Bank Service Providers," *Federal Register* 86, no. 223 (November 23, 2021), www.fdic.gov/news/board-matters/2021/2021-11-17-notational-fr.pdf.

6.3.3   Moving Forward

Once a victim decides to move forward with a breach investigation, the breach coach will typically take the following steps:

- Establish key questions for the investigative team to answer.
- Direct the investigative team to collect, analyze, and report on evidence.
- Evaluate the results.
- Assess the risk that the incident qualifies as a breach or meets other requirements for action based on relevant laws, regulations, or obligations.
- Provide clear direction for the response, as needed. This may include notification, risk management processes, additional investigation, or other activities.

6.3.4   Outcomes

Typically, the outcome of a breach investigation is a formal, legal determination of whether the incident under investigation triggers breach notification and reporting laws in a relevant jurisdiction. In "denial" extortion cases such as ransomware, the adversary may only intend to impact operations, but the mere fact that they accessed systems containing sensitive information may be enough to trigger a breach notification law.

If investigators are able to rule out unauthorized access to certain sensitive information through a careful review of relevant evidence, the victim may be able to minimize notifications or even avoid the need to notify altogether. Minimizing the number of notifications saves the organization money and can also reduce reputational harm.

Along the way, the investigative team should coordinate and communicate with public relations, leadership, and other key functions to inform other aspects of the response.

6.4   Evidence Preservation

Access to evidence is fundamental for all investigations. Unfortunately, the evidence needed to make informed decisions does not last forever. Digital evidence is like food: You need to freeze it fast, or it spoils. Evidence disappears as part of the normal use of a computer system. For example, it may be overwritten by new data, or purged after a set number of days, or lost when a system is rebooted.

Preserving evidence is the process of collecting and storing evidence in a format and location that will ensure the integrity and availability of the data as long as it is needed. When critical evidence is preserved in the early stages of a cyber extortion crisis, it dramatically improves the chances of identifying the adversary, scoping the incident, and properly investigating a breach, if needed. This, in turn, can minimize the risk of future compromise and potentially save the victim thousands or even millions of dollars in data breach–related costs.

Evidence preservation takes time and resources, which are in short supply in a crisis. Understanding potential sources of evidence and the order in which they should be preserved will prevent missteps that can result in lost, destroyed, or compromised evidence.

Before a cyber extortion event, and especially prior to preserving evidence, the organization should create a strategy to facilitate effective evidence preservation, and prevent accidental destruction, duplication, or contamination.

Case Study: Evidence Destroyed

All of the servers belonging to a school district were encrypted by ransomware. While the district had migrated to the cloud and stored most of its current data there, its servers contained files saved prior to 2018 that included medical and behavioral issues, as well as birth dates, home addresses, and other personally identifiable information of students and staff. The organization's insurance company insisted on a forensic investigation to determine if any of the data was accessed or exfiltrated prior to encryption. The authors of this book were asked to lead that investigation.

Early on, it became apparent that the IT team was opposed to the investigation primarily due to the time it would take to gather and preserve evidence from the impacted systems. Their focus was restoring systems and moving on. The IT staff decided among themselves that preserving one domain controller would be sufficient. They set it aside for us, then wiped and rebuilt the rest of the impacted servers.

As a result, evidence was limited. We were able to determine that the adversary had, in fact, accessed the network through a vulnerability in its Fortinet VPN, scraped the IT administrator's credentials, and successfully moved laterally to other hosts containing sensitive data. However, because the Windows Event logs and other filesystem artifacts were lost when the IT team reimaged the other impacted servers, artifacts that could have been used to narrow the scope of unauthorized access (or rule it out entirely) no longer existed on the network. We could not determine what the adversary did or did not access with enough certainty to rule out a data breach.

In the end, the school district had to notify thousands of individuals about their breach and the potential that their personal information had been viewed or stolen. If the other affected systems had been available, the school district might have potentially limited the number of people who needed to be notified (or avoided notification altogether), thereby saving time, money, and reputation.

6.4.1   Sources of Evidence

To a certain extent, the type of cyber extortion event determines where valuable evidence will be found. However, some common sources are valuable and should be preserved regardless of the type of event. Keep in mind that the evidence may reside with a third party (such as a managed service provider) outside of the impacted network. Here is a list of common types of evidence that are useful in a cyber extortion case:

- Security software and devices
- Ransom notes
- Encrypted file extensions
- Volatile evidence
- System artifacts
- Firewall logs
- Flow records
- Authentication logs
- Cloud-based evidence

Let's look at each of these in turn.

6.4.1.1 Security Software and Devices

Security software and devices such as intrusion detection and prevention systems, antivirus software, access control software, and more can provide insights into the intrusion. A successful detonation of ransomware indicates that security software and devices were not sufficient to stop a full attack, but it does not mean that they aren't useful to an investigator. Valuable artifacts such as behavioral alerts, additional malware detections, access violations, and much more may be contained within this log data. The investigator can also use this data to establish an early IoC list, which can provide a significant benefit to responders.

How to Get It

Acquisition methods for security software and devices will differ based on which types of elements exist within a network and how they are configured. In some cases, the data may be stored in a centralized location and can be easily accessed and exported if the storage location has not been encrypted. In other cases, the data may reside with a third-party provider, which will need to provide the data to the investigator at the request of the victim. The investigator should also be aware that some security software, such as antivirus or anti-malware applications, may store log data locally on their respective hosts.

6.4.1.2 Ransom Note Metadata

Ransom notes are left behind by the adversary primarily to provide information about how to contact them to pay the ransom. Ransom notes can contain much more information than a defender might originally think. Notes may contain information that is essential to the proper operation of decryption software if the goal is to decrypt data using a utility provided by an adversary. In general, the following information can potentially be gained from the ransom note:

- The time when encryption started
- Key information for decryption
- Contact information for the adversary
- Ransom amount information

While ransom notes may be named the same, contents of the notes may differ. In situations where the note is needed by the adversary to create a decryption utility, a defender needs to get all unique notes from an infected environment. When searching for individual notes, a cryptographic hash of the note file can be used to separate duplicate notes if needed.

How to Get It

Ransom notes will sometimes exist only on the desktop folder of the affected computer or in some other high-visibility area, or they may exist in every folder that the ransomware has touched. Ransom notes will often follow similar or identical naming conventions; so, once a single note is identified, it is usually easy to find the others. Writing a PowerShell or bash script to identify files by name is a trivial task, even for an inexperienced IT person. It is important, however, to keep note of where these notes were identified.

6.4.1.3 Encrypted File Extensions

File extensions are the letters or numbers appended to filenames that indicate the file type to the user's filesystem. While some ransomware strains encrypt all files on an impacted network with a single file extension, others use different extensions on each individual host, device, or file share they encrypt. A different file extension can indicate the use of a unique key used to encrypt just files with that extension, meaning a responder will need to identify changes in file extensions to ensure that decryption is possible if a utility is purchased from an adversary. Failure to identify changes in encryption can lead to repeated negotiations with an adversary and wasted time during recovery.

How to Get It

File extensions for encrypted files need to be identified and recorded by a responder. Extensions for impacted files can be found at the end of filenames on systems that have been encrypted.

6.4.1.4 Volatile Evidence

Volatile evidence includes artifacts from computers that are not stored long-term and will be lost once power is removed (or even sooner). This can include RAM, CPU cache, network connections and process listings, pagefiles, and so on. Volatile evidence can contain information showing live activities on the system, including active network connections, active processes and applications, decrypted versions of software, passwords, and even decryption keys. Volatile evidence should be captured very quickly to avoid evidence spoliation. See Section 6.4.2 for more information about the order of volatility.

How to Get It

Volatile evidence can be captured from any system on the network that is in a powered-on state and has not been powered off or rebooted since the incident started. Popular forensic tools that can capture such evidence include Volatility, Axiom by Magnet Forensics, and FTK Imager, among others.

6.4.1.5 System Artifacts

System artifacts include Windows Event logs, Windows Registry data, filesystem metadata, and other evidence stored on the hard drive of a computer system. They can also include deleted files or snippets of data stored outside the filesystem. These artifacts may contain crucial indicators of compromise that a responder can use to pinpoint malicious activities, potential file access, system modifications, or other evidence consistent with the adversary's activities during the incident.

How to Get It

System artifacts can be obtained from any computer system on the network and can be forensically preserved using specialized software like FTK Imager. Responders can take a full system image to forensically preserve all nonvolatile evidence, including metadata and deleted files. Unfortunately, this process can be time-consuming and take up large volumes of storage space.

In many instances, responders can use rapid, targeted captures (also known as "sparse acquisition") to preserve only relevant system-based artifacts. This dramatically reduces the time and storage space needed to preserve evidence, although there is always a risk that important evidence may be missed. If the original hard drive is not immediately needed for the recovery, responders should preserve the original hard drive of the impacted host by physically locking it up after performing a sparse acquisition. That way, responders can begin rapid analysis and recovery, while still maintaining a source for gathering additional evidence later, if needed.

6.4.1.6 Firewall Logs

Firewall logs may exist at the enterprise level, physical location level, or department location depending on the infrastructure model and maintain a record of all inbound and outbound traffic. Such logs can provide information about network activity during a period of compromise. As a common exit or entry point to a network, the firewall is in a unique position to capture data relating to most, if not all, network communication. In incidents where data exfiltration is a concern, the firewall log data can provide a very clear view of any suspicious connections or large data transfer events. The full timeline of compromise can also be identified using firewall logs, as the time between initial infection and ransomware detonation is often significant.

How to Get It

As their name suggests, firewall logs are normally found on perimeter firewall devices, or contained within central log aggregation systems. All available devices and log repositories on a network should be analyzed and all identified sources of log data should be preserved immediately.

6.4.1.7 Flow Records

Flow records are logs documenting the flow of information across a network and can contain both internal and external communications. Tracking network activity is a necessary part of any investigation. Flow records can be used to identify signs of lateral movement, unauthorized access, data exfiltration, and much more. As an added benefit, because flow records record only a summary of information about network activity, they take up a relatively small amount of storage space and can be quick to analyze. Their small footprint compared with their potentially high usefulness make flow records a very valuable source of evidence.

How to Get It

Flow records are conveniently generated by many different types of network hardware, from routers, to switches, to access points, and many more devices. Typically, network equipment does not include large volumes of built-in storage space, so flow records must be routinely exported from network equipment and sent to a separate collection system for retention.

6.4.1.8 Authentication Logs

Authentication logs ideally record all attempted, failed, and successful logins to devices or the infrastructure. Successful authentication events can provide a useful map of assets within a network that have been compromised or otherwise accessed without authorization, which provides a responder with information about which data may be at risk, which accounts may have been compromised, and how far an adversary made it into the network. Failed authentication events can alert responders to an attack, indicate that a system or account is compromised, or signal that malicious software is present on a network. For example, if a responder observes a series of failed logins from a specific source within the environment, this may indicate the presence of an adversary's brute-force utility, which helps a responder remove compromised endpoints from the environment and reduce the chance of reinfection.

How to Get It

Authentication logs can be found in multiple applications or devices within an enterprise network. This can include user applications, file servers, cloud services, network appliances, and many other locations. Authentication logs may roll over after a specific number of days or volume of used space, so collection and preservation should be a top priority during incident triage to avoid potential loss.

Tip: Time Zones

While preserving evidence, document the time zone and format that are currently in use on each source. For example, are the log files in UTC or are they set to a local time zone? If you are pulling logs from multiple locations, are they all in the same time zone? Does the system record time in 12- or 24-hour formats? Are the devices in sync or is time skewed? Correlating events based on timestamps gives you an accurate picture of the event, whereas if times are skewed or tracked differently, you may draw false conclusions.

6.4.1.9 Cloud-Based Evidence

Cloud-based evidence can include any artifacts stored within a cloud service or application—for example, email, file metadata, backup systems, application, or any other service that utilizes cloud-based infrastructure. Quite often in cyber extortion cases, cloud-based evidence is intact and reliable even when the local environment has been totally destroyed. While adversaries may attempt to encrypt or erase data within cloud environments in addition to the local network, this is a newer trend and typically requires extra effort. In the meantime, responders may be able to trace the initial point of entry back to a phishing email stored in the cloud or gain valuable insights by analyzing artifacts from cloud backup solutions. Responders can use cloud-based evidence to reconstruct the attack timeline and understand the full scope of the compromise.

How to Get It

Certain cloud-based applications have a built-in legal hold function. When this is available, responders may wish to immediately activate it to prevent evidence destruction.

Responders should export cloud-based evidence to a secure source for preservation and analysis. Be sure to quickly secure cloud repositories that may contain evidence (for example, by changing passwords), so that the adversary cannot modify evidence after the fact. Also, responders should avoid exporting cloud evidence to a host that is connected to the infected network. Often, retention times for cloud evidence can range anywhere from days to years, so local evidence preservation may take priority.

6.4.2   Order of Volatility

Evidence should be preserved quickly and methodically to minimize accidental loss and avoid potential contamination from active malware. Unfortunately, in the midst of a cyber extortion incident, particularly one involving ransomware detonation, access to evidence can be very unpredictable.

Volatility refers to the lifespan of digital evidence. Some types of evidence are naturally short-lived, or more "volatile," and need to be prioritized for collection over items that can safely be left for a period without the risk of data or information loss.

The *order of volatility* refers to the timing of evidence preservation. Responders should collect the most volatile evidence first, and work their way down to the least volatile, to maximize the success of evidence preservation efforts. A general order of volatility for digital evidence sources is as follows (in order from most to least volatile):

- **Volatile artifacts:** CPU cache, RAM, active network connections, and other sources of data that typically change quickly or may be lost if power is removed from a device.

- **Nonvolatile artifacts:** Hard drive images, local application logs, and other sources of evidence that will persist through a power cycle but may be overwritten during normal system operations.

- **Cloud-based evidence:** Artifacts contained within cloud infrastructure, services, or applications. (Note that this may vary greatly depending on the system and type of evidence.)

- **Centralized security artifacts:** Evidence contained on the hard drive of a central syslog server or SIEM.

- **Offline physical storage:** Secure, nonwritable storage devices or locations including offline backups, tape storage, and external media.

- **Archive media:** Data written to CDs/DVDs, paper media, and archived physical storage.

6.4.3   Third-Party Evidence Preservation

In some cases, evidence may be stored by third parties in a manner that is not directly accessible to the victim. This frequently occurs when data is hosted by cloud providers, but it can also occur with other third parties such as managed service providers and affiliates, particularly when the adversary gained access by leveraging one of these organizations.

When investigating a case that involves a third-party provider, ask legal counsel to compose letters of preservation and send them to the affected organization. A letter of preservation notifies the receiving party that they are to preserve any and all evidence related to the matter. If possible, the letter should outline specific types of evidence to be preserved.

Note that a letter of preservation does not require the third-party provider to actually produce the evidence; it merely notifies them of potential impending litigation and requests preservation. You may need to engage the services of an attorney and file a subpoena to actually require the third party to produce the evidence, unless a relevant law or contract in place requires it.

6.4.4   Storing Preserved Evidence

Once evidence has been preserved, it must be protected. Original copies should be put on removable media (such as hard drives or portable USB drives) and stored in a secure, fireproof location like a safe or safe deposit box.

Going forward, investigation should never take place using the original preserved evidence. Instead, the investigator should use a copy, while the original remains securely stored. In most situations, the copy used for investigation should be a forensic image. However, for log files, a simple copy is sufficient.

6.5   Conclusion

In this chapter, we discussed the purpose, strategy, and importance of an investigation after a cyber extortion incident. We also covered three types of investigations—adversary research, scoping the incident, and data breach investigation—and outlined expected outcomes for each.

In the next chapter, we will delve into techniques for negotiating with the adversary.

6.6   Your Turn!

Every cyber extortion incident is unique. The response team's options and priorities will vary depending on the victim organization's industry, size, and location, as well as the details of the incident itself.

Based on what you learned in this chapter, let's think through key elements of the investigation.

Step 1: Build Your Victim

Choose one characteristic from each of the three columns to describe your victim's organization:

Industry	Size	Location
Hospital	Large	Global
Financial institution	Midsized	United States
Manufacturer	Small	European Union
Law firm		Australia
University		India
Cloud service provider		Country/location of your choice
Organization of your choice		

Step 2: Choose Your Incident Scenario

Select from one of the following incident scenarios:

A	Ransomware strikes! All of the victim's files have been locked up, including central data repositories, servers, and workstations.
B	A well-known cyber extortion gang claims to have stolen all of the victim's most sensitive data and threatens to release it unless the victim pays a very large ransom demand. The gang posts the victim's name on their dark web leaks site, along with samples of supposedly stolen data.
C	Double extortion! Both A and B occur at the same time.
D	The victim is hit with a denial-of-service attack on its Internet-facing infrastructure that slows its access and services to a crawl. The adversary threatens to continue and even escalate the attack unless a ransom is paid.

Step 3: Discussion Time

The incident response team is ready to conduct their investigation. Given what you know of the victim and the scenario, answer the following questions:

1. Name two benefits of investigating a cyber extortion incident.

2. The victim's leadership is considering skipping evidence preservation to speed recovery. Do you think this is a reasonable idea? Describe the tradeoffs and your recommendation. Make sure to support your conclusions.

3. Which type of information can you expect to find when conducting adversary research? Are you likely to identify the person responsible for the attack?

4. Name three sources of evidence that may be useful in fully understanding this incident.

5. What obstacles might the victim face when attempting to preserve evidence held by a third party?

Chapter 7

Negotiation

A negotiator should observe everything. You must be part Sherlock Holmes, part Sigmund Freud.

—Victor Kiam

Learning Objectives

- Learn effective tactics for negotiating with cyber extortionists and achieving your objectives
- Understand the "proof of life" process with respect to cyber extortion
- Recognize and avoid common mistakes during negotiations

Negotiating with extortionists is a complex, powerful, and sometimes intimidating process. On the one hand, an experienced negotiator can often reduce ransom amounts, buy you time to recover data, reveal information about the extortionists, and help you bring an extortion case to a resolution. On the other hand, it is very easy to botch a ransom negotiation, and trigger irritated cybercriminals to raise their demands or abandon the conversation entirely, leaving the victim in dire straits.

Negotiations are valuable for several reasons beyond simply determining a ransom amount. During a cyber extortion incident, a responder might want to engage the adversary in conversation for many different reasons, including these:

- Acquire details about tactics, techniques, and procedures (TTPs) used by the adversary
- Determine the full volume and types of affected data
- Delay the public release of exfiltrated data
- Buy time to check the status of your backups

In this chapter, we provide tips for communication, discuss "haggling" and the proof-of-life process, and share common mistakes and ways to avoid them.

7.1   It's a Business

Adversaries typically view cyber extortion as a business. They consider themselves to be employees, contractors, or, in some cases, owners. For this reason, throughout this chapter, we will refer to the processes and practices of cyber extortionists using the terminology normally used to describe to legitimate businesses.

During negotiations, the authors of this book have received replies from adversaries that clearly demonstrate this ideology: "I'll have to run that by the boss" and "OK. Please wait. It will take me 20 minutes to get into the office." However, no one better exemplified the business mindset than an adversary we called James.

Case Study: Our Friend James

Employees of a small manufacturing company arrived one Monday morning to find their server and workstations encrypted. Their only backup consisted of an external hard drive connected to the main server that was also encrypted during the ransomware attack. The organization was at a standstill; production was halted. The authors of this book were called in to help the organization contain the outbreak and recover, as well as to negotiate the ransom. That is how we met James.

Our client's system was infected with Matrix ransomware, and a hallmark of that strain is the use of email addresses that begin with "JamesBaker," followed by numbers. So, while it's highly unlikely that the adversary's real name was James, that is how we referred to him.

After our first communication with James, we received a response that appeared to be a template that was likely used for all of this adversary's new extortion attempts:

Important! **We are always in touch and ready to help you as soon as possible!**

Attach up to 3 small encrypted files for free test decryption. Please note that the files you send us should not contain any valuable information. We will send you test decrypted files in our response for your confidence.
Of course you will receive all the necessary instructions how to decrypt your files!

Important!
Please note that we are professionals and just doing our job!
Please do not waste the time and do not try to deceive us - it will result only price increase!
We are always opened for dialog and ready to help you.

However, after that initial response, James's responses were no longer canned. While most adversaries remain very terse and abrupt in their communications, James was verbose. Throughout the negotiations, James continued to display his "customer"-focused attitude and service. Replying to our communications, he made comments such as "Don't worry we will help" and "We understand what you are talking about!" As negotiators, we used his eagerness to please in our communications, frequently referring to the victim as "our mutual client" when responding to James. During one impasse in the negotiations, we were honest with James and told him that our mutual client was "losing faith" and "no longer trusted him" to do the right thing. We got a quick response:

> WE DO NOT WANT TO DECEIVE YOU!!!!!! [sic] please trust!

We then received a longer email full of reassurances, including:

> We understand that you are in a difficult situation and we want to help you. you (sic) are our partner.

> This is the best deal that could be! your [sic] client is lucky that you are negotiating!

And finally ...

> ... in our business it is important to fulfill the conditions!

Ultimately, we settled negotiations at a generous discount of 60% off the initial demand, received a working decryption key, and recovered our client's files. When we discovered that the key would not decrypt all of the files, James provided us with additional keys at no charge. James even followed up to ask us how the decryption went. In the business of cyber extortion, James is likely employee of the month, every month!

7.2   Establish Negotiation Goals

Before you begin communicating with an adversary, take time to set goals, understand the adversary, and create a plan. This is a business negotiation, so make sure to approach it that way. What is your desired outcome?

Your goal may be to purchase a decryption key for the lowest price possible, or simply to use negotiation as a stall tactic to buy time while you assess the viability of data recovery. If the incident includes threats of data exposure, the goal of negotiation may be to prevent the release of data, or some combination of all of the above.

Take time to meet with the appropriate members of the incident response team and agree on the goal(s). Team members involved should include legal counsel, finance, and upper management.

Here are some examples of goals:

- Engage the adversary in dialogue in case payment needs to be made.

- Purchase a decryption key to restore data.

- Keep communication open until it can be determined if backups are viable and data is recoverable.

- Prevent the public release of data.

Let's look at considerations that should be taken into account during the goal setting process.

7.2.1   Budget

Make sure your team discusses a budget when establishing your goals. Ransom demands of five-, six-, and even seven-figure amounts are common. As a team, understand what the organization is willing and able to pay. If cyber insurance coverage is available, understand how much coverage can be applied toward the ransom payment, professional services, or other expenses.

Expenses you might incur during a cyber extortion incident include the following items:

- Ransom payment

- Insurance deductible

- Forensic services for containment and investigation

- IT/managed service provider assistance for recovery and rebuild

- Equipment, such as hard drives, for data recovery and rebuilding systems

- Third-party negotiation services

- Legal services

- Brokerage and exchange fees for cryptocurrency purchases

- Notification costs if personally identifiable information (PII) was exposed

- Credit monitoring for individuals whose personal data was exposed

If the victim has a cyber insurance policy, ensure that responders are familiar with any requirements that may impact the negotiation and payment process. For example, many insurers require victims to obtain their approval prior to incurring any expenses, and they may also require victims to choose from a list of approved vendors for negotiation, legal assistance, and payment. (See Section 8.5.2 for more details on the insurance approval process.)

In some cases, the ransom notes or accompanying portal will state the amount of the adversary's ransom demand, but keep in mind that those costs can go up if you delay or need to decrypt multiple systems. If you do not have information about the amount of the ransom being demanded up front, a bit of research goes a long way when budgeting for this expense prior to opening communications.

It is a good idea to conduct adversary research to understand the average ransom demand and final payment associated with the adversary, if available. See Chapter 6 for more details.

7.2.2 Time Frame

Recovery time largely depends on the number of endpoints infected, the number that need to be decrypted versus rebuilt, and the strain of ransomware. However, in general, recovery from ransomware is not a quick process. In 2021, victims of ransomware attacks experienced, on average, 22 days[1] of business interruption. Realistically, you need to plan on resuming full operations in a matter of weeks, not days.

7.2.2.1 Your Timeline

How long can you be without your data before there is no point in getting it back? Do you have backups? Do you need time to determine if they are viable? The answers to these questions will affect your negotiation approach.

If your organization needs its data as soon as possible to remain viable, negotiations must be aggressive, with quick responses to messages and realistic, transparent counteroffers. You may also be more inclined to pay the ransom rather than attempt to draw out discussions and buy time for data recovery.

Some organizations pay the ransom because they believe decryption will be faster than restoring from backups. The time required to restore from backups largely depends on the media used for and the availability of your backups. Depending on how backups have been configured, it's possible that centralized backup systems really store only just a part of the organization's data. In any event, either process will be time consuming. Depending on the number of files that must be restored and quite a few other factors, even decryption can be a long, drawn-out process. See Chapter 9 for details on the decryption process.

---

1. "Ransomware Attackers Down Shift to 'Mid-Game' Hunting in Q3 2021," Coveware (blog), October 21, 2021, www.coveware.com/blog/2021/10/20/ransomware-attacks-continue-as-pressure-mounts.

7.2.2.2 Your Adversary's Timeline

In general, the adversary wants to wrap discussions up quickly, receive their payment, and move on, for a couple of reasons:

- They want their money.

- They know that the longer they maintain contact, the more clues they leave that may be used to track them.

For these reasons, during the negotiations, the adversary will likely give the negotiator deadlines. For example, they may say, "If we do not receive payment by Tuesday, the price doubles" or "If we don't receive payment in 72 hours, we will post the data publicly." The negotiator can push back on or counter deadlines if they do not further the organization's goals.

7.2.3   Information Security

You might have specific regulatory or contractual requirements regarding information security that you are obligated to fulfill, or public relations objectives that may be impacted by the case. As you establish your goals, consider whether it is possible to reduce damage and minimize harm by negotiating with the adversary, and if so, whether you intend to try.

Information security goals can include the following:

- **Protecting confidentiality:** If you are actively being extorted, one goal may be to prevent public release of your data. While it's not possible to guarantee that your data has not been sold or otherwise shared once it has been stolen, one of your goals may be to demonstrate that you did everything possible to avoid letting your data be published or further exposed.

- **Ensuring integrity:** Once an adversary has accessed your network, systems, cloud-based instances, or mobile devices, it is always possible that the data has been altered in come way. During the restoration and recovery process, forensic investigations can be conducted to ensure that the data has not been altered, corrupted, or infected with further malware, regardless of whether the data is being restored from backups or decrypted. Addressing this goal will add time to the recovery process and should be considered when setting timelines.

- **Restoring availability:** In many cases, restoring access to services or data is critically important, and may require cooperation of the adversary.

  - **Services:** Your primary objective might be to resume normal operations, especially if your system normally has 24/7 uptime requirements, as is the case with hospitals and e-commerce sites. In this situation, you may need to restore system configurations, applications, and/or a limited subset of data to resume your organization's operations.

You should have a clear understanding of precisely what data/systems need to be restored prior to engaging in negotiation.

– **Data:** If your primary goal is to recover data repositories, keep in mind factors such as the state of backups, availability and reliability of free decryption tools, and resources needed to re-create data (if that is even an option). All of these variable may impact the goals of a negotiation.

7.3 Outcomes

Extortion is a crime that takes advantage of hope. Victims, in the midst of one of the worst days of their professional lives, hope that criminals are trustworthy. They hope that if they simply pay what the criminals ask, they will receive a decryption key that will unlock their data. They hope that if they pay, their data won't be released publicly or sold on the dark web.

The adversary manipulates the victim into believing that all is not lost, and that after the payment is received, they will get what they've been promised. Unfortunately, the outcome of cyber extortion cases is far from certain. But forewarned is forearmed—so let's look at some of the potential outcomes that differ from victim expectations. Specifically, we will review two scenarios:

- The victim hopes to purchase a decryptor.

- The victim hopes to prevent publication or sale of stolen data.

In both cases, once the victim has paid a ransom, they may be identified as a target for future extortion. During the response, make sure to identify the means of access and remediate all security issues on your network as quickly as possible to reduce the risk of future compromise. (See Chapter 5 for more details.)

7.3.1 Purchasing a Decryptor

Paying the ransom for a decryptor could result in the following unexpected outcomes:

- **The adversary doesn't send the key.** Victims that pay and do not receive a key may be less likely to report their experience due to embarrassment over being "duped." Always remember that you are dealing with criminals. The outcome in which some simply take your money and walk away without following through with delivery of a working decryption key is always a very real possibility.

- **The decryption key doesn't work.** Some adversaries will send keys that don't work. Perhaps the data was encrypted multiple times and a single key won't work, the adversary is not technically knowledgeable and produced a faulty tool, or the adversary sent the wrong key. Of course, it's also possible—and quite likely—that the adversary purposely set out to deceive the victim, in a slightly more elaborate version of the "take the money and run" scheme.

- **Follow-on infections occur.** Decryptors may contain additional malware, which can lead to future malware outbreaks or incidents. See Section 9.7 for details.

7.3.2   Preventing Publication or Sale of Data

Once the victim's data has been exfiltrated, they no longer have control over it. The following are possible unexpected outcomes of paying a ransom to prevent data publication or sale.

- **The adversary publishes your data anyway.** Adversaries have been known to occasionally publish data even after payment has been received. For example, the Netwalker and Mespinoza gangs both posted data stolen from companies after the victims paid to prevent publication.[2] Affiliates of the REvil gang have been observed "re-extorting" victims of exposure extortion weeks after they paid to prevent stolen data from being posted.

  For example, according to Coveware's *Quarter 3 2020 Ransomware Marketplace Report*,[3] at least five ransomware groups are known to have accepted payment and published the data anyway or extorted victims twice, and published data when their demands were not met a second time.

- **The adversary sells your data anyway.** Despite assurances to the contrary, it's entirely possible that the adversary will quietly sell your data on the dark web before or after receiving payment, so as to take advantage of the additional revenue opportunity.

- **The adversary doesn't delete your data.** The adversary may provide proof that stolen data has been securely deleted from their systems, by sending screenshots illustrating deletion or similar supporting evidence. In reality, it's impossible to know for sure that the data has actually been deleted. Even if it's removed from a specific location, you have no assurance that the adversary did not copy your data to another location or share it with a third party first. In the 2016 Uber cyber extortion case, adversaries gained access to the records of 57 million riders and drivers.[4] Uber paid the extortionists $100,000 after receiving proof that they deleted the stolen data. It was later revealed that the extortionists first shared the data with a third party. Reportedly,

---

2. "Ransomware Demands Continue to Rise as Data Exfiltration Becomes Common, and Maze Subdues," Coveware (blog), November 4, 2020, www.coveware.com/blog/q3-2020-ransomware-marketplace-report.

3. "Beazley Breach Briefing—2020," Beazley, March 23, 2020, www.beazley.com/news/2020/beazley_breach_briefing_2020.html.

4. Mike Isaac, Katie Benner, and Sheera Frenkel, "Uber Hid 2016 Breach, Paying Hackers to Delete Stolen Data," *The New York Times*, November 21, 2017, www.nytimes.com/2017/11/21/technology/uber-hack.html.

they later requested that the third party delete the data, but they didn't know if the third party actually did so.[5]

- **Your data is stolen from the adversary.** Adversaries care very little about carefully securing your data once it has been stolen. In many cases, the adversaries store stolen data in poorly secured dropboxes or cloud shares.

Tip: Choose Your Negotiator

While some victims prefer to handle the negotiations directly, others choose to work with a third-party negotiator. Here are some of the benefits of working with an outside negotiator during a cyber extortion event:

- **Experience:** A negotiator who specializes in cyber extortion already knows the process: how to communicate, how to get proof of life, and when and how to apply pressure.

- **Objectivity:** Successful negotiations require a calm, professional demeanor. A third-party negotiator does not have the same emotional stake in the outcome as an owner, executive, or employee of the affected organization, and is therefore better positioned to stay cool in the heat of the crisis.

- **Familiarity:** If you work with an experienced negotiator, they have likely already worked with the same or similar groups and know what to expect in terms of response times, potential discounts, and outcomes, including the viability of the decryptor.

7.4 Communication Methods

Interacting with an extortionist may seem scary or intimidating. The victim or someone working on their behalf must communicate with an unknown adversary, in an unknown location, who may hold the future of the organization in their hands. Responders may have no idea what to expect.

Let's remove the mystery, starting with the basics. In this section, we'll review the most common methods used by adversaries to communicate:

- Email
- Web portal
- Chat application

---

5. *United States of America v. Joseph Sullivan*, Case No. 3-20-71168 JCS, p. 17, www.justice.gov/usao-ndca/press-release/file/1306781/download.

We'll also provide tips for responders who choose to interact with the adversary through any of these mechanisms.

7.4.1   Email

Many criminals simply communicate using email, often leveraging anonymizing email services such as Protonmail and Tutanota. In one of the most popular communication methods, adversaries use free encrypted email services to communicate with their victims during negotiations.

If email is the required method of communication, it's wise to create a dedicated "throwaway" email address for the purposes of negotiation. This is an account created using a third-party service just for communication with the adversary.

Remember that while you are studying your adversary, your adversary is studying you. Don't use real names when creating the throwaway account. The less information you give to the adversary, the better. If you use a personal email address with your real name attached, you give your adversary two key pieces of information that could be used to further attack or extort you.

Once you use an email address to communicate with the adversary, that account may become a target, meaning that the adversary could try to gain access to the account. If you are using an account that you normally use for work or personal communications, and the adversary gains access, all of your email, including any that detail the organization's response to the cyber extortion incident, will be available to the adversary.

When choosing a third-party service to use, consider using one that offers encrypted email to limit the chances of your messages being intercepted by other adversaries. Use a strong password. Also, if available, use multifactor authentication to add a layer of protection against unauthenticated access.

The throwaway account should never be used for any purpose other than this negotiation. If somehow the adversary gains access to the account, you don't want to provide other email addresses involved in or details regarding the current incident. Once appropriate screenshots are taken or emails are downloaded, the account should be deleted, so that there is no trail for the adversary to follow after the incident is resolved.

7.4.2   Web Portal

Many extortion gangs communicate with victims using a web portal, which they often call a "Customer Service" or "Customer Support" portal (see Figure 7.1 for an example). The portal may even have a built-in chat function that lets you communicate with the adversary in real time. Often, though not always, portals are accessible on the dark web using a browser like Tor.

Even if the portal does not require an anonymizing browser like Tor, it's always advisable to use one. While common browsers that include an "incognito mode" or "privacy tabs" do erase browsing history when the browser is closed, they do not block the user's source IP address, traffic while connected, or information potentially related to the computer, operating system, or digital footprint. Using a browser like Tor prevents the adversary from using the session to learn more information about the negotiator or organization.

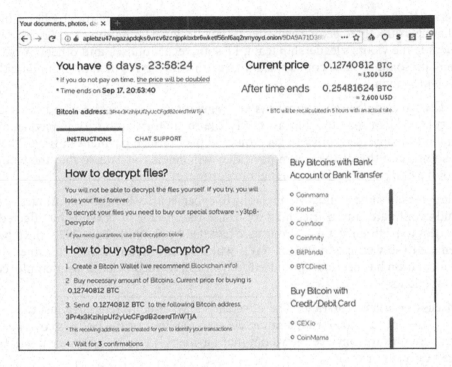

Figure 7.1 An example of a ransomware portal

(Screenshot taken by LMG Security, September 2019.)

7.4.3 Chat Application

Instead of a web-based chat portal, adversaries are increasingly choosing to use chat applications such as Telegram and Whatsapp. These services offer end-to-end encryption and, in some cases, the potential for anonymity. They are also very easy to access using mobile devices, providing flexibility for the adversary's staff.

When using chat applications, responders should take care not to reveal their actual phone number or contact information, so as to reduce the risk of follow-on targeted attacks.

7.5 Pressure Tactics

By the time the adversary has engaged in extortion, they have already gained leverage over the victim by threatening the confidentiality, integrity, and/or availability of information resources. Throughout the extortion process, the adversary may attempt to increase that leverage or engage in psychological tactics to maximize the pressure on the victim. These methods may include:

- **Personalize communications:** The adversary may reach out by email, phone, or other channels directly to people who may be involved in negotiation or response. This can include the victim's leadership team, IT staff, legal counsel, and others. Adversaries may personalize these communications in an effort to frighten or intimidate the victim into paying.

- **Reference compliance requirements and regulations:** Adversaries who have access to regulated data may threaten to notify the regulatory authority if payment is not made or, conversely, offer to keep quiet if they receive payment in time. They may also promise that if the victim pays, they will delete the data so that the victim will not have to pay hefty fines to regulators or report a data breach.

- **Threaten lawsuits:** As litigation relating to cybersecurity incidents continues to evolve and proliferate, adversaries may try to use the specter of lawsuits by affected third parties to frighten victims. In one case handled by the authors in 2020, the adversary emailed the victim and wrote: "[W]e will inform all your clients that their private information has been compromised . . . you will be sued by both your employees and your clients."

- **Discuss insurance coverage:** The adversary may directly reference insurance limits and attempt to settle for an amount close to the limit of the policy's coverage. They may attempt to convince the victim that payment is no big deal since it will be covered by insurance.

- **Publish a subset of stolen data:** The adversary may publish subsets of stolen data to draw media attention to the event and further turn up the pressure on victims. For example, in March 2021, the Cl0p group posted the names, Social Security numbers, and home addresses of the employees of a bank[6] on a dark web site in an attempt to pressure the bank to negotiate. The adversary then emailed a link to the site to the media saying, "It often motivates [sic] to reconsider the decision" and "This is advertising for future customers =)."

- **Taunt on social media:** In addition to publicizing their attacks, adversaries may use social media accounts to taunt or call out their latest victim. During the ransomware attack on the City of Baltimore, a Twitter account believed to belong to one of the adversaries published screenshots of documents purported to be stolen in the attack, and taunted the mayor in an attempt to pressure the city to pay.[7]

---

6. Lorenzo Franceschi-Bicchierai, "Ransomware Gang Fully Doxes Bank Employees in Extortion Attempt," Vice: Motherboard, March 8, 2021, www.vice.com/en/article/3an9vn/ransomware-gang-fully-doxes-bank-employees-in-extortion-attempt.

7. Kelly Jackson Higgins, "Baltimore Ransomware Attacker Was Behind Now-Suspended Twitter Account," Dark Reading, June 3, 2019, www.darkreading.com/threat-intelligence/baltimore-ransomware-attacker-was-behind-now-suspended-twitter-account-/d/d-id/1334860.

- **Directly contact third parties:** The adversary may reach out directly to customers, patients, data subjects, affiliates, or other third parties associated with the victim to indirectly increase the pressure.

While it might not seem like it, both sides actually have leverage in a cyber extortion incident. The adversary has a large portion of the leverage, because they are holding the victim hostage. However, the victim also has leverage: It has money or other resources that the adversary wants—typically as much as possible, as soon as possible.

Heads Up! The Perks of Being a Victim

Today's cyber extortion gangs often tout extra perks that they think will provide an incentive for the victim to accede to their demands. Here are a few examples of popular offerings:

- **Penetration test reports:** These "reports" usually consist of a text file with an informal description of the method of entry, which files were accessed, and/or what, if anything, was exfiltrated. The adversary may promise (falsely) that with this report, the organization will not have to pay for forensic analysis and investigation.

- **Antivirus or anti-malware recommendations:** Adversaries will offer suggestions, and in some cases instructions, for antivirus or anti-malware software that should be used to scan your systems after your files are decrypted or to avoid future incident.

- **PII alert:** If the adversary stole your data, they have likely already done a thorough search of it and may offer a list of the types of data they are holding, such as credit card numbers, particularly if the data contains personally identifiable information (PII). Of course, this also may be used in a manner meant to apply pressure.

- **Attestations of deletion:** If the adversary is holding your data, they will likely offer to send "proof" that they have deleted or destroyed it if you pay. They may even claim that their proof is a guarantee that you will not have to declare a data breach, which of course is not true. Only your legal counsel can advise you on whether a notification is required. Proof of deletion is discussed further in the next section.

- **Customer service:** Remember James? While being extorted is not something anyone would describe as pleasant, more extortionists are focusing on offering the "client" a "good" experience. Can Yelp reviews and surveys be far behind?

7.6   Tone, Timeliness, and Trust

Negotiation is a tricky business even under the best circumstances. A cyber extortion negotiator must communicate with an unknown party, absent any information about that person's background, identity, or location. The only thing that the negotiator knows for certain is that the person(s) on the other end engage(s) in cyber extortion. However, the adversary may not see their "work" as criminal; they may see it as nothing more than their "job." The negotiator must walk a fine line to get the best deal possible while not offending the adversary and causing a breakdown in negotiations.

To achieve the best results, take a businesslike approach. Negotiations should be based on logic and carried out with detached professionalism. In the following subsections, we discuss the three T's of negotiation: tone, timeliness, and trust.

7.6.1   Tone

A neutral tone of professionalism and respect should be used throughout the negotiation process. Respect does not equal agreement, admiration, or even understanding. In this situation, respect is simply saying, at this moment, "I'm going to let you do you." The adversary sees their "work" as a job, a valid business. A negotiation is not the time to point fingers, recriminate, or denigrate that perception. It's not necessary to openly state respect, but if the adversary refers to the extortion or encryption as their work, it's also not advisable to correct them.

Both the victim and the adversary have a mutual interest in obtaining a successful outcome. Building an atmosphere of teamwork may bring about quicker and more agreeable outcomes. Using words like "we" or "our" (as in "our mutual client") in conversation with the adversary reinforces this sentiment.

Ranting, expressing outrage, name calling, and despair do nothing to reduce the ransom or reach a mutually agreeable conclusion. Failure to maintain a respectful tone may offend or anger the adversary, which in turn may lead to them breaking off communications, deleting the decryption key, or immediately publishing stolen data. Regardless of the negotiator's tone, the adversary may choose to employ an aggressive style. The negotiator can and should remain calm, fair, and firm without resorting to the same.

7.6.2   Timeliness

It's important to regularly monitor the email account or portal being used during the negotiations. Adversaries will be checking in on their end, and if they have not received a response, they will likely begin setting deadlines or threatening exposure. Depending on your goals, such tactics may not require an immediate response, but the organization should be aware of them just the same.

If it appears an immediate response is required, an explanation of the delay may be enough to buy more time. For example, telling the adversary that the organization is considering payment, but needs time to determine if it's possible to get the funding together quickly, may be enough to keep the adversary from following through on any threats or new deadlines. Alternatively, the negotiator may say that the organization is waiting for a response from the leaders of the organization or from insurance.

7.6.3 Trust

As funny as it sounds, a certain level of mutual trust is required in a ransom negotiation. If the negotiator makes a promise to the adversary—such as wiring them money by a certain date—the victim should stick to it. Otherwise, the adversary may choose to stop responding, or even respond punitively by deleting the decryption keys or publishing the stolen data.

If some level of trust is established, the negotiator might be able to reduce the price or buy more time for the impacted organization. To build trust, make a point of repeatedly fulfilling small promises during the negotiation. For example, if you say you will respond at a particular time, do so. These small acts can go a long way toward building trust, and ultimately pay off.

Heads Up: Learning from Hostage Negotiation

Real-life hostage negotiation is a long-established industry with well-developed response tactics that have been refined over time. Cyber extortion responders can draw on some of these lessons, but it's important to recognize that some key differences also shape the negotiation process.

For example, in a traditional kidnapping/hostage incident, the adversary must actively keep the victim alive, which includes providing some kind of nourishment and shelter. This is inherently a drain on the kidnapper's resources, and a negotiator may choose to employ delaying tactics, such as breaking off communication for several days, in an effort to try to pressure the kidnapper into reducing the ransom or even walking away.

However, an adversary engaged in cyber extortion does not have the same challenge. The only item they must maintain is decryption keys and/or stolen data. This takes up space, of course, but the costs of data storage are relatively low.

Furthermore, cyber extortionists often negotiate with multiple victims at the same time. If they don't hear from a particular victim for a couple of days, or if the negotiator angers them unnecessarily, they may simply delete the organization's data and move on to the next victim. The promise of quick money is typically the adversary's primary motivator, and as a result the adversary holds most of the leverage in a negotiation. In consequence, a cyber extortion negotiator who delays or is unresponsive may place the victim at greater risk—a very different model compared with traditional hostage negotiation tactics.

7.7   First Contact

The negotiator's initial communication with the adversary sets the tone for the entire negotiation. The message should be concise, professional, and courteous. The goal of the first message is to establish contact and ask for the ransom demand, in addition to building trust.

In most cases, it's best practice to let the adversary name their price first. While it may be tempting to try to throw out a number to open the negotiations, until more is known about who the adversary is, the negotiator risks starting high and paying more than necessary to restore data.

> ### Tip: What's in a Name?
>
> If the email address provided for communications with the adversary includes a name or if later replies are signed, consider using that name in the greetings of emails sent to bring a sense of intimacy or camaraderie into the communications.

7.7.1   Initial Outreach

Here is an example of an initial message to the adversary:

> Hello,
>
> I am a neutral third party writing on behalf of an organization impacted by your work. My goal is to bring a quick and successful resolution for all of us. Can you please tell me the current price for data restoration?
>
> Thank you,
> J. Smith

In the preceding example, the negotiator maintains a neutral, detached, and professional tone and refers to the malicious infection as "work." No identifying information is given away. The negotiator shares a common goal, and then asks for a price—simple and to the point.

7.7.2   Initial Response

The adversary's initial response, as well as each subsequent reply, provides information about the adversary that may prove useful during the negotiation process. Here is a list of items to watch for and note:

- **How quick is the response?** When the initial email is sent, the negotiator should document the time, monitor the account, and note when a response is received.

The timing of responses can give clues about the location of the adversary as well as the type of criminal enterprise. For example, if a response is received in less than an hour, regardless of the time or day sent, it's more likely that the adversary is a professional criminal organization or nation-state. They likely have employees and the ability to monitor incoming email around the clock. In contrast, if a response is not received for several hours, or only at specific times of day, it is more likely that the adversary is a single individual or "amateur" criminal.

- **What style of communication is being used?** The style of communication also provides insight into the adversary. If English is used, does it appear to be non-native English? Does it sound like a native speaker, English as a second language, or someone using Google Translate? Which language do the email headers use? Again, this provides information that may be useful as the negotiation and later investigation move forward.

- **Is the adversary aggressive, rude, or abrupt?** The adversary's tone may provide insight into the feasibility and likely success of stalling tactics, aggressive offers, and potential tradeoffs during negotiations. While the negotiator may opt to mimic the adversary's style in a case where the adversary uses short sentences, mimicking aggression does not typically end well for the organization being extorted.

7.8 Sharing Information

As negotiations progress, it is often necessary to share information. However, that information should be limited, and some information should never be shared if possible. Try not to provide anything to the adversary that could later be used to further the attack.

> ### Case Study: LOL
>
> A manufacturing company was hit with ransomware. The authors of this book were acting as their ransom negotiators. It was the Egregor ransomware strain. We reached out through the criminals' portal to negotiate and identified ourselves as a third-party negotiator.
>
> "What is the name of your company?" the extortionist demanded.
>
> "I'm a third party. What's the current price?"
>
> "I hope you know what company do you [sic] represent," the extortionist replied. "Price for you is $800,000."

"I do know," I said. "But our mutual client has not authorized me to share that information."

"Share this information? LOL. We have broken your security perimeter and downloaded critical data and financial documents," implying that they already knew.

"Then why did you ask?" I wondered. When we asked for proof of exfiltrated data, all we received was a screenshot of a directory on our client's computer. This could easily have been taken while the criminals were actively in the network. The adversary never provided a sample file, and they never actually named the victim (even once) during our negotiations.

The adversary will try to play mind games, but quite often they don't have as much leverage as they want you to believe. Make sure you don't give them any more.

7.8.1   What Not to Share

Following is a list of the types of information that should never be shared during negotiations unless absolutely necessary:

- Name of the impacted organization
- Type of organization
- Extent of the impact
- Financial status
- The negotiator's real name or identifying characteristics

We'll discuss each of these in turn.

- **Name of the impacted organization:** In some cases, the adversary may already know the name of the impacted organization, which may be clear in the ransom note or file extensions on encrypted files. However, there is no reason to share the name of the organization if they do not have it, or to confirm it if they do. Your job is not to make theirs easier, and any information you provide gives them another piece to use for weaponization.

- **Type of organization:** Avoid disclosing the type of business infected by ransomware or being extorted. If the adversary discovers that they have impacted a critical service such as healthcare, they'll likely increase the amount of the ransom. Likewise, if they determine that the organization has deep pockets or is a well-known name, the ransom will increase accordingly, particularly if a threat to release data is involved.

- **Extent of the impact:** The ransomware may have encrypted a server, a dozen workstations, or thousands of endpoints. The data stolen may include medical records, Social Security numbers, or intellectual property. The adversary does not need to know that. Telling an adversary that your whole network is unusable provides additional leverage to increase the ransom. Lying and saying it's only one server when it's really 20 may lead to a later increase in the ransom demand or refusal to return data, especially if multiple decryption keys are needed.

- **Financial status:** Regardless of the organization's ability to pay a ransom either independently or through insurance, the negotiator should not share the organization's financial status during the initial dialogue. Once the adversary has named a price and negotiations begin in earnest, some financial information may be beneficial as leverage—but the less said in early communications, the better. Likewise, until the negotiator better understands which information the adversary already has, it is unwise to pose as something other than what the organization is. For example, a *Fortune* 500 company should not pretend to be a small, nonprofit organization. If the adversary knows or later determines that the negotiator is lying, settlement could be delayed, more costly, or even impossible. Keep communications direct and narrowly focused.

- **The negotiator's real name:** The negotiator should adopt a pseudonym and use it throughout communications. The adversary should never be given the real, full name of the negotiator. Providing that information not only provides the adversary more information related to the organization, but can also make the negotiator another target of the adversary.

Case Study: School District Snafu

A school district was held hostage by cyber extortionists. The IT staff followed the instructions on the ransom note and began communicating with the adversary before calling in a professional negotiator. Unbeknownst to the IT staff, the ransom notes were different on each workstation.

When the adversary said that the victim needed to provide a ransom note from each one of its computers, the IT staff wrote back, "But we have thousands of computers!" All of this happened before a price had been named.

Consequently, the extortionists knew that they were dealing with a large organization. They set the ransom demand very high—in fact, at the time, it was the highest ransom that the authors had ever seen.

After that, the school district called the authors in to engage in professional negotiations, and we were able to dramatically reduce the ransom demand.

7.8.2 What to Share

The following list describes the types of information that are typically important to share with the adversary during negotiations:

- **Multiple ransom notes, if present:** To decrypt some forms of ransomware, the adversary may require a copy of the ransom note. With some infections, each copy of the ransom note may be the same; however, depending on the strain, a ransom note may have several unique versions on the network or workstation. If the adversary requests a copy of the ransom note, the negotiator should make sure to ask if notes from each encrypted files location are needed or if a single note from any location is enough. If the adversary is using a portal rather than email for communications and negotiations, a copy of a ransom note may be required to gain access to the portal.

- **Desired outcome or goal:** A negotiator can create trust by stating the desired outcome. Naming the goal early in the conversation creates transparency and sets the tone for straightforward communication. Even better, the goal may be framed as a mutual goal: "We'd like to reach an agreement quickly so that you receive your payment, and we get back to business as usual." That can further increase the sense of teamwork.

7.8.3 What to Hold Back for Later Use

Some information that is initially held back can be used later during negotiations as leverage to reduce the ransom demand or come to an agreement more quickly. The following types of information are often used for this purpose:

- How quickly payment can be made
- Number of systems impacted
- Whether the organization has insurance
- Amount of readily available funds

We'll discuss how negotiators can leverage this information later, in Section 7.11.4.

7.9 Common Mistakes

When not handled correctly, negotiations with an adversary can take a cyber extortion incident from bad to worse. To avoid pitfalls, here are the most common mistakes made by inexperienced negotiators:

- **Pretending to be someone else:** In an early ransomware case we handled, the organization reached out to the adversary prior to contacting us for help. They told the adversary that they were "just a teenage girl trying to get her homework back before it's due tomorrow." The adversary had likely heard this type of story before. If the adversary had access to the organization's network during the attack, the adversary already knew it was a lie, and opening communications with outright, blatant lies did not set a good tone for the ongoing negotiations.

- **Playing on the adversary's sympathy:** In the preceding example, the organization hoped that by pretending to be a teenage girl they would accomplish two possible outcomes: (1) The adversary would set the ransom very low given that a teenage girl likely would not have the ability to pay much of a ransom or (2) the adversary would feel badly for the girl and provide the decryption key for no charge (the ideal outcome from the victim's perspective). However, most adversaries are not moved by sympathy for a target. Instead, they are skeptical and likely to set the initial demand much higher out of anger at the manipulation attempt. In the case outlined here, the adversary already had unauthorized access to the organization's network, financial statements, and email, so the lie was immediately called out and the adversary treated the organization very aggressively during initial negotiations.

- **Failing to provide factual information:** While some information can be omitted or glossed over, some factual information is critical to the recovery of the organization. If the adversary states that the organization needs to provide the number of systems infected, or copies of ransom notes from each infected system, the only reason not to provide accurate information is if the organization does not need to decrypt all systems. Otherwise, every system that has encrypted files that need to be recovered must be counted.

- **Using anger or recrimination:** As is true with most people, attacking the adversary's character, behavior, or moral compass only serves to put the adversary on the defensive. The organization should use a negotiator who can maintain an objective, unemotional demeanor throughout the process. While it's possible that the adversary will use an aggressive approach anyway, it's less likely that negotiations will break down if the negotiator remains calm.

7.10   Proof of Life

Any fan of TV crime dramas or novels knows that prior to paying a ransom, the kidnapper is asked to provide proof of life—that is, proof that the person being held hostage is still alive. "Proof of life" is demanded in cyber extortion incidents as well, so as to reassure the victim that the extortionist can deliver what they promise.

7.10.1   Goals and Limitations

In the context of cyber extortion cases, proof of life is typically aimed at accomplishing any or all of the following, depending on the type of attack:

- Demonstrating that the adversary is in possession of the correct decryption key, if the victim's data is encrypted

- Demonstrating that the adversary's decryption tools work and can successfully be used to recover data

- Illustrating that the extortionist actually possesses data that they are threatening to publish

- Showing that the adversary has the power to halt a denial-of-service attack

7.10.2   Denial Extortion Cases

When files are encrypted and inaccessible, proof of life is generally provided by sending two to three files to the adversary and asking them to send decrypted copies of the files back. Files should be chosen carefully, and to protect the organization and keep negotiations flowing smoothly, they should meet multiple criteria:

- **Innocuous files:** Most adversaries have policies in place about what type of file is acceptable for proof-of-life decryption. For example, most adversaries will not decrypt Excel files, large Word documents, database tables, or anything that seems "important" to the organization. They do not want to decrypt a file as proof of life only to find that it was the file the organization needed to get back up and running and they have lost their chance at a payoff. Many adversaries place file size limits on the requests as well, particularly if they are using email as a communication method, since most email clients place size limits on attachments.

- **No identifying information:** Choose files that have no logos or information identifying the organization and avoid non-stock photos. Be sure that the files chosen contain no PII. If you're uncertain, system files such as .jpeg files for operating system icons are always a safe bet. PDFs such as user manuals for common software or equipment are also a good solution—just make sure that they don't give away any trade secrets or confidential network information.

- **Multiple locations or devices:** Some strains of ransomware require a separate decryption key for each infected device and, depending on the method used to infect files on servers, may require multiple decryption keys for one device. Choose infected files from multiple locations, and if more than one device was encrypted, choose files from multiple devices. Depending on the strain, it may be necessary to include ransom notes from each file location. If uncertain, gather those at the same time so they are ready.

Note that an adversary may offer to provide proof of life before the negotiator requests it. Generally speaking, the offer will be to decrypt one file. While it is in the best interest of the organization to limit the number of files sent to unknown persons, it is also imperative to ensure that the adversary can decrypt files from more than one device or location. If the adversary offers to decrypt only one file, the negotiator should send three files, with a note stating exactly that. For example, "Thank you for your offer. I have attached three small files, as I want to ensure that the decryption key you have will work on files from more than one location. Please decrypt these three files and return them to me."

7.10.3 Exposure Extortion Cases

If the adversary claims to have exfiltrated or stolen the organization's data, a different approach to the proof-of-life process is necessary. Rather than simply assuming that the adversary is telling the truth and is actually in possession of the organization's data, it is reasonable to ask for evidence demonstrating this is true.

In this case, the negotiator should ask the adversary to prove that data was actually exfiltrated and the adversary is in possession of it. Some adversaries may attempt to do this by providing screenshots of directories of files. The organization should review and determine if the directory structure matches one of the impacted devices.

However, screenshots alone are not enough to prove that data was exfiltrated. The adversary could have taken the screenshots while breaching the organization's network and may not have actually exported the data. Therefore, a request should be made for copies of one or two files in a decrypted state. Ideally, these files should be chosen by the victim, not the adversary, to demonstrate that the adversary has stolen a repository and not just a couple of sample files.

The sample files should be different from those shared for the denial extortion proof of life, of course. If possible, the negotiator should provide a path to specific files, so as to reduce the risk of confidential information passing through email or being posted to file hosting sites.

7.10.4 What If the Adversary Refuses to Provide Proof of Life?

An adversary who encrypted or stole your data is typically willing to provide proof of life to get paid; that step has become common practice. If you request proof of life, and they refuse, the most likely explanation is that the adversary doesn't have the ability to provide it. If your data has been encrypted, failure to prove that they can decrypt it likely means that the adversary either does not have the decryption key or cannot make it work.

Likewise, if you've asked the adversary to provide proof of file exfiltration and they refuse, they likely do not have your files. As mentioned earlier, if all the adversary provides is a screenshot of files in a directory on one of your systems, request a copy of one of those files.

7.11 Haggling

Once the initial exchange of information and proof of life have been completed, it's time to start bargaining. In this section, we discuss when and how to haggle, and provide tips for getting the best deal.

Tip: Cryptocurrency Is Volatile

Whenever possible, negotiate the price of the ransom in the local currency. Cryptocurrency prices are volatile and can change rapidly in a matter of hours. If the adversary sends the initial demand in a cryptocurrency such as Bitcoin, the negotiator can ask—either at that time or at the end of negotiations—if agreement can be reached in U.S. dollars or the appropriate local currency.

If the adversary insists on setting the ransom demand in cryptocurrency, the victim should plan to pay an additional 1% to 10% to cover the cost of any fluctuations. (Review the fluctuations over the previous month and especially the previous week to try to determine what percentage is appropriate.)

To demonstrate using simple math, assume that an adversary insists on negotiating in Bitcoin, and at the time agreement is reached, 1 Bitcoin (BTC) equals $10,000. The agreed-upon price is 10 BTC and payment must be made in 24 hours. The organization makes arrangements and sends $100,000 to a broker to make payment. However, when $100,000 is sent 20 hours later, 1 BTC equals $11,000. The adversary is likely to refuse to deliver the decryption key until the additional $10,000 is sent. If the ransom had been negotiated explicitly in U.S. dollars, the $100,000 sent would have been correct.

7.11.1 Discounts

Can you get a discount on the price of a ransom? Often, the answer is yes! For example, in the Tesla 2020 cyber extortion case, the accused Russian agent, Egor Igorevich Kriuchkov, was indicted. According to an FBI Special Agent assigned to the case:

> KRIUCHKOV said that victim companies usually negotiate with the group to pay less ransom money than the group initially requests, for example [one] company was ransomed at US $6 million and ultimately paid US $4 million. He said only one company paid the full initial ransom.[8]

In general, cyber extortionists name their initial price with the expectation that their target will want to negotiate, so negotiators should always ask for a discount. It's rare to

---

8. *United States of America v. Egor Igorevich Kriuchkov*, Case No. 3:20-mj-83-WGC, Complaint for Violation of: Title 18, United States Code, Section 371, www.justice.gov/opa/press-release/file/1308766/download.

work with a cyber extortionist who will not bargain. While some adversaries are willing to drop their asking price by only 2% to 5%, others may, after some back and forth, agree to a 50% decrease (although a discount that large is rare).

To ask for a discount, use the direct approach but keep it realistic. If the adversary opens the negotiation with a demand in the millions, it's highly unlikely you will be able to settle on payment in the thousands.

Make your counteroffer, preferably in the local currency. Name the exact price you want to pay. Be prepared to justify your position.

7.11.2 Setting the Price

What amount should you counteroffer? This decision is usually a team effort involving the victim's executive team, in cooperation with insurance and legal counsel. Make sure to consider your goals before making a counteroffer. If the primary goal is to get the decryption key quickly, the counteroffer should be conservative. If the goal is to stall for time, the initial counteroffer can be more aggressive (although not so aggressive that the adversary will walk away). In all cases, take into account any information you have about the person or group extorting you. Some extortionists are more willing to provide discounts than others, and you may be able to leverage known patterns regarding specific groups.

You might also want to consider the adversary's communication style in their first messages. If the replies have been short, rude, aggressive, or threatening, and you make a lowball offer, be prepared for a swift and angry response, or in rare cases the cessation of communication.

> ### Tip: Starting Over
>
> If the adversary breaks off communication due to anger or a disagreement, the negotiator can set up a new throwaway email account and attempt to start negotiations from the beginning with a new pseudonym.

7.11.3 Making Your Counteroffer

The counteroffer should be straightforward:

> Thank you for the proof of life files, James. We are ready to move forward if we can come to agreement. Would you be willing to accept $200,000?

Most likely the first counteroffer will be rejected. If the organization decided to use an aggressive counteroffer, the adversary may come back angry or threatening, offended by such a low offer. In that situation, the negotiator will often address that in a follow-up response. For example:

Our intention was not to offend you. We simply want to be realistic with you about our budget.

If negotiations stall at any point, it's time to employ tradeoffs.

7.11.4   Tradeoffs

In Section 7.8.3, we identified types of information that can be held back to be used later in negotiations, including rapidness of payment, number of systems impacted, availability of insurance, and readily available funds. This information can be used to during the haggling process to try to improve the final outcome for the organization. Let's look at each individually.

- **How quickly payment can be made:** One bit of leverage that a negotiator has and can use is timeliness. When the impacted organization can make payment quickly, the negotiator can use that information if the give-and-take of negotiation stalls. If it's realistically possible for the organization, the negotiator can ask for a discount percentage if payment is made within a certain time frame. For example:

  Hi James,

  We'd like to wrap this up as quickly as possible. We'd like to offer payment within 48 hours, if you will agree to a 25% discount off of your last offered price of $X. Do we have an agreement?"

  Thank you,
  J. Smith

- **Number of systems impacted:** Early in negotiations, organizations generally understate or obfuscate the number of systems infected and downplay the impact on their business to the adversary in an attempt to keep ransom demands lower. However, some strains of ransomware require a unique decryption key for each infected system. Once the opening demand has been made and negotiating begins, the negotiator should ask the adversary if the decryption key offered will decrypt all systems and documents. If the question isn't asked and answered, the organization may find itself in the difficult position of having to go back to the adversary after purchasing the key and request more decryptors. That will usually result in further extortion, and more time and money lost.

- **Insurance:** If the organization does not have cybersecurity insurance, a negotiator can attempt to use that information in the late stages of negotiations. For example, if the adversary offers only minimal reductions in price, it may be worthwhile to share that the organization has no insurance, so the payment will be coming directly from the organization and therefore needs to be reasonable and reflect its budget.

This method may backfire if the adversary had access to the organization's network and time to review financial statements, account information, or insurance status.

- **Readily available funds:** Another tactic to reduce the ransom demand is to focus on the amount of readily available funds. If the organization has quick access to $100,000 but would require a week or more to gain access to $200,000, let the adversary know that. We have worked on cases with public organizations that had spending limits. One organization had policies in place that stated the head of the organization was able to spend up to $50,000 without further review, but anything beyond $50,000 required a public meeting of the board of directors. We used that as a negotiating tactic to let the adversary know that if they were willing to accept $50,000, the victim could pay within 24 hours. In contrast, if they continued to insist on $75,000, that outlay would require a public meeting, which would take approximately a week to arrange, and chances were that the board would not approve payment at all. The adversary quickly settled for $50,000.

7.12   Closing the Deal

If the adversary agrees to a price that is acceptable to the victim, and they have determined that they want to pay, it's time to close the deal.

7.12.1   How to Close the Deal

When closing the deal, start by getting written confirmation of agreement from the adversary. This typically includes the agreed-upon price, form of payment, timing, and deliverables received in return. For example:

Thank you, James –

Yes, we agree to the price of $X payable in Bitcoin, and will send the funds within 24 hours. In exchange you will provide the key(s) that will decrypt all of our files. Do you agree?

It might seem odd to restate the agreement and ask for confirmation when this is not a contractual obligation that could ever be enforced in a court of law, but it can help to prevent misunderstandings. Also, remember that there really is honor among thieves. Because extortion is the adversary's business, they often honor their agreements. They know that if they don't, word might get around—and victims will be less likely to pay if the adversary has a reputation for not holding up their end of the bargain.

See Chapter 8 for more details about forms of payment and intermediaries, including potential surcharges and handling fees.

7.12.2 Changing Your Mind

Whether the goal of the negotiations is to stall for time or the organizational leaders change their mind about making payment, the negotiation process can be halted at any time. (Make sure the extortionists no longer have access to the victim's information resources by the time you make this decision.)

As long as there is a chance that the organization will decide to pay, the negotiator should maintain contact with the adversary. That doesn't mean that each new communication has to include a counteroffer. Stalling tactics may work just as well. Consider telling the adversary that it is taking time to get buy-in from the executive members of the organization, to gather that much money, or to figure out where to purchase cryptocurrency. In general, it is a good idea to maintain a regular communication cadence with the adversary.

Once the decision has been made that no payment will be made, the victim typically breaks off contact. It is not necessary to tell the adversary that the organization doesn't intend to pay, and often best to simply stop communicating. This can prevent the situation from escalating. The negotiator may want to continue to monitor the email account used for negotiations for another week or so to ensure that there are no additional threats or further extortion attempts, but once messages from the interactions have been saved and documented, typically the account can be closed.

7.12.3 After the Deal Is Closed

To make payment to the adversary once price has been agreed upon, the negotiator will need to ask the adversary for a cryptocurrency wallet address. That address is used to direct payment to the adversary's cryptocurrency account. Depending on the type of cryptocurrency used, the wallet address will likely be a long string of alphanumeric characters.

Once the wallet address is received, crucial steps must be taken to verify that payment can be made to the adversary. Those steps will be covered in Chapter 8, which focuses on payment.

7.13 Conclusion

Cyber extortion is a business, and a successful ransom negotiation should be treated like a business deal. In this chapter, we outlined that process, including the first and most important step: setting goals. We discussed how the negotiator should use a professional tone, maintain a calm demeanor, and communicate clearly and logically. We delved into "proof of life" methodologies, provided tips for obtaining discounts, discussed which information to share and when to share it, and described how to close the deal. In the next chapter, we'll cover how to make payment once agreement has been reached.

7.14   Your Turn!

Every cyber extortion incident is unique. The response team's options and priorities will vary depending on the victim organization's industry, size, and location, as well as the details of the incident itself.

Based on what you learned in this chapter, let's think through key elements of the negotiation process.

Step 1: Build Your Victim

Choose one characteristic from each of the three columns to describe your victim's organization:

Industry	Size	Location
Hospital	Large	Global
Financial institution	Midsized	United States
Manufacturer	Small	European Union
Law firm		Australia
University		India
Cloud service provider		Country/location of your choice
Organization of your choice		

Step 2: Choose Your Incident Scenario

Select from one of the following incident scenarios:

A	Ransomware strikes! All of the victim's files have been locked up, including central data repositories, servers, and workstations.
B	A well-known cyber extortion gang claims to have stolen all of the victim's most sensitive data and threatens to release it unless the victim pays a very large ransom demand. The gang posts the victim's name on their dark web leaks site, along with samples of supposedly stolen data.
C	Double extortion! Both A and B occur at the same time.
D	The victim is hit with a denial-of-service attack on its Internet-facing infrastructure that slows its access and services to a crawl. The adversary threatens to continue and even escalate the attack unless a ransom is paid.

Step 3: Discussion Time

Your victim has decided to enter into negotiations with the adversary. Given what you know of the victim and the scenario, answer the following questions:

1. What steps should the victim organization take before communicating with the adversary?

2. The president of the victim organization wants to lead negotiations. Is this a good idea? What are the pros and cons?

3. The victim organization receives a message from the adversary. What characteristics can they look for to learn more about the adversary? What types of information can they learn?

4. The adversary states that the ransom demand is $5 million. Name one factor that the victim can use as leverage to convince the adversary to lower their price.

5. The victim organization needs proof that the adversary can actually deliver on their promises. Describe an appropriate proof-of-life process in this incident.

Chapter 8

Payment

Yesterday's price is not today's price!

—Fat Joe

Learning Objectives

- Know the risks and potential outcomes associated with ransom payments
- Gain familiarity with key regulatory issues surrounding ransom payments that can place victims in legal jeopardy and at risk of government enforcement actions
- Understand the cryptocurrency payment process, including the strategy, timeline, and typical steps
- Learn how to gain access to large volumes of cryptocurrency quickly, and coordinate with third parties to ensure a smooth payment process

---

In the fictional worlds of television and movies, paying a digital ransom seems easy. Ask the criminals for their account number, open a payment app, press "Send," and watch while the bad guys confirm that the funds immediately appear in their account.

Reality is not nearly that quick or straightforward. Under normal circumstances, it can take weeks or months to procure large volumes of cryptocurrency—but as we will see, there are ways to access funds quickly in a cyber extortion crisis. Making payments to criminals can also place you at risk of potential civil or criminal penalties, even if you work through experienced third parties. In addition, victims may need to obtain approval for making such payments from a cyber insurance company. One mistake can result in the loss of hundreds of thousands (if not millions) of dollars, or lead to civil charges, fines, or even a prison sentence for those involved.

In this chapter, we discuss the ransom payment process from beginning to end, including the decision of whether to pay, how to make the payment, regulatory issues, compliance and reporting requirements, common mistakes, and tips for success.

8.1 To Pay or Not to Pay?

One of the big decisions that victims need to make is whether to pay the ransom. In the following sections, we'll look closely at the arguments for and against paying a ransom demand.

8.1.1 Is Payment Even an Option?

Before considering a ransom payment, the victim should determine whether there are any relevant laws, contractual obligations, or organizational policies that restrict ransom payment. For example, in the United States, several states have proposed banning ransomware payments (although none of these laws had passed at the time of this writing).[1] In some cases, victim organizations may have preestablished policies banning ransom payments. This is often the case for public-sector entities such as government agencies, police departments, and school districts, where leadership has established that ransom payments are not an acceptable use of taxpayer dollars.

8.1.2 The Argument Against Paying

Cyber extortionists are criminals, and ransom payments fund their operations. By paying ransoms, victims unwillingly perpetuate crime. In some cases, the money is used to fund other criminal enterprises or terrorist organizations.

What's more, criminals may not fulfill their end of the bargain after the ransom is paid, or their decryption tools may not work effectively. According to a 2021 whitepaper, victims that paid a ransom were able to recover, on average, just 65% of their encrypted data.[2] In the infamous Colonial Pipeline ransomware case, the victim paid nearly $5 million for a decryption utility, only to find that the tools were so slow the company was better off restoring from backups.[3]

Repeated extortion attempts are not uncommon. For example, in 2016, Kansas Heart Hospital fell victim to ransomware. The hospital paid the initial ransom, but the adversary refused to send the decryption key and instead demanded a second payment. The victim did not pay again.[4]

---

1. Cynthia Brumfield, "Four States Propose Laws to Ban Ransomware Payments," CSO, June 28, 2021, www.csoonline.com/article/3622888/four-states-propose-laws-to-ban-ransomware-payments.html.

2. Sophos, *State of Ransomware 2021*, April 2021, p. 11.

3. William Turton, Michael Riley, and Jennifer Jacobs, "Colonial Pipeline Paid Hackers Nearly $5 Million in Ransom," *Bloomberg*, May 13, 2021, www.bloomberg.com/news/articles/2021-05-13/colonial-pipeline-paid-hackers-nearly-5-million-in-ransom.

4. Ms. Smith, "Kansas Heart Hospital Hit with Ransomware; Attackers Demand Two Ransoms," CSO, May 22, 2018, www.csoonline.com/article/3073495/kansas-heart-hospital-hit-with-ransomware-paid-but-attackers-demanded-2nd-ransom.html.

In a more recent case, the United Kingdom's National Cyber Security Centre reported in 2021 that an unnamed victim had paid £6.5 million (roughly $8.9 million at the time) and received a decryptor. The victim decrypted their data and got back to work. They did not take the time to analyze their network and determine how the adversary got in or further secure the network. Two weeks later, their data was encrypted a second time in an attack attributed to the same adversary.

Because cryptocurrency payments are nonreversible, there is no money-back guarantee if the criminal does not keep their word. The risk that the adversary will take the payment without fulfilling their end of the bargain is very real.

The city of Baltimore chose not to pay an $80,000 ransom in May 2019, when the city's network was crippled by a ransomware attack (see Chapter 2 for details).[5] Mayor Bernard C. Jack Young released a video explaining why the city chose to recover rather than pay the ransom.[6] He listed multiple reasons:

- The city was advised by the Secret Service and FBI not to pay.

- Paying criminals was not in line with the city's mission, and it would not reward criminal behavior. Mayor Young said, "That is not the way we operate."

- There was no guarantee the adversary could or would unlock the data.

- It was not possible to track the payment or identify the recipient.

- The city had no way of knowing if the adversary left other malware on the system to extort the city again later.

"Ultimately, we would still have to take all of the steps we've taken to assure a safe and secure environment," said Young. "I'm confident we have taken the best course of action."

8.1.3 The Argument for Paying

Nobody likes paying a ransom, but there are cases where it may realistically be the least damaging outcome. Although formally the U.S. government "strongly discourages all private companies and citizens from paying ransom or extortion demands,"[7] officials nonetheless tacitly acknowledge that there are valid reasons for paying.

In the Colonial Pipeline case, U.S. Deputy National Security Adviser Anne Neuberger said, "We recognize … that companies are often in a difficult position if their data is

---

5. Angela Moscaritolo, "Ransomware Attack Strikes Baltimore City Government." *PCMag*, May 8, 2019, www.pcmag.com/news/ransomware-attack-strikes-baltimore-city-government.

6. Mayor Bernard C. Jack Young (tweet), June 5, 2019, https://twitter.com/mayorbcyoung/status/1136377418325864448?s=20.

7. "Updated Advisory on Potential Sanctions Risks for Facilitating Ransomware Payments," U.S. Department of the Treasury, September 21, 2021, https://home.treasury.gov/system/files/126/ofac_ransomware_advisory.pdf.

encrypted and they do not have backups and cannot recover their data."[8] The adversary has even greater leverage when the security of patients, students, customers, or other third-party data is threatened.

At Hollywood Presbyterian Medical Center in 2016, adversaries detonated ransomware, taking the hospital offline and causing patients who needed emergency care to be diverted to other facilities. The ransom demand was 40 Bitcoins, equal to approximately $17,000 at the time. "The quickest and most efficient way to restore our systems and administrative functions was to pay the ransom and obtain the decryption key," said President and CEO Allen Stefanek in a public statement. "In the best interest of restoring normal operations, we did this."[9]

While some victims pay ransoms because their backups have been destroyed, other cases are not as simple. Often, speed of recovery and the costs of restoring from backups are two key considerations. Even when backups are available, the costs of recovery can be steep. As previously mentioned, the City of Baltimore (which did not pay the ransom) spent at least $18 million to recover its data from backups.[10] A large portion of this money was pulled from a fund devoted to parks and recreation. Similarly, the City of Atlanta spent at least $12.1 million[11] to recover from a ransomware attack, and ultimately was not able to recover all data from backups. Indeed, the attack resulted in the permanent loss of police dashcam videos and other data.[12]

In exposure extortion cases, victims may choose to pay the ransom because they want to demonstrate that they did everything possible to protect their clients' or employees' data and prevent it from being published or sold on the dark web. For example, when cloud provider Blackbaud was hit with a cyber extortion attack in 2020, the company issued the following statement: "Because protecting our customers' data is our top priority, we paid the cybercriminal's demand with confirmation that the copy they removed had been destroyed."[13]

---

8. William Turton, Michael Riley, and Jennifer Jacobs, "Colonial Pipeline Paid Hackers Nearly $5 Million in Ransom," Bloomberg, May 13, 2021, www.bloomberg.com/news/articles/2021-05-13/colonial-pipeline-paid-hackers-nearly-5-million-in-ransom.

9. Hollywood Presbyterian Medical Center (memo), February 17, 2016, https://web.archive.org/web/20160221115251/http://www.hollywoodpresbyterian.com/default/assets/File/20160217%20Memo%20from%20the%20CEO%20v2.pdf.

10. Ian Duncan, "Baltimore Estimates Cost of Ransomware Attack at $18.2 Million as Government Begins to Restore Email Accounts," The Baltimore Sun, May 29, 2019, www.baltimoresun.com/maryland/baltimore-city/bs-md-ci-ransomware-email-20190529-story.html.

11. Reuters Staff, "Atlanta Officials Reveal Worsening Effects of Cyber Attack," Reuters, June 6, 2018, www.reuters.com/article/us-usa-cyber-atlanta-budget/atlanta-officials-reveal-worsening-effects-of-cyber-attack-idUSKCN1J231M?feedType=RSS&feedName=technologyNews.

12. "Atlanta Ransomware Attack Destroyed Years of Police Dashcam Video," Sophos: Naked Security, June 8, 2018, https://nakedsecurity.sophos.com/2018/06/08/atlanta-ransomware-attack-destroyed-years-of-police-dashcam-video/.

13. "Security," Blackbaud, www.blackbaud.com/securityincident.

While distasteful, some victims decide to pay a ransom to protect their organizations, those they serve, or other third parties from suffering even greater damage.

> ### Heads Up! The Role of Cyber Insurers in the Payment Process
>
> Cyber insurers that offer extortion coverage typically cover the cost of a ransom payment (subject to sublimits, retentions, and/or deductibles). The victim's coverage (or lack thereof) can be a huge factor in deciding whether to pay a ransom.
>
> Many insurers require that ransom payments be approved by the claims adjustor *before* payment is made if the insured wants to be reimbursed. Typically, victims notify their cyber insurer prior to making a payment, and the cyber insurer approves the amount in advance of payment.
>
> Insurers may also have restrictions on the type of cryptocurrency used for payment. Thus, victims should familiarize themselves with the details of their coverage and the insurer's policies in advance.

8.2 Forms of Payment

Paying a ransom demand is not like paying for a hamburger or even a new car. Today, the vast majority of cyber extortion payments are made using cryptocurrency. As discussed in Chapter 2, cryptocurrency provides the adversary with anonymity (at least, in theory) and nonreversible payments while facilitating fast, online transactions. In fact, the emergence of cryptocurrency was a key invention that facilitated the growth of the cyber extortion industry.

Initially, Bitcoin was the digital currency of choice for cyber extortionists, since it was the most widely adopted cryptocurrency and generally accessible to victims. However, while Bitcoin transactions are theoretically anonymous, the ledger is public. Over time, law enforcement developed effective techniques for identifying fraudulent transactions and tracing cybercriminals, using a combination of the public ledger, identifying information provided by exchanges, and other factors.

In response, adversaries began adopting different types of cryptocurrency that afforded more privacy. In April 2020, the REvil group announced that they would begin moving toward Monero for their payments, with the intention of making it more difficult for law enforcement agencies to track the payments.

The combination of an anonymous browser Tor and Monero can quite successfully make a person's financial activity completely invisible to the police and government agencies. We are extremely worried about the anonymity and security of our adverts, so we began a "forced" transition from the BTC to Monero.[14]

Despite REvil's statement, Bitcoin remains in widespread use for ransom payments. According to Marc Grens, founder and president of DigitalMint, in 2021 approximately 95% of ransom payments were made using Bitcoin and 4.5% in Monero.[15]

While many cyber extortionists still accept Bitcoin, they now offer incentives for victims to use privacy tokens. For example, in January 2022, the authors handled a case involving the BlackCat extortion gang. The criminals agreed to a payment of $185,000 in Monero (XMR), but demanded a 15% surcharge if the victim paid in Bitcoin (BTC). Ultimately, the parties settled for $200,000 in BTC.

In 2022, a data leak revealed that the infamous Conti ransomware gang had planned to develop their own cryptocurrency system to facilitate money laundering and reduce the risk of law enforcement takedowns.[16]

Tip: Nonreversible Transactions

Once a cryptocurrency payment is sent, it cannot be reversed. A payment creates a transaction. The transaction is added to a block in the blockchain and encrypted, and becomes irretrievable. For this reason, when sending or authorizing an extortion payment, it is critical to get the adversary's wallet address precisely right. Getting even one character wrong means that the payment will be sent to the wrong recipient. The only way a cryptocurrency payment can be refunded is if the new owner who received the payment decides to sends it back by initiating a new transaction.

8.3   Prohibited Payments

Nations around the world, as well as the United Nations, maintain lists of parties that cannot be engaged in financial transactions. For example, the U.S. Department of Treasury's Office of Foreign Assets Control (OFAC) maintains a range of different sanctions

14. Lawrence Abrams, "Sodinokibi Ransomware to Stop Taking Bitcoin to Hide Money Trail," *Bleeping Computer*, April 11, 2020, www.bleepingcomputer.com/news/security/sodinokibi-ransomware-to-stop-taking-bitcoin-to-hide-money-trail/.

15. Interview with Marc Grens, conducted by Sherri Davidoff on February 13, 2022.

16. Matt Burgess, "The Big, Baffling Crypto Dreams of a $180 Million Ransomware Gang," *Wired*, March 17, 2022, www.wired.com/story/conti-ransomware-crypto-payments/.

programs, including the well-known "Specially Designated Nationals and Blocked Persons List" (SDN list). According to OFAC, all U.S. persons are "responsible for ensuring they do not engage in unauthorized transactions or dealings with sanctioned persons or jurisdictions."[17] Violations can result in millions of dollars of fines and potentially prison sentences of 20 years or more.[18]

Not surprisingly, there is a high risk that cyber extortionists may be associated with a sanctions nexus. The United States and many other countries have added "malicious cyber actors" to their sanctions lists, including criminals associated with Cryptolocker, SamSam, WannaCry 2.0, and other ransomware strains. In 2021, the United States put its first cryptocurrency exchange, SUEX, on the SDN list in part because it was used to facilitate financial transactions for at least eight ransomware strains.[19]

"Ransomware payments benefit illicit actors and can undermine the national security and foreign policy objectives of the United States," cautioned OFAC in its 2021 *Updated Advisory on Potential Sanctions Risk for Facilitating Ransomware Payments*.

8.3.1 Compliance

Prior to making any ransom payment, it is critical for the victim to conduct a comprehensive check to determine whether the recipient is associated with a sanctions nexus. Unfortunately, this is not an easy task. Sanctions lists are updated frequently and include individual names, business entities, countries, cryptocurrency wallet addresses, and more.

It is not enough to specifically check for a precise match. Keep in mind that adversaries are also familiar with these lists—so if one of their names or cryptocurrency wallet addresses appears on a sanctions list, they will stop using it. Victims need to do their due diligence to determine whether there is a risk that the adversary is associated with an entity on the list based on characteristics such as malware strain, communications content, or other factors.

Due to the risk and complexity associated with potentially sanctioned payments, it is wise for victims to engage a professional third-party specialist to conduct due diligence before paying a ransom demand. For example, DigitalMint, a leading provider of ransom settlement services,[20] currently checks more than 60 lists for a sanctions nexus.[21]

Experienced and reputable cryptocurrency payment processors maintain a formal, risk-based sanctions compliance program. They will conduct rigorous checks to ensure

---

17. *Sanctions Compliance Guidance for the Virtual Currency Industry* (U.S. Department of the Treasury, Office of Foreign Assets Control, October 2021), https://home.treasury.gov/system/files/126/virtual_currency_guidance_brochure.pdf.

18. Thomas McVey, "Understanding the OFAC Sanctions Laws: Requirements for U.S. Companies," JDSupra, December 18, 2020, www.jdsupra.com/legalnews/understanding-the-ofac-sanctions-laws-66379/.

19. "Updated Advisory on Potential Sanctions Risks for Facilitating Ransomware Payments."

20. DigitalMint, https://cyber.digitalmint.io/.

21. Interview with Marc Grens.

that an adversary is not associated with a sanctions nexus prior to facilitating a cryptocurrency payment.

Victims that engage a third-party compliance specialist should request and review documentation of the sanctions due diligence check prior to approving the payment. Remember, even if a third party facilitates a payment on your behalf, ultimately you are responsible for ensuring that the recipient is not sanctioned.

Heads Up! "Know Your Customer" Screening

Reputable finance firms that specialize in cryptocurrency settlement services also perform due diligence on the victim organization and the signer on the agreements, including background checks. This process, referred to as "know your customer" (KYC), is designed to reduce the risk of fraud.

"Are there companies perhaps that are faking getting hit by ransom so they can launder illicit proceeds overseas?" commented Marc Grens, founder and president of DigitalMint, in an interview with the authors. This possibility creates the need for intermediaries to conduct due diligence not just on the ransom payment recipient, but also on the alleged victim.

8.3.2   Exceptions

If the victim feels compelled to pay a ransom demand but the recipient is associated with a sanctions nexus, it may be possible to apply for a waiver. For example, the U.S. Department of the Treasury has stated that "license applications involving ransomware payments demanded as a result of malicious cyber-enabled activities will be reviewed by OFAC on a case-by-case basis." However, these applications may take quite a while to review, and there is "a presumption of denial," meaning victims should proceed assuming that their request will be denied.[22]

8.3.3   Mitigating Factors

There are many reasons to report cyber extortion attacks to law enforcement: It can help agencies understand the scope of the threat, identify adversary tactics, track down criminals and bring them to justice, and more. In some cases, law enforcement agencies may be able to provide victims with nonpublic tools or information that can facilitate recovery.

Victims that actively reach out to law enforcement and government agencies may reduce their risk of negative consequences in the event that they pay an adversary that is

---

22. "Updated Advisory on Potential Sanctions Risks for Facilitating Ransomware Payments."

sanctioned. As stated in the *Updated Advisory on Potential Sanctions Risk for Facilitating Ransomware Payments*:

> In the case of ransomware payments that may have a sanctions nexus, OFAC will consider a company's self-initiated and complete report of a ransomware attack to law enforcement or other relevant U.S. government agencies, such as CISA or the U.S. Department of the Treasury's Office of Cybersecurity and Critical Infrastructure Protection (OCCIP), made as soon as possible after discovery of an attack, to be a voluntary self-disclosure and a significant mitigating factor in determining an appropriate enforcement response. OFAC will also consider a company's full and ongoing cooperation with law enforcement both during and after a ransomware attack—e.g., providing all relevant information such as technical details, ransom payment demand, and ransom payment instructions as soon as possible—to be a significant mitigating factor.

In addition, victims that have taken proactive steps to reduce the risk of cyber extortion are likely to receive less severe enforcement penalties.[23]

8.4 Payment Intermediaries

Paying ransom demands can pose special logistical challenges for a couple of reasons. First, the amount is typically quite high (today it is common to see six- or even seven-figure ransom payments). Second, the payment must be made quickly (usually within days).

Obtaining and moving large volumes of cryptocurrency fast can be tricky. Typically, cyber extortion victims turn to one of three types of organizations: miners, exchanges, and ransom settlement processors.

- **Miners:** Miners are exactly what they sound like—individuals or corporations that actively mine cryptocurrency. A miner may be a person with one computer, or an organization with thousands of computers in a data farm. Larger mining operations may be willing to sell cryptocurrency, but depending on the valuation and market volatility, transaction and processing fees will likely be higher through miners. The only limit on purchases from miners is the amount that they are willing to sell.

- **Exchanges:** Exchanges offer a wide variety of cryptocurrency choices and are primarily meant for trading different types of government-issued currency. Some exchanges will not accept government-issued currency, such as U.S. dollars, for cryptocurrency purchases. Fees tend to be high and will likely include commissions. Deposit fees will be charged when new purchases are made. The other element at play is that most centralized exchanges limit purchases made with your account until you have verified your identity. Once a purchaser is verified, the exchange brings limits up slowly over time, based on criteria such as purchase history, payment type, and country of origin.

---

23. "Updated Advisory on Potential Sanctions Risks for Facilitating Ransomware Payments," pp. 4–5.

- **Ransom settlement processor:** Cyber extortion has become so prolific that some third-party vendors actually specialize in ransom payments. Ransom settlement processors such as DigitalMint offer a specialized service in which they facilitate payments for victims of cyber extortion.[24] Typically, they perform due diligence and document the results, make the payment in the required cryptocurrency, and provide the victim with proof of payment and transactional confirmation. Some ransomware settlement processors will float payments up to a certain amount without waiting to receive the cash in advance of the payment. If time is of the essence, a ransom settlement processor is typically the best choice for victims of cyber extortion because of its specialized expertise.

Cyber insurers may have preferred intermediaries that they recommend (or require) for ransom payments. These preexisting relationships can simplify the payment and reimbursement process and may also lead to reduced fees.

> ### Heads Up! Transaction and Processing Fees
>
> Victims need to pay transaction fees as well as additional processing fees, no matter which type of intermediary is used. The amount of the fee depends on the intermediary. Remember that any ransom payment creates risk and additional future work for the intermediary (such as monitoring additions to sanctions lists and later reporting if appropriate). As a result, intermediaries may charge extra fees to compensate for the risk and administrative overhead of transferring ransom payments on a victim's behalf.

8.5   Timing Issues

All extortion cases involve time pressure. The adversary typically sets a specific deadline for receiving payment. After this deadline passes, the ransom demand may go up (sometimes double the original price). The adversary may also go silent and stop responding or may punitively delete the decryption key.

Delays during a ransom payment process are not just frustrating: They can dramatically increase the damage to the victim and decrease the chances of a successful recovery. Be aware of these common pitfalls and plan accordingly.

---

24. DigitalMint, https://cyber.digitalmint.io.

8.5.1 Funds Transfer Delays

Many intermediaries require cash to back the purchase of cryptocurrency, particularly for high-dollar amounts. While some accept credit cards, they place limits on the amount of cryptocurrency that can be purchased via credit cards, and of course, the cards themselves have a credit limit.

If a large amount of cryptocurrency is needed, the organization may need to wire funds to the person or place from which it is acquiring the cryptocurrency, or to the third-party paying on its behalf. It is important for the victim to understand their bank's time frames. Typically, a wire transfer will be much faster than an Automated Clearing House (ACH) payment. Even so, wire transfers can take 24 hours or more to process. If the negotiation included a payment deadline, or a specific timeline for payment, remember to allow time for the payment to clear.

8.5.2 Insurance Approval Process

In some cases, the victim's cyber insurance company must approve a ransom payment before it is made for the funds to be reimbursable. Red tape within the victim's cyber insurance company can cause delays in the approval process, placing the victim at greater risk. Make sure to consider the cyber insurance company's response and approval times when selecting a cyber insurance provider and know your insurer's approval process and payment policies before you find yourself in the midst of a cyber extortion crisis.

8.5.3 Fluctuating Cryptocurrency Prices

The value of a particular cryptocurrency, such as Bitcoin, is volatile and can vary by thousands of dollars in a short period of time. When preparing to pay a ransom, it's important to understand cryptocurrency fluctuations and try to determine if the value is fairly stable over short periods of time or changing rapidly. Confirm with the adversary the exact amount of cryptocurrency or fiat currency to be sent, and complete the transaction promptly to reduce the risk associated with value fluctuations.

Case Study: Cryptocurrency Volatility

A large software provider arrived after a long holiday weekend to discover that the majority of its 800 servers were infected with Ryuk ransomware. While the organization was able to recover a lot of its data from backups, it was missing six key databases. The organization decided that it needed to pay a ransom for a decryption key, and the authors of this book were asked to negotiate. The software provider had already filed a claim with its insurance company.

We contacted the adversary. The initial ransom demand was for 37 BTC, which at the time was equivalent to approximately $2.5 million. After receiving proof of life and exchanging several messages over a few days, an agreement was reached at 17 BTC (approximately $950,000). The insurance company approved the settlement and placed an order for the Bitcoins with a broker. Not surprisingly, the impacted organization did not have access to enough cash to make a purchase of that size, so it asked the insurance provider to make the payment directly to the broker. Their claim adjustor agreed and unknown to us, approved an order with the broker for 17 BTC, which the broker purchased. As a result of a series of miscommunications, the payment center at the insurance company marked the payment as a reimbursement rather than a ransom payment, meaning that it was not fast tracked.

Since brokers understandably will not release payments until they have received payment, the Bitcoins sat in a wallet for two weeks while the payment request worked its way through the insurance company's internal approval systems. We continued to reach out to the adversary, trying to assure them that payment was on the way. After 16 days, the broker received the payment. We were ready.

Unfortunately, during the delay, the value of Bitcoins plummeted. The agreed-upon settlement of 17 BTC now had a value of about $780,000. The adversary wanted to start negotiations over at 37 BTC. After much back and forth, we reached a revised agreement with the adversary at 22 BTC (approximately $860,000). That's when we learned that the insurance company had approved the original order broker 16 days prior, and the broker purchased the Bitcoins when the value was higher. The broker required more money to purchase 5 additional Bitcoins, but the insurer refused, saying that it had already paid $950,000—an amount more than the current settlement agreement, but less than what was required to purchase the additional Bitcoins. Meanwhile, the ransomware victim continued to struggle without access to its critical files.

8.6 After Payment

Once the payment has been made, it's time to sit back and wait, right? Not exactly. The organization needs to follow through on several more steps, not only related to acquiring the key, but also to ensure that the business accounts for the incident going forward.

Cryptocurrency payments are not instantaneous. Blockchain confirmations can take hours to complete. After payment has been sent, it is often a good idea to notify the adversary that the payment has been made, and to send the link used to monitor the transaction or take a screenshot of the transaction showing the details of the payment.

Once the payment has reached its destination, typically both parties can confirm its arrival by monitoring the recipient's wallet. The adversary may simply reach out after seeing payment. If not, then it's time for the negotiator to touch base and ask for the deliverables that the adversary had promised.

The victim may be required to notify a government agency or other parties within a specific period of time after a ransom payment has been made. Consult with an experienced attorney to ensure that as the victim, your organization meets the notification obligations in a timely manner.

Eventually, the victim will need to account for the expenses incurred, including the ransom payment. While the Internal Revenue Service (IRS) does not specifically address the issue of ransom payments, consensus among tax professionals is that they are a business expense and therefore tax-deductible. "I would counsel a client to take a deduction for it," said tax attorney Scott Harty of the firm Alston & Bird.[25]

In the United States, business expenses "must be both ordinary and necessary" to be deductible, according to the IRS.[26] As cyber extortion payments reach epidemic proportions, accountants have said this trend strengthens the argument that they are tax-deductible. According to Don Williamson, a tax professional at the Kogod School of Business at American University," It's becoming more common, so therefore it becomes more ordinary."[27]

8.7 Conclusion

Paying a ransom is never desirable, but in the event that it becomes necessary, an understanding of the payment process and the pitfalls that can occur during that process is crucial. In this chapter, we discussed the decision-making process, learned about complying with sanctions and the potential penalties for violations, discussed payment intermediaries, stepped through the payment process, discussed potential timing issues, and reviewed the steps to take after payment is made.

In Chapter 9, we'll delve into the recovery process, showcasing strategies for restoring data and operations, and transitioning the victim from "crisis mode" back to a "new normal."

---

25. Alan Suderman and Marcy Gordon, "Hit by a Ransomware Attack? Your Payment May Be Deductible," Bloomberg, June 19, 2021, www.bloomberg.com/news/articles/2021-06-19/hit-by-a-ransomware-attack-your-payment-may-be-deductible.

26. *Publication 535 (2021), Business Expenses,* Internal Revenue Service, 2021, www.irs.gov/publications/p535.

27. Suderman and Gordon, "Hit by a Ransomware Attack?"

8.8   Your Turn!

Every cyber extortion incident is unique. The response team's options and priorities will vary depending on the victim organization's industry, size, and location, as well as the details of the incident itself.

Based on what you learned in this chapter, let's think through key elements of the payment process.

Step 1: Build Your Victim

Choose one characteristic from each of the three columns to describe your victim's organization:

Industry	Size	Location
Hospital	Large	Global
Financial institution	Midsized	United States
Manufacturer	Small	European Union
Law firm		Australia
University		India
Cloud service provider		Country/location of your choice
Organization of your choice		

Step 2: Choose Your Incident Scenario

Select from one of the following incident scenarios:

A	Ransomware strikes! All of the victim's files have been locked up, including central data repositories, servers, and workstations.
B	A well-known cyber extortion gang claims to have stolen all of the victim's most sensitive data and threatens to release it unless the victim pays a very large ransom demand. The gang posts the victim's name on their dark web leaks site, along with samples of supposedly stolen data.
C	Double extortion! Both A and B occur at the same time.
D	The victim is hit with a denial-of-service attack on its Internet-facing infrastructure that slows its access and services to a crawl. The adversary threatens to continue and even escalate the attack unless a ransom is paid.

Step 3: Discussion Time

The victim is considering paying the ransom. Given what you know about the victim and the scenario, answer the following questions:

1. List one reason the victim might want to pay the ransom, and one reason it might not want to pay. Do you have a recommendation either way? Describe your rationale.

2. The adversary demands an extra 10% surcharge if the victim decides to pay in Bitcoin instead of Monero. Explain why the adversary might prefer Monero cryptocurrency.

3. The victim pays the ransom, but then later discovers that it made an error and the recipient was a sanctioned entity. Which actions can the victim take that may help to mitigate potential enforcement actions?

4. If the victim has cybersecurity insurance, which questions should it ask about its coverage before paying a ransom?

5. Name one common timing-related issue that could impact the payment process.

Chapter 9

Recovery

To achieve great things, two things are needed; a plan, and not quite enough time.
—Leonard Bernstein

> ### *Learning Objectives*
>
> - Understand strategies for effectively restoring operations
> - Learn about processes for recovering data
> - Reduce the risk of data loss and potential reinfection
> - Effectively transition from crisis mode back to a "new normal"

Cyber extortion attacks can have a negative impact on the victim's operations, either as a direct consequence (for example, in ransomware cases) or indirectly as a result of the containment and response activities. Throughout the entire crisis, responders must keep in mind the ultimate end goal: recovery.

"Recovery" in the context of this book is the process of regaining normal functionality to support operations. Typically, responders work on recovery efforts in parallel along with containment, investigation, negotiation, payment, and other time-sensitive response activities. Recovery efforts typically include the following steps:

- **Back up important data**, including key configuration settings, encrypted files, and data repositories.

- **Restore operations**, including the following phases:

  - Build your recovery environment

  - Implement monitoring/logging

  - Establish your process for restoring computers

  - Restore functionality based on the order of operations described in Section 9.5

- **Restore data** that may have been encrypted, deleted, or simply rendered unavailable.

- **Clean up any changes** made during the crisis and transition to a new normal.

To restore operations as efficiently as possible, make sure to follow a methodical restoration process. Woe to the response team that skips steps and accidentally tramples on critical evidence or makes an erroneous change that can't be reverted! There is always pressure to resume normal business operations as quickly as possible. As we will see, the order of operations and timing matter enormously. Seemingly small decisions can make or break your recovery plan.

In this chapter, we dig into logistics for rebuilding your technology environment, restoring data, evaluating and implementing improvements, and cleaning up from the response process. Along the way, we share real-life examples and point out common mistakes that can help you recover more quickly and with lower risk.

9.1   Back up Your Important Data

Expect the unexpected during a cyber extortion recovery. The process is risky, especially when you are dealing with an environment that has been compromised. Adversaries may have planted a backdoor in your environment or set up stealthy malware that detonates at predetermined times. The risk of a ransomware reinfection or follow-on compromise is high.

Compounding this is the fact that recovery during a crisis is typically unplanned, rushed, and fraught with pressure. Rarely is documentation of the previous environment complete before you are thrown into the crisis. Often, responders discover unexpected dependencies throughout the recovery and have to backtrack and redo work.

Make sure to back up and/or image important data before starting your recovery process. This may include data that isn't immediately intuitive, such as the following items:

- **Configuration files:** Before you modify the system or network configuration, back it up so you can reference it or roll back if needed. Configuration files may also be useful for forensic investigations (see Chapter 6 for details).

- **Data repositories (including encrypted data):** Make sure you have a complete backup of all important data before you attempt to restore it. You should always have at least one version of important data stored offline at all times. Don't attempt to restore data using the sole existing copy. At any point during the recovery process, your data may become corrupted or re-encrypted. Make a copy and attempt restoration from that copy. Keep the original offline and safely stored so that you can go back to it if something happens.

  Make sure to include a backup of your encrypted data if you have already been hit with ransomware. If you are hit with a secondary ransomware attack during the recovery process, your data will be encrypted with new keys. You want to be able to roll back to the previous encrypted version, so that you can use keys you have already purchased or obtained. Otherwise, you may have to negotiate with the adversary, purchase new keys, and start the recovery process all over again.

- **Critical systems, such as domain controllers, file servers, etc.** It is usually not appropriate to do a full image or backup of every single device in the environment, due to time and resource constraints. However, you may wish to make a backup or forensic image of key systems, such as the domain controller, core file servers, or others. Even if you start from scratch and build the systems anew, having backups can be invaluable for reference, or for recovering data or configurations that you might not have realized are important.

Tip: Back up Before Making Changes

One of the most common mistakes occurs when responders simply do not take the time to back up configurations, operating systems, or encrypted files. In the triage phase, the pressure to restore normal business operations quickly can sometimes trump this critical best practice. However, the risk of data loss during an unplanned and messy recovery is very high.

Never put your organization in a position where responders may make a change that cannot be reverted to the prior state. Make sure *all* important files in your cyber extortion incident are backed up, in case you need to get back to the starting point.

9.2 Build Your Recovery Environment

The victim's recovery environment is a stripped-down network designed to minimize the risk of reinfection or compromise, while facilitating an efficient recovery. While it takes time to set up a recovery environment properly, the payoff in terms of risk reduction is huge. Skipping this step may lead to reinfection or an ongoing compromise.

In this section, we present a typical architecture for a recovery environment, which is used when there has been a widespread compromise of the victim's normal production environment. The goal of the recovery environment in these cases is to provide an infrastructure to restore and monitor systems and minimize the risk of a lingering infection.

Keep in mind that every recovery is unique. This section provides general guidance, which you should thoughtfully customize as needed for a specific incident.

9.2.1   Network Segments

Typically, the recovery environment requires at least three separate, isolated network segments:

- **Clean network:** Where the new, production environment will ultimately live. When you set up your "clean" network, make sure to minimize the attack surface by keeping services off and ports closed until they are needed. Never connect a potentially compromised system directly to your "clean" network.

- **Dirty network:** Where responders initially connect potentially compromised systems and/or data repositories that may contain malware. The "dirty" network should be fully isolated to the greatest extent possible. If you connect a compromised system to the Internet, an adversary may continue to siphon off data or add additional malware. To the greatest extent that you can, keep the dirty network contained. Assume that everything on it is compromised. If possible, systems on the "dirty" network should not be allowed to communicate with each other.

- **Transition network:** An intermediary subnet used for transferring data/systems between the clean and dirty networks. The transition network should be heavily instrumented and monitored, so that you can detect any unexpected malware or signs of residual compromise that may have been missed when the system was cleaned.

The precise architecture of your recovery environment will depend on your unique environment, resources, and needs. If you have the ability to segment your environment using separate virtual LANs (VLANs), this is an easy and effective approach. Recovering a cloud environment such as Azure or Amazon Web Services (AWS) can be surprisingly straightforward, since VLAN segmentation options are built in natively. At other times, it is necessary to put hands on cables and segment a network using IP addressing.

Often remote access is configured early on to support IT effort. In such a case, the access must be highly restricted and filtered, to minimize the risk of additional compromise and data exposure.

Whatever your strategy, take the time to think it through and document your setup before beginning the restoration process. Make sure to use a minimum of three separate environments, as outlined earlier: one for "dirty" systems, a transition environment for monitoring, and the final "clean" network.

9.2.2   Network Devices

The recovery environment can be much simpler than a full-scale production network. As a result, responders typically need only a few network devices to get it up and running.

If you are reusing network devices from the victim's existing infrastructure, make sure to perform these actions:

- Back up the configuration and logs from each device prior to making changes.

- Simplify the configuration as much as possible to support the recovery environment only. Most of the time, you will want to erase the existing configuration (after backing it up) so that you start with a clean slate.

- Change any usernames/passwords or access strings. Make sure to select strong new credentials and store them securely.

- Configure the devices to support your recovery needs (i.e., three segments with limited Internet access). It is wise to start by denying all access between segments and to the Internet, and then grant access on a case-by-case basis. You will also want to configure support for detailed logging/monitoring.

Later, responders will update the network configuration to support a more complex architecture. For now, in the recovery phase, the primary goal is to create a secure, clean environment that will minimize the risk of reinfection or ongoing adversary access during the recovery process.

Tip: Improve the Technology Environment

Victims usually have no choice but to improve their technology environment when recovering from a cyber extortion attack. Typically the adversary has gained access to the environment by leveraging weaknesses that must be addressed, or else the crisis will repeat itself. In some cases, it is faster and cheaper to purchase new hardware than to fully clean and restore every system from scratch (especially if there is a strong need for evidence preservation).

In addition, the aftermath of a cyber extortion event can present a uniquely unimpeded environment for implementing changes. For example, in ransomware cases, the victim's local network may already be offline or in a state of partial operation. This is a perfect opportunity for the victim to implement badly needed architectural improvements or infrastructure changes that might normally cause disruption.

In much the same way that forest fires clear out space for new growth, the devastation caused by a major outage can provide political capital and downtime that facilitate implementation of key technology improvements. When going this route, it is important to make changes consciously. The organization may have suddenly shifted to the cloud or personal devices in the wake of a cyber extortion event. During the response, leadership should consider whether to continue use of these new processes and technologies, or shift back to a more traditional approach. The decisions made during the recovery process will have long-lasting effects on the overall technology environment, the user experience, and the potential for additional cybersecurity incidents in the future.

Every crisis is an opportunity, and a cyber extortion event is no exception. Take advantage of it where you can.

9.3   Set up Monitoring and Logging

Once the victim has been compromised, they are at elevated risk of a future infection—and probably always will be. Why? An adversary has learned extensive details about the victim's environment, and may have exfiltrated passwords, network information, supplier details, user lists, and other information that can be leveraged for future attacks.

In addition, the adversary may have planted malware in the environment, which may or may not be active right away. As an example, in the SolarWinds compromise (discussed in Chapter 1), the adversary installed a backdoor in the SolarWinds Orion network monitoring product, which was pushed out to 18,000 customers beginning in March 2020. The malware did not send out its first beacon until it had been installed for 12 to 14 days. Instead, it lay dormant, evading detection by security analysts or researchers who typically analyze malware in sandboxes for shorter periods of time when checking for malicious activity.[1]

Effective monitoring is critical for detecting threats early and minimizing the risk and damage of a compromise. In the following sections, we discuss the goals of monitoring (both short-term and long-term), the key components of your monitoring infrastructure, and processes for detection and response.

9.3.1   Goals of Monitoring

The importance of implementing an effective monitoring program quickly cannot be overstated. Without it, the victim may suffer additional compromises that could have been avoided by implementing appropriate detection capabilities. Monitoring is important both for short-term and long-term reasons:

- **Short term:** During the recovery process, responders aim to detect malware and other signs of compromise on the dirty network and the transition network, to ensure that they have effectively removed any threats from systems before they are moved to the clean network. This will reduce the risk of reinfection during recovery.

- **Long term:** An effective, ongoing monitoring program will reduce the risk of future compromise. This is especially important because, as previously discussed, after falling victim to a major cyber extortion event, the organization will typically remain at an elevated risk.

Quite often, the victim's monitoring capabilities prior to the compromise were inadequate, which contributes to the risk. When that is the case, it is important to allocate additional budget and resources to design and implement effective monitoring.

---

1. Fire Eye, "Highly Evasive Attacker Leverages SolarWinds Supply Chain to Compromise Multiple Global Victims with SUNBURST Backdoor," Mandiant, December 13, 2020, www.fireeye.com/blog/threat-research/2020/12/evasive-attacker-leverages-solarwinds-supply-chain-compromises-with-sunburst-backdoor.html.

9.3.2 Timing

Monitoring capabilities should be implemented as early as possible during the recovery process. The good news is that the beginning of the recovery process is often an ideal time to make major changes to the monitoring architecture, which might otherwise require scheduled downtime. For example, while network devices are being configured, responders have the opportunity to add logging and monitoring capabilities. There may even be a need to purchase some new network hardware, which can be carefully chosen to better support an integrated monitoring program. Since the environment is usually down during this time already, changes can be quickly tested without concern for impacting ongoing operations.

Likewise, as workstations and servers are rebuilt, the response team should consider adding or upgrading endpoint monitoring software so that it is consistently deployed and configured throughout the environment.

9.3.3 Components

An effective monitoring architecture relies on an integrated selection of complementary tools, which have been carefully chosen to provide visibility throughout the technology environment. The following areas typically should be monitored:

- Individual workstations and servers
- Network (internal and perimeter)
- Cloud
- Mobile devices

Here are some important components to include in a robust monitoring program:

- **Antivirus software:** Make sure that effective, properly licensed antivirus software is installed on all endpoint systems. This should include both signature- and behavior-based detection methods. Ensure that antivirus software runs regularly, updates frequently, and reports back to a central location.

- **Flow records:** These summaries of network traffic are typically already generated by network equipment, but not always collected. Flow records can be extremely useful for tracking malicious activity, identifying attempted lateral movements, and determining whether an adversary exfiltrated data.

- **Intrusion detection/prevention system (IDS/IPS):** These security products automatically detect and prevent threats. Host-based IDS/IPS are installed on endpoints, whereas network-based IDS/IPS are designed to monitor network traffic (network). To be effective, these tools typically need to be carefully tuned to detect threats relevant to the local environment and reduce false positives.

- **Endpoint detection and response (EDR) software:** EDR tools are designed for use by an experienced professional to hunt for malicious activity that can evade automated antivirus software. They are especially useful during the recovery process, as a means to identify more subtle malware on the dirty network and transition network, and to monitor the clean network carefully in the days and weeks following the recovery. The victim may or may not choose to integrate EDR and similar software into their environment on a long-term basis.

- **Logs (including firewall logs, application logs, workstation logs, and cloud systems):** All modern network devices, operating systems, and major applications are designed to output activity logs, which can be extremely useful for scoping security incidents. These can include authentication logs, records of privileged use, and even logs of specific commands. Make sure that you enable appropriate logging for your environment and collect logs in one central location to facilitate quick access.

- **Centralized long-term storage and analysis:** A centralized platform can be used to aggregate and analyze monitoring information from many sources, including all the sources just listed. Traditionally this is implemented as a SIEM or syslog server. Responders can access the centralized platform to obtain historical telemetry data and/or real-time, actionable intelligence regarding potential network threats and activities.

When selecting monitoring components, responders should consider both the immediate, short-term needs of the recovery process and the organization's longer-term monitoring processes. Whenever possible, components should be selected to support the recovery process as well as the organization's long-term needs, so as to minimize waste and use resources as efficiently as possible.

9.3.4   Detection and Response Processes

Setting up a monitoring program isn't enough: Humans need to actively review alerts and investigate suspicious activity. All too often, organizations invest heavily in monitoring tools, only to skimp on the human resources required to actually analyze the intelligence and respond.

Monitoring needs to be maintained at all steps during the recovery—and beyond. It is critical during the first days and weeks, when the likelihood of an ongoing malware infection or compromise is high. Even after the recovery phase has passed, monitoring must continue as part of the daily hygiene of the technology environment. It is a new normal. (See Section 10.3.4 for more details about establishing continuous monitoring processes on a long-term basis.)

Case Study: An Ounce of Monitoring Is Worth a Pound of Reinfection

A midsized accounting firm reached out for assistance following a ransomware attack against its network. An adversary had gained access to its domain controller and used the PSEXEC toolkit to distribute the Dharma ransomware variant to the firm's primary file servers. Backups for the network were not new enough to be valuable, so purchasing a decryptor was the only way to recover sensitive client information.

The authors were brought in to facilitate negotiation for the decryptor, test its functionality, and deliver the software to a private IT contractor who would handle decryption. Once the transaction and testing were complete, the decryptor was sent to the firm's IT staff and decryption began. The victim was advised to back up all of its encrypted data prior to attempting to use the adversary's tool, and thankfully it did.

The first panicked call from the victim came about 3 hours after the firm received the decryptor. Everything seemed to be working fine, but after about 30 minutes all the files they had decrypted were suddenly re-encrypted with a new encryption key.

It turned out that the victim's IT staff, feeling pressured for time, had decided to simply run Windows Defender on the firm's servers and then decrypt the data without setting up any additional monitoring or detection capabilities. Unfortunately, the ransomware was still active in their production environment. Absent any advanced detection capabilities, staff did not identify the residual infection until it was too late.

After three failed attempts to decrypt the data over the next two days, all data was shipped to LMG's lab. There, staff securely decrypted the data in a recovery environment while the victim's IT staff fully rebuilt the network from the ground up and added monitoring capabilities.

9.4 Establish Your Process for Restoring Individual Computers

Once you have built your recovery environment, it is time to start recovering individual computers. Carefully think through this process and make sure to document it, so that all responders are on the same page. Whether you are restoring servers, workstations, mobile devices, or other systems, here are some key steps to address for every system:

- **Preserve evidence, if needed.** (See Chapter 6 for details.) Make sure to develop an evidence preservation strategy, with input from the victim's legal counsel.

There is always a tug-of-war between the need for a fast recovery and the drive for evidence preservation. Responders need to consider the most efficient ways to gather evidence and clearly communicate the necessary tradeoffs with leadership and legal counsel. Take into account each system's criticality and the classification of data stored on it, as well as the potential needs of a breach investigation.

For some high-priority systems, a full forensic image of the hard drive may be critically important. For other systems, responders may be able to gather a subset of evidence using targeted imaging techniques, such as Custom Content Captures in FTK.

- **Restore normal functionality.** If you can fully rebuild the system from scratch, this minimizes the risk of reinfection. New systems should be built from the ground up on the clean network. In many cases, however, a full rebuild takes too much time. When documentation of configuration and dependencies are scarce, rebuilding from scratch can be especially challenging.

  If a full rebuild is not practical, responders can restore functionality of the existing infected system and use security tools to eradicate malware, as detailed next.

- **Eradicate malware.** All potentially infected systems should be placed on the "dirty" network segment when they are first reconnected. While on the "dirty" network, make sure to:

  - **Scan with effective antivirus software** (it never hurts to use more than one).

  - **Leverage endpoint detection software**, such as threat hunting tools, host-based IDS/IPS, and endpoint detection and response (EDR) toolkits.

- **Minimize the risk of a future security incident.** Responders should proactively implement host-based security and configuration improvements, such as the following:

  - Install software updates and patches.

  - Change all passwords associated with the system.

  - Harden the operating system, using widely accepted benchmarks and standards.

- **Monitor to reduce the risk of an undetected infection.** Normal user workstations should be monitored on the dirty network for at least 24 hours before transfer; more critical systems such as domain controllers may be monitored for 72 hours or more.

Once the initial monitoring is complete, responders can transfer each system to the clean network, typically by way of the transition network. All systems should be subjected to careful, ongoing monitoring, particularly within the first 90 days after the infection.

9.5 Restore Based on an Order of Operations

Now you're ready to get your technology environment back up and running! The order in which you restore devices and services is critically important for ensuring a smooth transition.

In general, responders should begin by establishing the core of the network, which will serve as the backbone for the rest of the environment. Once the core is up and running smoothly, you can configure the remaining network and bring up peripheral servers and workstations. Here is a simple restoration checklist, in order:

1. Domain controllers (DCs)

2. High-value servers

3. Network architecture

4. Workstations

There are significant benefits to restoring the environment incrementally instead of all at once. First, every recovery effort has limited resources. Breaking the restoration into chunks and taking a methodical approach enables the recovery team to stay organized and verify that each component is free of malware and operating correctly before other systems are connected.

In addition, if responders bring everything up at the same time, it can be very challenging to identify a single piece of the infrastructure that is causing an issue. Taking the time to verify that each component is functioning correctly reduces the risk of repetition and widespread reinfection.

In the subsections that follow, we provide tips for each component of the restoration. Every environment is different, and your unique needs may vary. Consider the information presented here as a foundation, and modify it as needed to suit your specific situation.

The only hard-and-fast rule is to make conscious decisions about the restoration process, rather than blindly moving forward.

9.5.1 Domain Controllers

It's usually a good idea to start by recovering the DCs. They must be up and running if you are to properly manage your users, permissions, devices, policies, access controls, and more.

Unfortunately, because DCs are so critical, they are often targeted by the adversary. Access to a DC gives hackers the keys to the kingdom—access to all user settings, all access controls, and more. If there is any system that can traverse individual VLANs, it is the DC.

Responders must balance two competing interests: the need to get the DCs up and running fast and the risk that they may be compromised. It is wise to assume your DCs are compromised unless you have very strong evidence to the contrary. If you restore an infected DC, you will almost certainly have to rebuild the network again a second time. Play it safe and do not trust the integrity of your DCs.

Here are steps to restore a DC that may be compromised:

1. **Preserve evidence.** Image the whole operating system if you can. That way, you can check carefully for signs of compromise and trace the adversary's access after the fact. Capture RAM and other volatile evidence, if possible.

2. **Export data.** Extract key data from the old DC, including users, groups, group policies, and any other items that your specific domain configuration will require.

3. **Audit the configuration.** Adversaries often add user accounts or leverage misconfiguration/lax permissions. Carefully review all accounts and remove any that are unnecessary or suspicious. Tighten permissions and align them with a zero-trust model whenever practical.

4. **Change all passwords.** Adversaries often steal passwords with the aim of breaking into the environment or moving laterally. A full, immediate, system-wide password reset is the safest approach. This includes every account, from system administrators to users. Ensure that old passwords cannot be reused.

5. **Do a Kerberos reset.** Adversaries will frequently compromise Kerberos tokens to elevate their privileges and maintain persistence. Responders should include a full Kerberos reset and the revocation of active access tokens. This can be done via PowerShell from the DC.

6. **Build the new system.** If possible, use new hard drives for high-priority systems to speed the recovery. Otherwise, wipe and reinstall the operating system to ensure that no malware remains. Then import key data from the old DC, after it has been carefully audited and updated.

7. **Restore key network services.** If your DC will be responsible for DNS or WINS services, begin configuration of the services so that servers and workstations in the following steps can connect to each other without requiring a static IP address.

Start by following these steps for your primary DC, and then replicate this process to build your secondary DCs. It is a time-consuming process—but far less time-consuming than dealing with a reinfection.

If the victim chooses not to fully rebuild the DC and instead opts to restore using the existing software:

- Follow the steps from Section 9.4 to minimize risk of a residual infection on the system.

- Audit the configuration and change passwords, as described in this section.

- Perform a double Kerberos reset from the DC to avoid a "golden ticket" attack.[2]

---

2. Mike Pilkington, "Kerberos in the Crosshairs: Golden Tickets, Silver Tickets, MITM, and More," SANS (blog), November 24, 2014, www.sans.org/blog/kerberos-in-the-crosshairs-golden-tickets-silver-tickets-mitm-and-more/.

9.5.2 High-Value Servers

The next step is to connect the victim's high-value servers to the domain. These are the key devices and applications that the organization *needs* to operate. They will be different for each organization, but typically include the following servers:

- Database servers

- Application servers

- Other peripheral servers

Take a measured and planned approach. Start by identifying high-value servers, and then recover as discussed in Section 9.4. Ensure that high-value servers are restored in a hardened, secure configuration, so as to minimize risk.

In many cases, the system may include complex dependencies that are not well documented. For example, the database server may need to be brought online first, before an application server is brought online. Review any existing documentation prior to attempting restoration, so as to minimize roadblocks. If a full map of connected servers, their dependencies, and overall network connections is not available, now is a great time to create one that can be referred to later if problems present themselves.

> ### Tip: Preserve Evidence on High-Value Servers
>
> Typically, it is wise to take a forensic image of high-value servers that have been running in a compromised environment, particularly if they store sensitive data or can be leveraged to access other key repositories. These systems are often primary targets of attackers.
>
> Make sure to preserve, at a minimum, the operating system and event logs. When possible, preserve metadata and logs from any repositories containing sensitive data. This evidence can be critical during a breach investigation (see Chapter 6 for details).
>
> Finally, if the system contains data that was encrypted by an adversary, back up the encrypted data.

9.5.3 Network Architecture

Up to this point, the recovery process has been conducted using a simple skeleton network designed specifically to facilitate restoration, with multiple segments that support monitoring and isolate potentially compromised systems. Once the core servers have been brought online and verified to be clean, it is typically a good time to fully restore the overall enterprise network that will support normal operations. This includes adding segments for workstations and servers, implementing port forwarding, establishing internal NAT, setting up VPNs, and so on.

> ### Tip: Don't Let a Good Crisis Go to Waste
>
> This is a rare opportunity to review your architecture and make improvements, because the network is already down. Take advantage of it!
>
> Often, a cyber extortion event occurs in part because an adversary was able to move laterally throughout the network undetected for an extended period of time. Now is the time to implement effective segmentation and monitoring, as a means to reduce the risk of future compromise.
>
> Review your architecture carefully and document any changes that you intend to make, so that the recovery team is aligned. Implement proper segmentation, as well as additional monitoring capabilities that will enable you to detect any latent threats. At a minimum, make sure to capture flow records and logs for network devices, and tie these into a central monitoring service.

When bringing the network online, most responders reuse existing hardware, though they may supplement it with additional purchases as needed to support upgrades. The first decision to make is whether network devices need to be fully rebuilt or simply audited and updated. For expediency, the less you need to fully rebuild, the better. However, this convenience always needs to be balanced with risk. If there is a risk that a network device was subjected to unauthorized access, you may want to do a factory reset and reconfigure the device.

Whichever you choose:

- Back up the device configuration. This is important for two reasons: (1) It can help you revert changes as needed and (2) it is important evidence that can be later used to support the investigation. See Chapter 5 for more details.

- Collect any logs that may reside locally on the device.

- Change device passwords and access strings to minimize the risk of ongoing compromise.

- Check the configuration to identify any suspicious rules.

- Configure the new device. If you are reusing existing configurations, audit them carefully to identify any suspicious rules or insecure configurations and update as needed.

Take a zero-trust approach whenever possible. As you design and configure the network, consider the scenario in which an adversary has access to a compromised workstation or server. A well-designed network architecture can limit the spread of compromise, slow down the attacker, and facilitate early detection.

9.5.4 Workstations

The victim's fleet of workstations is normally the last part of the infrastructure to fully come back online. Up to this point, only the workstations needed to configure essential services and collect evidence have been available. Now it's time to bring the remaining devices back online—a process that presents unique challenges due to the number of new devices that need to be cleaned and transferred. This is where the rubber hits the road.

If possible, it's best for responders to create new workstations using a "golden" image installed on a completely formatted hard drive. It might be tempting to just start plugging in the workstations that were already on the network, but spending appropriate time here greatly reduces the chances of a follow-on infection. Computers that were potentially exposed to malicious activity during the cybersecurity incident may have undiscovered malware, backdoors, vulnerable configuration, outdated patches, and other security risks. The golden image created to build new systems should already be up-to-date on security patches, have antivirus software preinstalled, and be hardened against exploitation.

If the victim opts to bring previously active workstations back on to the network without installing a fresh operating system, make sure to install and run updated antivirus and monitoring software prior to connecting the workstations to the production network.

It's a good idea to bring workstations online in stages. Connecting too many simultaneously can overwhelm your monitoring capabilities and malicious activity might be missed. Here is a sample order for prioritizing your workstation recovery:

1. **Mission-critical personnel:** Workstations used by critical IT and support staff. These members of the organization may be responsible for additional network and server configurations, technical support, or other essential tasks.

2. **Executives:** High-level members of the executive staff, who need to take priority. These members of the organization are responsible for maintaining business operations, making high-impact decisions, and guiding the overall direction of the organization. This step also takes pressure off IT staff members, who have undoubtedly been bombarded with questions from executives about when their workstations will be back online.

3. **Secondary IT staff:** Members of the organization who are responsible for lower-level user support. These users will need to be in place and ready when the primary workforce comes online so issues with performance and configuration can be addressed without removing resources from the response team.

4. **Other mid/high-level staff members:** Members of the organization who are necessary for maintaining day-to-day operations. This group will typically include depart-
mental managers, service dispatchers, administrative support staff, and others who
require system access to maintain organizational flow.

5. **Everyone else:** The remaining members of the organization, who may not require
full access to the network as a part of their job duties. These users rely on the system
only for tasks like email, general communication, and other tasks that can either be
completed without network access or are not time sensitive.

Breaking the workstation recovery into these stages enables responders to test, maintain, and correct monitoring issues, antivirus alerts, connection issues, and other potential
network problems. Any workstations that show indications of malicious activity need to
be immediately removed from the production network and quarantined. If malware is discovered, antivirus and monitoring software can be configured with updated signatures to
prevent further activity. The isolated workstation should be given to responders for evidence preservation, formatting, and installation of a new operating system.

Heads Up! Missing Documentation Is Costly

Planning a potential recovery strategy before an incident can save significant
amounts of time if the network needs to be rebuilt from the ground up. Many
organizations do not have a full data inventory, network map, dependency
map, and other essential documentation describing how the network is configured. When responders have to figure this out in the midst of a crisis, it leads
to stress, wasted time, and frustration. Work with your IT staff to develop
these documents now, because you will *not* have time during a real emergency.

9.6   Restoring Data

Data restoration can be done in several ways depending on the type of incident, its severity, the impacts, and other factors. A balance needs to be achieved among considerations
such as speed, completeness, cost, and resources required.

To effectively restore your data, you need to have a solid understanding of which data
is missing. Refer to your data inventory if you maintain one.

In this section, we begin by describing techniques for transferring data while minimizing risk. Then, we discuss each of the following strategies for recovering data after a catastrophic cyber extortion incident:

• Backups

• Gathering from current production systems

- Reentering and re-creating data
  - Paper files
  - Other sources (e.g., does a patient have records on file at a different nearby hospital?)
  - Interviews
- Decryption

9.6.1 Transferring Data

Data recovered from a "dirty" (or potentially compromised) system needs to be tested and verified before it is restored to the production environment. This careful transfer is accomplished in different ways depending on where the data in the dirty system is located. Data is commonly transferred using one of the following methods:

- **Physical data transfer:** Data contained on physical devices in the network can be moved by transferring the data to external media (e.g., USB-connected storage) or by physically moving the drives containing data to the transition network.

- **Virtual device storage:** Virtual hard drives containing data can be moved to a transition segment within the virtual environment by disconnecting them from their virtual host and attaching them to a scanning system. Do not move live virtual machines out of the dirty network if possible.

- **Cloud storage:** Data contained within cloud archives can be downloaded to the transition network for scanning and verification. The data can be uploaded again after scanning is complete.

The separation between the transition environment and the clean environment should be maintained at all times. After data is scanned on the transition network, it can be moved to the clean network, assuming that no malicious items were detected. The clean network should then be monitored closely to ensure that no indicators of malicious activity are present. Make every effort possible to avoid cross-contamination.

The way data is reintroduced to the production network needs to be planned for the purposes of efficiency, as well as risk reduction. Responders will potentially be moving terabytes of data into the new environment, and just starting a top-to-bottom copy operation can take a significant amount of time. Prioritize data that has high value or is necessary for business operations first. Items such as older archived files, backup data, or other elements of the filesystem that are not immediately needed can be placed at the back of the line.

9.6.2   Restoring from Backups

If backup files are available and intact, then restoring from backups is typically the preferred approach. This is normally done right after evidence is collected.

Unfortunately, restoring from backups is not always a quick process. If your network is virtualized and you can just roll back to a previous snapshot, this will often take significantly less time than a bare-metal restoration—but it will still take time. If you have cloud-based backups, the time needed to download those backups must be factored into the recovery timeline. Some backups may be very large and will take time to prep. Responders also need media with enough space to house the files during this process.

Another consideration is the integrity of the backups. It is always wise to assume that the victim's backups may be infected, even if responders are relatively sure they date from a time prior to the system's compromise. An adversary could have been accessing the environment for months before deciding to pull the trigger on their extortion plot, so the backups may be laced with malware or otherwise compromised. Restoring the environment to a compromised state opens the door for a follow-on infection and the negation of all the progress made to this point.

Finally, the age and frequency of the backups need to be evaluated. In almost any restoration from backups, some data loss will be encountered. Responders need to decide if the amount of data lost is significant enough to trigger a change in the recovery strategy.

Case Study: Time Is Not on Your Side

In a 2019 case handled by the authors, a midsized municipal city government was taken offline by a Ryuk ransomware attack. Bills could not be sent or paid, taxes could not be addressed, and local residents were angry.

The government office did have full backups for all the encrypted data, so paying a ransom for decryption was not a concern. The problem was where the backups were stored.

As part of the city's VEEAM environment, automated cloud backups were taken frequently and uploaded to a storage location in AWS. The backups were then transferred to long-term storage for retention. The city had never done a full test of its backup system, so the time to download and prep all of the images was a complete unknown. City services were already significantly impacted and would continue to suffer until at least the core infrastructure could be brought back online, so time was of the essence.

Unfortunately, the city realized quickly that getting backups for its environment was not going to be a fast process. Between downloading the backups (1.5 weeks), transferring data between systems (5 days), and restoring servers (2 weeks), the network was offline for almost an entire month.

9.6.3   Current Production Systems

In some cases, data may still be intact on segments of your network. If the adversary was unable to fully access systems, or for whatever reason did not destroy everything, the victim may be able to simply collect the data from various sources. This does not mean you can just plug unencrypted data repositories back into the production environment, however.

This data needs to be evaluated for the presence of malicious files, as well as for integrity and completeness. Remember, any data being transferred from the dirty environment to the clean production environment should be treated as if it is potentially infected.

A data inventory should always be part of your overall response program. If data was corrupted, deleted, or otherwise compromised, responders should document any missing items and adjust the recovery plan accordingly.

9.6.4   Re-creating Data

An often-overlooked method of data recovery is the manual reentry and re-creation of data. In organizations that maintain paper copies of sensitive data, such as hospitals, the opportunity may exist to add this data back to the digital storage in the network by hand. This data may be recovered from multiple sources:

- Paper files

- Archive media (CDs, DVDs)

- Interviews with users/clients

- Other sources (e.g., does a patient have records on file at a different nearby hospital?)

This can be a very long and tedious process. If your intention is to re-create your data in this manner, consider hiring a data entry firm to do the job for you. It may cost your organization money to hire them, but your staff will be free to do their normal jobs and the time it takes to complete the process will likely be much shorter.

9.7   Decryption

Decryption is usually the last resort for recovering data from a network impacted by a ransomware incident, but it is an unfortunately common scenario. In many cases, the data that is needed to bring a victim's environment back to life is simply not available from any other source. If primary systems are encrypted and no backup data is available, or if the backup data is old enough to lead to significant data loss, then a response team may find themselves in a situation where a decryption utility is their only hope. This approach comes with its own significant risk to the network.

Responders need to take a methodical and cautious approach to avoid potential setbacks—or even worse, a complete reinfection of the network. In this section, we discuss:

- The decryption process
- Types of decryption tools
- Risks of decryption tools
- Testing
- Decryption

Tip: Backup ALL Valuable Data

Before *any* recovery is attempted on a network, make sure to back up *all* data that needs to be decrypted in its current state. This means files, folders, ransom notes … everything. This is the most commonly skipped step during recovery, but it is perhaps the most important safeguard a defender can have in play in case something goes wrong.

9.7.1   Overview of the Decryption Process

The decryption process can be divided into an easy-to-follow series of subtasks, with each providing its own unique benefit and potential tripping point. Responders need to pay close attention at each phase to make sure that appropriate steps are being taken. A missed item on the response checklist can cause delays, issues with data integrity, and other much worse issues. Overall, the steps for decryption can be broken down like this:

1. Obtain a decryptor.
2. Test the decryptor.
3. Decrypt! (Use an isolated dirty network.)
4. Transfer data to the transition network.
5. Verify integrity.
6. Check for malware.
7. Transfer data to the production network.

In Section 9.2.1, the concept of separated networks was introduced as a key aspect of the recovery environment. The dirty, clean, and transition components described in that section are the primary network segments that will be used to facilitate decryption, file verification, and final transfer to the clean network. Responders need to keep the following principles in mind throughout the process:

- The decryptor should never touch the clean network.

- Data decrypted from the dirty network should not move directly to the clean network.

- Data types extracted from the dirty network after decryption should not include executable applications unless new versions of the application cannot be installed.

- Data from the transition network should not move to the clean network prior to completion of multiple passes of virus and malware scanning and verification.

- No network communication should exist between any of the three network segments. All data should be transferred through the use of removable media such as external hard drives.

9.7.2   Types of Decryption Tools

Decryption tools can come from a variety of sources, including the adversary, antivirus or anti-malware vendors, other victims, or law enforcement. However, not all tools can be trusted. Here is a look at the different types that may be available.

9.7.2.1 Free Decryption Tools

A Google search for free ransomware decryption software will return hundreds of thousands of results, and a search for a free utility should be the first thing a responder does. Depending on the strain of ransomware involved, there may be a solution to the encryption problem that does not involve sending copious amounts of cryptocurrency to a cybercriminal gang. Nevertheless, responders need to be careful with free decryptors and treat them the same way they would treat other malicious software, regardless of their source.

A responder will probably find two main types of free decryption utilities:

- **Legitimate commercial decryptors:** Multiple antivirus software vendors, and the occasional government agency, may create and distribute decryption software for specific strains of ransomware. Organizations like Emsisoft, McAfee, and others may offer these products free of charge. Most of these decryptors are only effective against older ransomware that has been removed from the playing field by law enforcement, or against previous versions of ransomware that contained a programmatic flaw that allowed for breaking their encryption. For modern ransomware, this option has become exceedingly rare.

- **Spam/malware/infected decryptors:** For every legitimate decryption utility available for free, there are several others designed to take advantage of the confusion and stress of a ransomware incident. As an example, in Chapter 3, we described a poisoned decryptor for the STOP ransomware variant. Once executed, the "decryptor" would re-encrypt files on the system.

How does a responder tell the difference between a legitimate and a potentially malicious free decryptor? The source is the most dependable piece of information a responder can evaluate. Using a service like NoMoreRansom.org[3] or other similar services can provide you with information about the exact strain of ransomware responsible for encryption, and identify whether a commercial utility exists that can decrypt it. Above all else, don't just download and run any free decryptor that pops up on the Internet!

9.7.2.2 Adversary Decryption Tools

The other option for obtaining a decryptor is to purchase one from the adversary who encrypted the network in the first place. This type of decryptor will be specific to the exact variant and encryption used to lock files on the network, and ideally should decrypt all files on the network.

In any scenario, the decryptor you plan to use should be treated like malicious software. Maintain network separation, proper scanning and monitoring, and secure data backups when you apply any decryption tool, even if it comes from a trusted source.

9.7.3   Risks of Decryption Tools

If you do obtain a decryption tool from an adversary and intend to use it, keep in mind that there are no guarantees that it will work correctly. In fact, the tool may be deliberately designed not to work as advertised. You'll need to take precautions to ensure that you don't accidentally make a bad situation worse.

Here are some potential risks to consider when using an adversary's decryption tool:

- Secondary infection
- Data corruption
- Delays

9.7.3.1 Secondary Infection

In some cases, the decryptor that is meant to unlock files on your system might contain additional malicious software designed to further compromise your network or provide a remote access point for an adversary to sell off to another cybercriminal.

In an interesting twist, some cases involving poisoned decryptors suggest that the adversary who deployed the ransomware may not be the one who implanted malware in the decryptor. Ransomware-as-a-Service operators will often include these malicious

---

3. No More Ransom, www.nomoreransom.org/.

additions without telling their affiliates, intending to further monetize the cyberattacks that affiliates carry out by offering up follow-on remote compromise victims to other groups.

9.7.3.2 Data Corruption

The utility needed to decrypt this data will directly alter the contents of files on the computers it runs on, and there is no guarantee of quality from an adversary when it comes to the software provided for this purpose. The adversary is also not obligated to provide a fully functional decryptor. Once you have paid, the adversary often could care less about how happy you are with the performance of the decryptor. If you lose data because of a faulty decryptor, the adversary is unlikely to care. This is another reason why maintaining backups of your encrypted data is essential.

9.7.3.3 Delays

The decryptor is unlikely to be a high-performance piece of software and may take a significant amount of time to complete its decryption cycle. This can lead to serious delays in recovery if a large database is set up for decryption first, and files should not be extracted from a computer while the decryptor is running. Instead, using the data backups, selected high-value data can be extracted in its encrypted format and decrypted first. Taking this approach can save valuable time in the recovery of primary systems, while leaving less important data for subsequent decryption after essential systems are brought online.

9.7.4 Test the Decryptor

Before using the decryptor on real data, responders should thoroughly test and analyze the software. This step is necessary to ensure that any potential adverse effects associated with the software can be identified and compensated for prior to making any changes to essential files within the infected network. Failure to complete this step can lead to severely adverse effects, including potential malware reinfection and data corruption.

Testing the decryptor involves two steps:

1. Check for malicious or unexpected behavior.
2. Test functionality in an isolated environment.

If the decryptor does not function as expected, responders can take steps to modify the decryptor, or simply change tactics. In some cases, a skilled programmer may be able to decompile and remove the malicious components of the software. A more likely outcome will be that you as the responder need to be aware of the behavior and compensate for it by blocking outbound traffic to a suspicious IP address or taking other steps to neutralize the malicious activity.

9.7.4.1 Check for Malicious or Unexpected Behavior

Any decryptor to be used on the network should be treated as an infected piece of software. This software usually requires the user to disable antivirus protection and run the utility with administrative privileges. As a result, the software, once executed, can perform almost any task imaginable, including re-encrypting the files that have already been impacted, installing additional malicious backdoors, and more. Decryptors, regardless of their source, should be tested in an isolated environment and verified before they come anywhere near the real encrypted shares on the network.

Software is available to analyze behavior and check for malicious activity. For example, Cuckoo[4] is an open-source toolkit that can be used to safely execute an unknown piece of software and provide a behavioral report for analysis. Online services can also perform these tasks, although caution should be exercised when using a public analysis engine. Information about the software you execute may be made available to all users, which may lead to disclosure of your incident if the software contains specific information about your environment.

A responder needs to look out for a few specific behaviors when a decryptor is running, and the best place to spot these types of activities is a malware "sandbox." In essence, a sandbox is an isolated and closely monitored computer system that can be used to safely execute unknown software and provide a report of specific activity. In general, the following pieces of the decryptor's operation, at a minimum, should be evaluated:

- Does the decryptor make any external network connections during operation?
- Does the decryptor install any files on the computer?
- Does the decryptor attempt to encrypt files on the computer?

9.7.4.2 Test Functionality in an Isolated Environment

The decryptor has one job: to decrypt files. This functionality needs to be verified, albeit very carefully. The dirty network can be used for this purpose. Using a small subset of files, execute the decryptor on an isolated computer and verify that it does, in fact, restore the files to their original condition.

Move your subset of files into a directory structure that matches their original configuration, and include a ransom note from the same folder. The ransom note may be needed to decrypt the files. Some ransomware decryptors look for the ransom note as an indicator that the contents of a folder need to be decrypted, while other ransom notes contain information necessary to decrypt files. Make sure the test environment is as close to the original file structure as possible to ensure that results are accurate.

This test can also give you an indication of how fast the decryption may work. If the decryptor runs slowly on a small subset of files, makes the computer unresponsive, uses

---

4. Cuckoo Sandbox, https://cuckoosandbox.org/.

excessive system resources, or has any other performance issues, knowing that fact early in the process can help you maximize the efficiency of decryption.

9.7.5 Decrypt!

Stage the data to be decrypted on a host within the dirty network. This data can consist of complete computer systems or simply subsets of data that are deemed to be a priority for recovery efforts. Backed-up data should not be connected. The data to be decrypted should be a copy of the original.

Next, execute the decryptor and observe its activities. It should be obvious within a few seconds if the decryptor is functioning as intended. If files are not decrypting, stop the utility and verify that the environment is configured correctly and the proper decryptor for the specific target data is being used (if more than one decryptor has been provided). Significant time can be saved by troubleshooting early instead of waiting for a full decryption cycle to complete before identifying issues.

Decryption is not particularly difficult, but it can be time consuming. It is important that proper expectations are set with management and tech staff on the amount of time it will take to complete decryption.

Remember, while an adversary may provide you with the software to decrypt your files, they have likely not put much time into optimizing this software. Plan your decryption efforts around critical data first, then move on to less important items.

9.7.6 Verify Integrity

Make sure the files you've recovered are complete and accurate. In most cases, changes made to files during the encryption process cannot be fully identified before the files are decrypted. That means the adversary responsible for encrypting the files could have potentially altered the contents of impacted files or planted malicious software in the file structure prior to encryption.

If the original file listing from the impacted hosts is available, verify that filenames, sizes, and any other pieces of metadata that can be identified are accurate. If these data points are not available, you will need to open the files and inspect them. If they have decrypted properly, standard file viewers should open the file contents without issue. Test a random assortment of files and file types to verify, to the greatest extent possible, that they are usable.

Be aware that custom file types, large files, database files, and other items may not decrypt correctly. Some ransomware variants will add padding or other data to files during the encryption process that may cause issues with proper recovery after decryption. If files are encountered that do not properly decrypt, copy the encrypted versions from your data backup and attempt decryption again. If the files are still not usable, you may need to contact the vendor that created the software for assistance.

9.7.7   Check for Malware

First, transfer the decrypted data to the transition network. This task is essential to maintain the integrity of the clean network. For physical networks, this may involve copying the data to external media for transfer and scanning. For virtual networks, a responder can copy the data to a mounted drive, disconnect the drive from the dirty host, and reconnect the drive to the transition host as an additional disk. This also gives the responder the opportunity to select only the data that is necessary for reintroduction to the clean network. This can greatly speed up the recovery process by eliminating unnecessary file transfer and scanning time. If the data is not needed, leave it on the dirty system and move on.

Much like decryption software, any data that has been impacted by a ransomware attack should be treated as a potential point of reinfection. The risk of infection from non-executable programs is low, but significant enough that additional verification is needed. Connect the decrypted data to the transition network and scan it with multiple antivirus software applications. If available, scan the data with both signature- and behavior-based antivirus software. The transition network should also be monitored closely at this point to determine if any malicious activity has managed to escape the dirty network.

9.7.8   Transfer Data to the Production Network

Once the data has been scanned and tested, you can begin moving the data to your production network. This process should follow the steps for transferring data to the transition network outlined in Section 9.7.7. Once data has been returned, continue monitoring for any signs of malicious activity. Malware can be very good at avoiding detection when observation times are short.

9.8   It's Not Over

Cyber extortion is a traumatic event. It takes time for individuals, and the victim's organization as a whole, to process and fully recover from it. The mid- and long-term effects of cyber extortion can include litigation, regulatory investigations, data loss, consequences of data exposure, negative media attention, challenges in obtaining insurance coverage, and damaged relationships with customers, shareholders, staff, and more—not to mention the personal trauma for individuals involved.

When faced with a cyber extortion incident, most victims view restoring operations as their finish line. They put all of their time, energy, budget, and effort into that one goal, but fail to look beyond it. In reality, restoration of operations is a milestone (and yes, a big one!), but it is not the finish line.

Over the long term, maintaining an appropriate response to cyber extortion may require changes to budgeting, staffing, and resource allocation. The victim may need to invest in several types of ongoing activities:

- **Legal response:** Lawsuits are becoming increasingly common following a cyber extortion crisis. They can include data breach lawsuits filed by affected subjects, derivative lawsuits filed by shareholders, conflicts with cyber insurers that end up going to court, and other types of litigation.

- **Regulatory investigations:** Similarly, regulatory agencies around the globe are becoming more aware of cyber extortion risks and are increasingly empowered to investigate such attacks. Following an attack, regulators may require a full analysis and demand information about the root cause, the victim's response, and any improvements that can or should be made. If gaps are identified, this can result in steep fines, depending on the industry and regulatory agency involved.

- **Public relations campaigns:** Cyber extortion incidents can gravely damage a victim's reputation, particularly when the adversary has a sophisticated relationship with the media and uses it as leverage. Long-term image repair campaigns and customer relationship efforts may be needed to restore goodwill and reverse any negative impacts on sales or revenue.

9.9 Adapt

In the best-case scenario, the victim will learn from a cyber extortion crisis and adapt to reduce its risk of attacks in the future. Once an organization has been hit with a cyber extortion attack, it will always be at an elevated risk of future attack, so it becomes even more important to grow and improve.

Key activities during this phase include the following:

- **Conduct a postmortem analysis.** Take the time to analyze the cause of the cyber extortion crisis and your response. Identify areas of success and deficiencies, and develop a prioritized action plan for improvement.

- **Update documentation.** Update the organization's documentation to account for any changes made to the environment during the response. In addition, update its response processes to account for any lessons learned. Once the dust has started to settle, it's wise to formally review all changes made to the environment and ensure that they are properly documented.

- **Revert changes.** During the emergency response, major changes may have been made to the organization's technical infrastructure. These can include architectural changes, new security controls, updated configurations, or even completely new technology environments. Unfortunately, when faced with the hectic pace and urgency of a crisis, many responders forget to document those changes—or simply don't have time.

- **Improve the cybersecurity program.** Ensure that key takeaways are used to improve the victim's cybersecurity program, and thereby to reduce the risk of future cyber extortion crises. This may include implementation of stronger controls, such as multifactor authentication, proactive threat hunting, or other updates. See Chapter 10 for a detailed discussion of cyber extortion prevention.

- **Fine-tune your response.** Review and update the organization's response procedures following a cyber extortion attack, ensuring that any gaps or changes have been addressed.

Remember, every crisis is an opportunity. In the best-case scenarios, victims learn from the experience and become stronger.

9.10   Conclusion

Recovering from a major cybersecurity incident is a complex and time-consuming task, which generally takes place under enormous time pressure. While speed is necessary, responders must be methodical. Failure to follow a carefully thought-out plan to recover both data and systems may lead to a secondary or reintroduction of the cyber extortion attack. Changes to configurations, processes, or images made during recovery should be documented. Ensure that sufficient monitoring and logging are in place to give you good visibility as operations come back online.

Remember that recovery from an incident is not the end of the road. It's an important milestone, but there is still a sobering element of truth to consider: Once your organization has been the target of a cyber extortion attack, it will likely be at a higher risk for additional attacks in the future. The changes made during recovery will strengthen your organization's cybersecurity posture, but your cybersecurity team will need to remain vigilant and ready to respond in the event of a future attack.

Even after operations return to "normal," the organization will continue to face fallout from the incident. Recovery is a marathon, not a sprint, and the organization should be prepared to budget the appropriate time, money, and personnel to ensure success.

9.11   Your Turn!

Every cyber extortion incident is unique. The response team's options and successful recovery will vary depending on the victim organization's industry, size, and location, as well as the details of the incident itself.

Based on what you learned in this chapter, let's think through key elements of the short-term and long-term recovery.

Step 1: Build Your Victim

Choose one characteristic from each of the three columns to describe your victim's organization:

Industry	Size	Location
Hospital	Large	Global
Financial institution	Midsized	United States
Manufacturer	Small	European Union
Law firm		Australia
University		India
Cloud service provider		Country/location of your choice
Organization of your choice		

Step 2: Choose Your Incident Scenario

Select from one of the following incident scenarios:

A	Ransomware strikes! All of the victim's files have been locked up, including central data repositories, servers, and workstations.
B	A well-known cyber extortion gang claims to have stolen all of the victim's most sensitive data and threatens to release it unless the victim pays a very large ransom demand. The gang posts the victim's name on their dark web leaks site, along with samples of supposedly stolen data.
C	Double extortion! Both A and B occur at the same time.
D	The victim is hit with a denial-of-service attack on its Internet-facing infrastructure that slows its access and services to a crawl. The adversary threatens to continue and even escalate the attack unless a ransom is paid.

Step 3: Discussion Time

Your victim organization must recover from their extortion event. Given what you know about the victim and the scenario, answer the following questions:

1. What are four types of activities commonly included in the cyber extortion recovery process?

2. Describe one reason why responders might want to back up critical configuration files and data before making changes in this situation.

3. How long should the victim monitor their environment to ensure that it is secure?

4. Describe two potential long-term effects of the incident, along with ways that the victim can address them.

5. Name one topic that you recommend the victim organization discuss during a post-mortem analysis.

Chapter 10

Prevention

Let's think the unthinkable, let's do the undoable. Let us prepare to grapple with the ineffable itself, and see if we may not eff it after all.

—Douglas Adams

Learning Objectives

- Identify the keys to building an effective cybersecurity program
- Describe key security technologies that can prevent initial entry
- Learn techniques and strategies for catching cyberattackers early, before an incident metastasizes into cyber extortion
- Know how to reduce attackers' leverage by increasing your operational resilience and decreasing the risk of data theft
- Understand that cyber extortion is a systemic challenge that requires a coordinated, global response

---

Extortion is the end of a journey; the last phase of a cyberattack. The adversaries' path to cyber extortion may take any number of routes. Recall that cyber extortionists attempt to obtain something of value by threatening the confidentiality, integrity, and/or availability of information technology resources. They can accomplish this in a myriad of ways: by stealing confidential data and publishing it, detonating ransomware, launching denial-of-service attacks, or many other malevolently creative means.

As a result, to effectively defend against cyber extortion, organizations must essentially defend against all types of cybersecurity incidents. This starts with building and maintaining strong cybersecurity program.

As we learned in Chapter 3, the adversary's journey can be broken down into entry, expansion, appraisal, priming, leverage, and finally extortion. Defenders have opportunities to thwart the attack at every phase by implementing effective security technologies, detection mechanisms, and response processes.

While a full treatment of cybersecurity defense can easily expand to fill a book (or a whole series), in this chapter we highlight the keys to building a strong, holistic cybersecurity program. Then, we delve into specific security technologies that help to reduce the risk of compromise. Organizations can further minimize the damage of cybersecurity incidents through early detection and monitoring, reducing the risk of data theft, and increasing their operational resilience.

Cyber extortion is a global challenge, and not one that any individual organization can solve alone. We conclude this chapter by discussing strategies for reducing adversaries' leverage through far-reaching policy changes.

10.1 Running an Effective Cybersecurity Program

Cybersecurity was the top spending priority for CIOs in 2021, according to Gartner, with a predicted growth rate of 12.4% for such expenditures by the end of the year.[1] Not all spending is equally effective, however. "How a security program is planned, executed, and governed is likely as important as how much money is devoted to cybersecurity," noted a 2020 Deloitte analysis.[2] Even mature organizations that have invested heavily in cybersecurity need to continually refine and tune their program as new risks emerge and the technology landscape evolves.

Here are the four keys to running an effective and efficient cybersecurity program:

1. Know what you're trying to protect.

2. Understand your obligations.

3. Manage your risk.

4. Monitor your risk.

By tackling these four areas, organizations can reduce the risk associated with cyber extortion attacks, as well as all cybersecurity risks.

10.1.1 Know What You're Trying to Protect

Many victims of cyber extortion are shocked by the amount of data that adversaries steal—often because the victims didn't know they were storing all that data in the first place. An inventory is the foundation of every strong cybersecurity program. It's also

---

1. "Gartner Forecasts Worldwide Security and Risk Management Spending to Exceed $150 Billion in 2021," Gartner, May 17, 2021, www.gartner.com/en/newsroom/press-releases/2021-05-17-gartner-forecasts-worldwide-security-and-risk-managem.

2. Julie Bernard and Mark Nicholson, "Reshaping the Cybersecurity Landscape," *Deloitte Insights*, July 24, 2020, www2.deloitte.com/us/en/insights/industry/financial-services/cybersecurity-maturity-financial-institutions-cyber-risk.html.

critical for responding quickly to cyber extortion events, particularly when concerns arise about potential data exfiltration and/or publication.

Emergency inventories are extremely expensive and are never as effective as a proactive, ongoing inventory process. All organizations should conduct routine, proactive inventories of sensitive data to understand the scope of their cybersecurity program, identify risks, and prepare for response.

10.1.1.1 Why Take an Inventory?

When you think about it, the importance of an inventory is obvious: You need to know what you're trying to protect, and where it is located, to effectively secure it.

All too often, organizations invest huge amounts of time, effort, and money into their cybersecurity programs without taking an accurate inventory. The result is that sensitive data is left sitting in places that are unprotected; vulnerable systems are overlooked; misconfigured cloud shares go unexamined; there are gaps in compliance; and insurance coverage is not aligned with the risks. Cybersecurity risks that are unseen cannot be properly addressed.

To build an effective cybersecurity program, you must first understand which information resources you are trying to protect. This includes identifying and tracking sensitive data throughout the organization, as well as IT assets such as servers, workstations, network equipment, cloud applications, and more.

It's not enough to take an inventory once and then forget about it; every organization is constantly evolving. Classifying data into three to five general categories can help; see the authors' website for a sample data classification policy (ransombook.com).

10.1.1.2 Why an Inventory Is Critical for Cyber Extortion Response

An inventory of information resources is critical for effective cyber extortion response specifically. Consider the all-too-common case of exposure extortion, in which an adversary threatens to publish a cache of stolen data. The last thing the victim needs is to scramble about trying to figure out exactly which data could have been in the stolen repository.

For example, in ransomware cases, there is nearly always a risk of unauthorized access to sensitive data. After all, to encrypt data, the adversary first must access it. To meet legal, contractual, and ethical obligations, the victim typically needs to figure out precisely which data may have been stolen to assess the risk and determine whether cybersecurity or breach notification laws have been triggered.

Responders also need to know precisely which systems and data to restore. That can be a painstaking challenge, particularly during the early and more chaotic portions of the response to a major compromise. Maintaining an up-to-date inventory of data and assets can dramatically reduce response costs and damage in the event of a cyber extortion incident.

10.1.2 Understand Your Obligations

The potential costs and ramifications of cyber extortion incidents depend, in part, on the victims' legal, regulatory, and contractual obligations. Cyber extortionists often remind victims that they may suffer lawsuits, regulatory investigation, and shame if third parties are notified or impacted.

What's more, these obligations may directly or indirectly require victims to conduct an investigation, perform a risk analysis, make notifications to data subjects, or take other actions.

Common obligations include the following:

- Federal, state, and local cybersecurity incident and data breach notification laws

- Cybersecurity and privacy laws and regulations (such as the General Data Protection Regulation [GDPR] in the European Union, or the Health Information Portability and Accountability Act [HIPAA] and the Cyber Incident Reporting for Critical Infrastructure Act of 2022 [CIRCIA] in the United States)

- Industry-specific regulations (such as HIPAA/HITECH in the United States)

- Contractual obligations (such as merchant agreements that require adherence to the Payment Card Industry Data Security Standard [PCI/DSS])

Well before an attack occurs, a qualified cyber attorney should evaluate the organization's regulatory and contractual obligations with respect to cybersecurity. This assessment should consider the organization's industry, geographic areas of service, type and volume of information stored, key existing contracts, insurance coverage, and any other factors that counsel believes are relevant. The results should be used to inform incident response processes, as well as proactive cybersecurity investments.

Cybersecurity-related laws are emerging rapidly, the regulatory landscape is constantly evolving, and new contracts increasingly include cybersecurity-related clauses. All organizations should have a process for continuously tracking laws, regulations, and contractual obligations, and updating policies and procedures as needed.

10.1.3 Manage Your Risk

Whole books have been written on managing cybersecurity risks—and even then, it's impossible to capture every nuance of an effective cybersecurity program. Every organization is unique, and therefore every cybersecurity program is different.

Here are high-level steps that every organization needs to take to effectively manage cybersecurity risks:

- Assign roles and responsibilities.

- Build your cybersecurity program.

- Choose and use a cybersecurity controls framework.

- Budget for cybersecurity.

- Develop your risk management plan.

- Engage in training and awareness.

- Fund your cybersecurity program.

- Get cyber insurance.

10.1.3.1 Assign Roles and Responsibilities

Ultimately, it is people who will design, build, and implement your cybersecurity program. Make sure you have trained and qualified people on your team. This starts with strong leadership!

Ideally, the person designing and overseeing an organization's cybersecurity program should have extensive cybersecurity experience, including familiarity with control frameworks, as well as a strong IT background. All too often, an IT generalist becomes the de facto cybersecurity program leader. This is like asking a family physician to act as a neurosurgeon. You don't necessarily need to hire a full-time employee to fill this role; it is becoming increasingly common to outsource a fractional chief information security officer (CISO).

Because cybersecurity is a relatively new field, experienced professionals are notoriously difficult to hire, with industry professionals reporting a "zero percent unemployment rate"[3] in cybersecurity and a dire lack of qualified candidates. Consider outsourcing when necessary to fill gaps and keep workloads at a reasonable level.

10.1.3.2 Choose and Use a Cybersecurity Controls Framework

A cybersecurity controls framework is essentially a checklist for your cybersecurity program. It serves as the foundation for the organization's cybersecurity efforts, ensuring that the organization takes a methodical approach that is in line with industry standard best practices. Rather than reinvent the wheel, most organizations choose a widely used framework such as the NIST Cybersecurity Framework or ISO 27001, customizing it as needed to fit their organization's unique needs.

---

3. Steve Morgan, "Cybersecurity Talent Crunch to Create 3.5 Million Unfilled Jobs Globally by 2021," *Cybercrime Magazine*, October 24, 2019, https://cybersecurityventures.com/cybersecurity-jobs-report-2019/.

Definition: "Security Control"

According to the U.S. National Institute for Security and Technology (NIST), a "security control" is defined as follows:[4]

> A safeguard or countermeasure prescribed for an information system, or an organization designed to protect the confidentiality, integrity, and availability of its information and to meet a set of defined security requirements.

Once the framework is selected and customized, you can use it as the basis for defining the cybersecurity program, planning investments, identifying gaps, and informing risk assessments (see Section 10.1.4).

10.1.3.3 Build Your Cybersecurity Program

Every organization should have a formal, written cybersecurity program, which is designed to comply with relevant laws, regulations, and other obligations. The program's documentation should include clear assignment of responsibilities, the scope of data and assets to be protected (see Section 10.1.1), a summary of obligations (see Section 10.1.2), and details on how the program will be maintained and monitored (see Sections 10.1.3 and 10.1.4, respectively). This document (or suite of documents) should be reviewed and updated at least annually, or more frequently as needed.

All too often, cybersecurity program documentation sits on a dusty shelf (virtually speaking), untouched until an auditor or third party requests access. Make sure to include your cybersecurity program elements in training and awareness programs so that the written materials are translated into action (see Section 10.1.3).

Metrics and reports are also key. As discussed in Section 10.1.4, it's important to conduct routine assessments to understand the effectiveness of the cybersecurity program. These results should be summarized into easily digested dashboards and provided to leadership routinely, along with any recommendations for program updates.

10.1.3.4 Develop Your Risk Management Plan

There is no such thing as "perfect" security—it is all about risk management. To develop a truly effective and efficient cybersecurity program, each organization should implement and maintain a plan for prioritizing and addressing risks so that the residual risk is aligned with the leadership team's appetite. This plan should be updated as often as practicable to take into account evolving risks and the state of the organization's cybersecurity controls.

Historically, many organizations conducted an annual risk assessment (particularly in highly regulated industries such as healthcare or finance). As cybersecurity tools mature, more organizations are embracing continuous risk management, using centralized

---

4. "Security Control," U.S. National Institute for Security and Technology, Computer Security Resource Center, https://csrc.nist.gov/glossary/term/security_control.

risk-tracking tools to identify and document risks on an ongoing basis. This, in turn, facilitates the development and maintenance of ongoing risk management plans that are routinely kept up-to-date as new threats and vulnerabilities are identified.

Sections 10.2 and 10.3 provide details on specific high-impact security technologies that should be considered for inclusion in every organization's risk management plan.

Tip: Proactively Manage Supplier Risks

Supply-chain risks are a growing area of concern, as we have seen throughout this book. The Kaseya ransomware attacks described in Chapter 1 perfectly illustrate how criminals can leverage technology suppliers to launch cyber extortion attacks against thousands of organizations in one fell swoop. In this case, the adversary exploited a vulnerability in the Kaseya remote management product, which was often deployed by third-party managed services providers (MSPs) on behalf of their customers.

For cybercriminals, attacks against the technology supply chain have proved to be an effective strategy, enabling them to maximize their reach and profit. It's critical for every organization to proactively monitor and manage supplier cybersecurity risks. To implement effective supplier cybersecurity risk management:

- Start by clearly assigning responsibility for vetting and follow-up.

- Establish clear requirements for supplier cybersecurity and include these in vendor selection processes.

- Enumerate all suppliers.

- Assign a risk rating to suppliers based on factors such as volume of confidential data that the supplier can access and criticality of the supplier for day-to-day operations.

- Ensure that supplier contracts clearly articulate cybersecurity requirements such as proactive cybersecurity measures, routine assessment and reporting, and incident notification.

- Vet suppliers routinely, prioritizing them based on their potential risk to the organization's cybersecurity posture.

- Monitor and follow up consistently on any areas of concern.

- Include key suppliers in the organization's cybersecurity incident response processes.

Supplier risk management has become an integral part of every effective cybersecurity program.

10.1.3.5 Engage in Training and Awareness

Effective cybersecurity programs include training and awareness programs that routinely communicate relevant program information to appropriate persons, including IT staff, security team members, legal counsel, general employees, and others. It is not enough to communicate information once: Effective training programs offer consistent, regular knowledge reinforcement.

On-demand cybersecurity training platforms have grown in maturity and popularity in recent years, particularly for general employee education. These systems can provide short training videos and games that adult learners can digest routinely, at convenient times. When paired with phishing test programs, these platforms can be very effective at reducing human-based cybersecurity risks across the enterprise.

Make sure to invest in specialized training for IT personnel, security professionals, and incident responders. Especially in a tight job market when workers are scarce, organizations need to invest in routine training for technical staff.

The executive team and board of directors also need routine education and awareness regarding security threats. A combination of short, on-demand awareness videos, supplemented by live training and interactive expert sessions, can help leadership teams understand the current threats and make smart decisions on behalf of their organization.

10.1.3.6 Fund Your Cybersecurity Program

No cybersecurity program can address every risk. On a regular basis, leadership should review the results of risk assessments (see Section 10.1.4) and use this information to prioritize their investments in cybersecurity.

This might include allocating funds for human resources, equipment, services, and more. By aligning investments to address the highest-risk areas, organizations can make the most effective use of their resources. Since cybersecurity evolves quickly, it's important to review and update your budget routinely, and ensure your investments remain in line with leadership's risk appetite.

10.1.3.7 Get Cyber Insurance

Cyber insurance has evolved to play a critical role in cyber extortion risk mitigation and response. First, like other types of insurance, cyber insurance is a vehicle for transferring residual risk to a third party. Certain types of coverage are especially useful for transferring risks relating to cyber extortion:

- **Business interruption**, which covers lost revenue due to technology outage.
- **Data recovery**, which can cover costs associated with restoring data from backups, decrypting data, manually recreating lost data, and more.

- **Cyber incident and breach response**, which typically covers costs for investigating and responding to a potential breach. This can include legal guidance, incident response consulting, threat hunting, forensic investigation, notification costs, and more.

- **Information security and privacy liability,** which can cover litigation expenses in the event of lawsuits, regulatory fines, and more.

Cyber insurers are also key players in the extortion response process. Insurers have a vested interest in supporting effective response practices and minimizing damage, since they foot a portion of the bill in the event of a claim. Unlike with car accidents, in cyber extortion cases the insurer has time to influence the outcome of the incident by providing support and guidance in the response process.

Many organizations do not have the resources to maintain their own trained and experienced cyber incident response staff in-house. To fill this gap, cyber insurers have put together cyber incident response teams and provide valuable services during the response process. These services often include, but are not limited to:

- Hotline for reporting cyberattacks
- Panel of vendors (often vetted) that provide:
  - Incident response services
  - Ransom negotiation
  - Legal guidance (especially important for breach investigations)
  - Public relations
  - Crisis management support
- Funding for response/recovery services and ransom payment
- Business interruption coverage

As a result of this kind of support, victims of cyber extortion often fare much better when cyber insurers are involved. Indeed, victims with cyber insurance coverage are more likely to have access to experienced professionals who can provide them with proper guidance and support, as well as the funds needed to engage these providers during a crisis.

Once cyber insurance coverage is selected, it's important to integrate it into the organization's incident response programs. Make sure to document the appropriate contact information and processes for notifying your cyber insurance carrier and assign responsibility for notifying the carrier (including after hours and on weekends, if needed). Include your cyber insurer in tabletop exercises and incident response training.

Heads Up! Cyber Insurers Incentivize Effective Security Controls

Because cyber insurers have a vested interest in reducing risk, they often provide valuable risk-reduction resources for insureds, and play a pivotal role in incentivizing the adoption of effective cybersecurity measures.

"Insurance historically helps set standards and we are doing the same now for cyber," said Bob Wice, Head of Underwriting Management, Cyber and Tech at Beazley,[5] in an interview with the authors. "We are in a prime spot to be able to evaluate where organizations are having problems and are seeing losses … and then we transparently inform the prospective insureds and current buyers."

Cyber insurers often offer value-added services, such as training, policy templates, or proactive scanning, which can be useful for IT staff and leadership. The terms of your cyber insurance policy may also inform aspects of your proactive cybersecurity program. Ensure that any requirements needed to maximize the value of your policy are communicated to IT leadership, such as documentation or technologies that should be implemented.

10.1.4   Monitor Your Risk

Cyber extortion risks are constantly evolving. It's important for every organization to maintain an accurate understanding of current risks, so that it can effectively protect its information resources.

"Monitoring risk" refers to the process of evaluating threats and vulnerabilities, assessing the potential impact and likelihood of a negative event, and determining the effect of security controls in place.

An effective risk monitoring program typically includes at least three components: cybersecurity controls assessment, technical security testing, and risk assessment. The organization should also track, evaluate, and report on any cybersecurity incident to identify gaps and the costs associated with security issues.

By accurately understanding the organization's risk profile, leadership can effectively invest funds where they are needed most and make efficient use of limited resources.

---

5. Interview with the author via Zoom, August 11, 2021.

10.1.4.1 Cybersecurity Controls Assessment

A controls assessment is an evaluation of the organization's actual cybersecurity program compared with a list of controls. Typically, the controls assessment is based on a widely accepted framework, such as the NIST Cybersecurity Framework or ISO 27001, although it may be customized to meet an individual organization's needs. The selected framework should be chosen to align with applicable laws, regulations, standards, and contractual obligations.

10.1.4.2 Technical Security Testing

Technical testing is conducted to identify known vulnerabilities, configuration weaknesses, policy issues, or any other gaps in the actual technical security profile of an organization's systems. Appropriate testing varies based on each organization's unique technology environment, but typically includes vulnerability scans, configuration reviews, penetration testing, phishing tests, and other technical security assessments.

10.1.4.3 Risk Assessment

A cybersecurity risk assessment is a methodical evaluation of potential threats and vulnerabilities, which the assessor maps to controls in place to determine the residual risk to the organization. Ideally, the results of the controls assessment and technical testing will be used as input in the risk assessment.

Because the cybersecurity threat landscape changes rapidly, it is wise to conduct all three types of assessments regularly. Modern risk management software can support continuous data discovery and data mapping, as well as regular controls assessments and risk assessments that take into account risks identified during routine technical testing.

10.1.4.4 Track and Analyze Cybersecurity Incidents

In addition to ongoing assessments, it's important to track ongoing cybersecurity incidents, routinely analyze root causes, and provide reports and metrics to upper management. This way, the organization can learn from incidents and identify effective measures for reducing the risk of future issues. In addition, incident reports can help leadership better understand the risks and evaluate the potential return on investment for cybersecurity controls.

10.2　Preventing Entry

Cyber extortion attacks are highly preventable, starting at the point of unauthorized entry into the victim's environment. As noted in Chapter 3, common entry vectors include the following:

- **Phishing:** The adversary sends an email, text, or other message designed to trick the victim into taking an action that gives the adversary information and/or access to the victim's environment.

- **Remote login:** The adversary successfully initiates an interactive session via a remote login interface such as RDP, using credentials that have been guessed, stolen, purchased, or otherwise obtained.

- **Software vulnerability:** A vulnerability in the victim's Internet-facing applications, servers, or network equipment is exploited by the adversary and allows them to gain access.

- **Technology supplier attack:** The adversary has access to a supplier's technology resources (such as a software provider or MSP), whether legitimately or through compromise, and leverages it to gain access to the victim's environment.

By implementing specific security technologies, organizations can dramatically reduce the risk of an intrusion that might metastasize into a cyber extortion incident. At the time of this writing, some of the most effective security technologies for preventing entry include the following:

- Phishing defenses, including spam filtering, web proxies, and training

- Strong authentication, such as multifactor authentication tools and password managers

- Secure remote access solutions

- Patch management

In this section, we consider how each of these technologies can be leveraged to prevent cyber extortion attacks and the intrusions that lead up to them. In many cases, these same technologies can also help to limit the damage even if attackers do gain entry.

10.2.1　Phishing Defenses

Phishing attacks have consistently been among the top vectors of entry for adversaries for the better part of two decades. Although most people associate "phishing" with emails, adversaries can leverage any medium for communication, including SMS ("smishing"), voice ("vishing"), social media, fax, and more. Ultimately, the adversary's goal is to trick the recipient into taking an action that will give the adversary information or access, typically by clicking on a link, opening a malicious attachment, or responding to a request for information.

Phishing is often paired with a malicious website designed to steal the victim's credentials or install malware. As the Verizon *Data Breach Investigation Report* (DBIR) explained, "Phishing continues to walk hand-in-hand with [use] of stolen credentials in breaches as it has in the past."[6]

Many tools and techniques are available to thwart phishing attacks. Among the most commonly used options are the following:

- Spam filtering

- Web proxies

- Training platforms

We will discuss each of these in turn.

10.2.1.1 Spam Filtering

A strong spam filtering system can block malicious links and attachments and prevent them from ever reaching the intended recipient. Systems may be stand-alone applications that serve a specific purpose, such as the Barracuda Spam Firewall, or they may be integrated with email systems, such as Exchange Online Protection (EOP) for Microsoft 365. No system is 100% effective; however, a good spam filtering system will greatly reduce the number of malicious (and junk) emails that your staff receives.

10.2.1.2 Web Proxies

In the simplest terms, a web proxy is an intermediary that sits between a client and a web server. Web proxies can be used for many purposes, including caching, filtering, and tracking of web traffic.

Web proxies can be configured to filter a user's web traffic and block access to known malicious sites. This capability is especially useful in the event that a user clicks on a link in a phishing email, because it can stop a malicious site from loading.

Many malware infections include a command-and-control (C2) component in which the infected computer reaches out to a server controlled by the adversary to receive further instructions or updates. Web proxies can be configured to monitor for this type of traffic and block it if it occurs. They can also alert on higher-than-normal outbound data transfers, which may indicate that data is being exfiltrated.

Web proxy logs are a rich source of evidence if an attack does take place. Like spam filters, no web proxy is 100% accurate, but every layer of security helps.

---

6. Verizon, *Data Breach Investigations Report*, May 2021, p. 16, www.verizon.com/business/resources/reports/dbir/2021/masters-guide/summary-of-findings/.

10.2.1.3 Training

"The most vulnerable hardware on a network is the human mind," wrote noted Twitter cybersecurity contributor, @swiftonsecurity.[7] Users need to be taught how to recognize phishing emails as malicious, how to report them, and most importantly, not to click on any links or attachments the messages may contain.

User training is a key component of phishing defense. Training is most effective when it is provided regularly and can take many forms. On-demand cybersecurity training subscription platforms such as KnowBe4[8] and Ninjio[9] provide a library of short videos, quizzes, interactive games, and more. Some of these services offer a broader awareness program that includes email templates, posters, and other supports.

The most effective training and awareness programs also include phishing tests, in which fake phishing emails are sent to an organization's users to evaluate the organization's risk and raise awareness. These phishing test platforms can be stand-alone systems (such as the open-source Gophish[10]) or integrated with cybersecurity training platforms.

To successfully manage the risk of phishing, organizations need to create a culture of cybersecurity awareness. A key element is encouraging users to report both suspicious emails and their own mistakes if they do fall for an adversary's ruse, without fear of reprisal. Mistakes happen, after all. In the hustle and bustle of the average workday, users may react without thinking and click the wrong thing—a link in an email, an attachment on the email, a suspicious website. Rewarding users who self-report (or at least encouraging them to) not only promotes a healthy cybersecurity culture, but also enables the security team to respond to potential threats more quickly and may prevent an incident altogether.

10.2.2 Strong Authentication

Cyber extortion attacks often begin with credential theft. Adversaries may steal user credentials through phishing attacks, or simply purchase stolen credentials on the dark web from an initial access broker (as discussed in Chapter 3). They may then use these stolen credentials to access remote login interfaces and gain a foothold to install malware within the victim's network or break into cloud storage and download repositories of sensitive data.

Multifactor authentication and password managers are two key technologies that can help foil credential theft.

---

7. SwiftOnSecurity (tweet), August 9, 2015, https://twitter.com/SwiftOnSecurity/status/630530012102262784?s=20.

8. KnowBe4, www.knowbe4.com/.

9. Ninjio, https://ninjio.com/.

10. "Open-Source Phishing Framework," Gophish, https://getgophish.com/.

10.2.2.1 Multifactor Authentication

Authentication is the process of verifying a person's identity. Three different types of authentication are commonly used in cybersecurity today:

- Something you know (for example, a password)
- Something you have (for example, a smartphone or hardware token)
- Something you are (for example, a fingerprint)

Multifactor authentication is the process of verifying a person's identity using two or more of these methods combined. For example, a password combined with approval using a smartphone app would combine "something you know" with "something you have." This way, even if an adversary has stolen a user's password, they couldn't immediately access the user's accounts without access to the user's smartphone app as well.

Because password theft is so rampant, single-factor authentication using passwords is risky, particularly for Internet-facing accounts. Happily, today strong multifactor authentication can be implemented using a free or low-cost smartphone app (available from Microsoft, Google, Duo, and many more) or hardware tokens (such as Yubikey, RSA, and many others). In particular, the emergence of authenticator apps for smartphones has facilitated adoption of multifactor authentication on a wide scale, for both corporate and consumer use.[11]

10.2.2.2 Password Managers

"Humans … have only a limited ability to memorize complex, arbitrary secrets, so they often choose passwords that can be easily guessed,"[12] explained NIST in an analysis of the strength of "memorized secrets" when used for authentication. This simple fact underlies the weakness of passwords as an authentication mechanism and has led to countless cyber extortion incidents.

What's more, humans have difficulty memorizing many different passwords, and often reuse the same or similar passwords across multiple systems. The result is that an adversary who steals a victim's Twitter password may be able to reuse that information to break into their bank account and work email. This phenomenon has led to a rise in "credential stuffing" attacks.

Password managers can effectively reduce the risk of password reuse and weak passwords, when used properly. Essentially, a password manager is specialized software designed to help users generate strong passwords and store them in an encrypted,

---

11. Sherri Davidoff, "Not All Two-Factor Authentication Is Created Equal," LMG Security, December 12, 2019, www.LMGsecurity.com/not-all-two-factor-authentication-is-created-equal/.

12. U.S. National Institute for Security and Technology, *Special Publication 800-63B: Digital Identity Guidelines*, June 2017, Appendix A.1, https://pages.nist.gov/800-63-3/sp800-63b.html.

attack-resistant vault. Cloud-based password managers such as LastPass, Dashlane, and 1Password can enable users to access stored passwords from multiple devices. The vault itself is protected with one master password, and ideally multifactor authentication, particularly if it is stored in the cloud.

Unfortunately, password managers are one of the most underutilized security tools. While many organizations train users to choose long and unique passwords, they don't always acknowledge that the human brain is simply not designed to remember long, complex passwords. Absent a password manager, users tend to reuse passwords or store passwords in documents on their computers, which can facilitate attacks. Deploying an effective password manager—and training users to leverage it—can reduce the risk of cybersecurity incidents, and therefore cyber extortion attacks.

10.2.3   Secure Remote Access Solutions

Unfortunately, many cyber extortion attacks begin with the adversary accessing the victim network through remote access services. Remote access is a necessity for staff, IT administrators, and vendors at organizations around the world.

Attackers constantly scan the Internet for available remote access interfaces such as RDP (as discussed in Chapter 3). Armed with a list of accessible remote access services, they can target these services with authentication attacks such as credential stuffing or vulnerability exploits. Adversaries can also leverage trust relationships between technology vendors and customers to leapfrog between environments.

Many organizations allow employees to use LogMeIn, GoToMyPC, or similar tools to connect directly to their workstations from their home computers. However, this practice introduces significant risk: If the user's personal computer becomes compromised, the adversary can then use these same tools to access the organization's internal network and hold it hostage.

Here are three popular ways to facilitate remote access while reducing risk:

- **Disable less secure remote access services such as RDP, particularly for Internet-facing systems.** Simply disabling these services can prevent compromise and dramatically reduce the risk of cyber extortion incidents.

- **Deploy virtual private network (VPN) software.** Modern VPN clients offer critical security features, such as a hardened operating system designed to resist attacks. Many VPNs can also be configured to scan remote systems for security issues before allowing connectivity.

- **Use virtual desktop infrastructure (VDI).** VDI consists of virtual workstations that are accessible via the Internet. VDI environments can be designed to limit user access and offer only specific applications. In this manner, they can reduce the risk associated with a compromised remote endpoint and facilitate quick containment of cybersecurity incidents.

By disabling less secure remote access models such as RDP in favor of tools such as VPNs and VDI suites, organizations can prevent cybersecurity incidents and thereby reduce their risk of cyber extortion.

10.2.4 Patch Management

Adversaries constantly scan and search for vulnerable software across the Internet. As discussed in Chapter 3, software vulnerabilities are often used to quickly gain a foothold inside the victim's environment. Once access is gained, the adversary may sell access to other cybercriminals or take advantage themselves. Since cyber extortion is so profitable, it is often the end result of a cyberattack, whether or not it is the initial intent of the adversary who gains access.

Cyber extortion gangs also directly leverage software vulnerabilities to escalate privileges once inside an environment. For example, the Conti gang's playbook, leaked by a disgruntled affiliate in 2021[13] and reviewed by the authors of this book, included step-by-step instructions for taking advantage of the common "PrintNightmare," "ZeroLogon," and "EternalBlue" flaws. At the time of the leak, the Microsoft patch to fix "PrintNightmare" had been available for less than a month—yet it had already been incorporated into the step-by-step instructions distributed to Conti affiliates.

To counter these sophisticated adversary training and distribution processes, defenders need to patch effectively and routinely.

Case Study: Unpatched Exchange Server

In 2021, a cyber extortion group named AvosLocker attacked a local government entity. The adversary had gained access to the victim's network, detonated ransomware on all the hosts and servers within the environment, and demanded a ransom of $3 million to restore the files and prevent data exposure.

The authors of this book were called in to assist. As the investigation moved forward, all signs of malicious activity within the network seemed to point to one server: the Microsoft Exchange 2016 server that the victim used for email. At the time of the investigation, Exchange servers across the world were routinely falling victim to the infamous "ProxyShell" and "ProxyLogon" vulnerabilities, which Microsoft announced and patched in the first few months of 2021. Cybercriminals were actively taking advantage of this widespread vulnerability and using it to gain access to networks.

---

13. Lawrence Abrams, "Angry Conti Ransomware Affiliate Leaks Gang's Attack Playbook," *Bleeping Computer*, August 5, 2021, www.bleepingcomputer.com/news/security/angry-conti-ransomware-affiliate-leaks-gangs-attack-playbook/.

Further investigation confirmed the authors' suspicions that the Exchange server had been the initial point of entry into the network. The evidence showed the adversary had deployed malicious web shells on the server and then leveraged that access to install the AnyDesk remote management software suite, which in turn gave them persistent remote access.

The victim wanted to know how the hackers got in, because it did apply patches routinely. Ultimately, after scanning the server and interviewing IT staff, investigators determined that when the patch was installed, it generated multiple errors and was never fully applied. Unfortunately, while the victim had manually attempted to install the patches, it did not have a process for verifying that the installation was successful. The result was a costly—and avoidable—disaster.

Let's discuss what makes a patch management program successful.

- **Know what to patch.** All too often, software remains unpatched because the organization's IT staff is simply not aware that it is deployed in the environment. For this reason, it's important to maintain an accurate inventory of software and dependencies. Depending on the size and complexity of an organization, tracking may be accomplished using a simple spreadsheet or a sophisticated asset management system. Make sure to include application software, operating systems, and firmware in your program. Devices such as firewalls, routers, and VPNs must be updated regularly as well.

- **Patch quickly.** Many organizations have monthly or bimonthly patching cycles. However, when a critical vulnerability is announced, hackers may actively try to exploit your server within hours or days—not weeks. By the time a patch is applied, the system has already been hacked. Make sure to document standard patch time frames and audit routinely to confirm that they are consistently applied. Carefully consider the risks of waiting versus the time needed to fully test and deploy a patch.

- **Use supported software.** These days, it is common to have software running on a network even after the vendor has stopped releasing patches. Such software is highly vulnerable to exploitation. Of course, it is best to discontinue the use of outdated software, but in some cases the organization must keep running it, at least for some period of time, to support critical business processes. In these cases, defenders can reduce their risks by placing outdated software on an isolated or highly segmented part of the network with very limited traffic. Carefully track this software and regularly review its usage.

- **Make time to patch.** Many organizations don't apply patches regularly because it is difficult (or even impossible) to find a good time to apply patches and restart critical systems. Architect your infrastructure with redundancy, so that you can reboot a critical system to install a patch without impacting the ongoing operations.

Remember that planned downtime is better than emergency downtime in the event of a cybersecurity incident.

- **Plan for the unexpected.** Even the most well-tested patch deployments can cause problems. Fear of "breaking something" can cause system administrators to delay patching. To alleviate this issue, develop and implement a software patch test plan whenever possible, to increase the likelihood of a successful deployment. Have a strategy for rolling back patches quickly in the event that a patch impacts system functionality.

- **Monitor patch status.** As seen in the "Unpatched Exchange Server" case study, often victims are taken by surprise because they thought a patch was fully installed and it was not, due to error or oversight. Patch verification is a critical component of every successful software patch process. Make sure to routinely check systems' patch status using automated patch verification software. Alert IT staff of issues and correct failed patch deployments quickly.

Heads Up! Software Bill of Materials

Tracking software products is a challenging but achievable task for IT teams. Tracking dependencies, however, is far more complex—yet equally important. In many instances, adversaries leverage vulnerabilities in shared libraries or software that was quietly incorporated into vendor products, and then used by end customers without their direct knowledge. When a major vulnerability hits (such as Log4j), defenders are left scrambling to figure out which of their myriad of products are vulnerable. By the time they find out, it may be too late.

In May 2021, the U.S. federal government issued an executive order requiring software providers that do business with the federal government to provide, among other information, a "software bill of materials" (SBOM).[14] This is conceptually equivalent to a list of ingredients in food products. While specific information may vary, an SBOM typically includes details about software dependencies, required packages, vendor agents, software development kits (SDKs), application programming interfaces (APIs), and more.

By collecting and tracking SBOMs, defenders can quickly determine whether they are affected by a new vulnerability, which in turn facilitates a quick response. Over the coming years, the distribution and use of SBOMs will likely become more common. Since tracking SBOMs and responding to vulnerability announcements involves managing thousands of software products, defenders will need tools that incorporate SBOMs into their software management and incident response. These tools barely exist at the time of this writing but will likely become widespread in the coming years.

10.3   Detecting and Blocking Threats

Even when an adversary successfully enters the victim's technology environment, speedy detection can enable victims to quash a cyberattack before significant damage is done and prevent the extortion attempt. As detailed in Chapter 3, there are many points at which the victim can identify, mitigate, and block the precursors to a cyber extortion attack.[14]

Effective threat detection programs typically include the following components (among others):

- Endpoint detection and response

- Network detection and response

- Threat hunting

Detection tools must be carefully tuned prior to their deployment to ensure that the systems accurately detect indicators of a potential cybersecurity incident. Even so, there will always be "false negative" events, in which detection systems fail to alert on malicious activity, as well as "false positive" events, which are triggered by benign activity and cause unnecessary work for responders.

Cybersecurity leaders should establish goals and metrics for detection systems and ensure that false-positive and false-negative events are aligned with leadership's risk appetite. To provide consistent value, detection tools and alerting systems also need to be subject to continuous monitoring.

10.3.1   Endpoint Detection and Response

Endpoint detection and response (EDR) software represents the latest evolution in endpoint protection. It typically includes features from traditional antivirus tools, host-based intrusion detection/prevention systems, vulnerability scanners, and more. A hallmark of modern EDR software is that all alerts are reported back to a central console, and the EDR software includes built-in features to facilitate the response.

A growing cyber extortion trend is for adversaries to leverage normal IT tools to exfiltrate data and prime the victim's environment, thereby enabling the adversary to evade traditional signature-based detection mechanisms. Modern EDR software can facilitate detection even when the adversary uses legitimate IT tools, by leveraging behavior-based detection methods in combination with more straightforward signature-based solutions.

Responders can leverage features of EDR software to quickly take action, such as proactively blocking and isolating remote workstations. This ability makes EDR software uniquely valuable in the event of a ransomware attack. As detailed in Chapter 5, EDR

---

14. "Executive Order on Improving the Nation's Cybersecurity," The White House, May 12, 2021, www.whitehouse. gov/briefing-room/presidential-actions/2021/05/12/executive-order-on-improving-the-nations-cybersecurity/.

software is a critical tool that can be used to isolate infected systems, halt ransomware encryption/data destruction, stop data exfiltration, and lock out the adversary.

When selecting EDR software, consider the ease of deployment, compatibility with existing software, and availability of support, in addition to cost and features. A centralized EDR system can also be monitored by an external vendor to increase the effectiveness and speed of the response.

Case Study: Saved by the EDR

In 2019, a professional services firm in the northwest United States suffered a ransomware attack at the hands of the GlobeImposter ransomware group. IT staff received a call from the FBI on a Wednesday evening. The FBI's cybercrime division had identified potentially malicious network traffic originating from the victim's network. The IT team was advised to respond immediately, because this was a strong indicator of an impending attack against the organization's network.

Unfortunately, the IT team decided to respond in the morning. By the time staff arrived at their offices, all of their workstations and servers were encrypted with the GlobeImposter ransomware. The adversary had even encrypted the backups, which were now useless.

The authors' firm was engaged and immediately flew to the victim's offices and deployed an EDR toolkit to all hosts on the network. It didn't take long to identify the Dridex banking Trojan on the network, which at the time was one of the most dangerous pieces of malware on the planet. One of the hallmarks of this malware was the ability to provide persistent network access to the adversary controlling it.

Upon analysis, the authors identified indicators of compromise going back at least 60 days prior to the ransomware detonation. The authors quickly eradicated the threat from the network and closed off the adversary's access point.

Surprisingly, on the very same day, the EDR dashboard indicated that a new infection was attempting to take hold on the network. This time, it originated from the computer used by the CIO. Upon further investigation, it turned out that an employee had recently received a phishing email with an infected document attached. The employee forwarded the email to the CIO and asked if it was legitimate. The CIO had opened the document on his workstation and enabled macros, nearly infecting his own computer with the malware.

Fortunately, because effective EDR software had been deployed, the malware was contained this time.

10.3.2   Network Detection and Response

Network detection and response (NDR) tools provide capabilities that complement EDR software. A modern adversary that has compromised an endpoint can obscure much of their activity by leveraging commonly used IT software, encrypting payloads, and blending their actions into the system's normal behavior. As a result, EDR or antivirus software may fail to alert on malicious activity—but traffic moving between hosts can contain clues a responder needs to detect unauthorized access, stop lateral spread, determine the incident scope, and prevent further compromise.

Enter NDR solutions, which monitor network activity and facilitate real-time response. Products such as ExtraHop's Reveal(x) and Cisco's Stealthwatch often utilize machine learning to establish normal activity profiles, then identify potentially malicious activity that deviates from that baseline. The features included in traditional IDS/IPS have been incorporated into modern NDR solutions, which now include more behavioral detection capabilities and tools to facilitate real-time response.

Like EDR software, many of today's NDR tools are available as cloud services. This enables responders to access the data even if the internal network is completely down.

10.3.3   Threat Hunting

Threat hunting, as described in previous chapters, refers to the process of proactively and manually searching a technology environment for indications of threats. While threat hunting is an essential part of cyber extortion response, it can also be used proactively to identify and prevent cyber extortion attacks.

Recall that a primary use of threat hunting is to root out malicious activity before a full network takeover occurs. Often, EDR software is used both to conduct routine threat hunting and to facilitate a quick response. Additionally, threat hunters need to be specially trained to detect these subtle indicators of compromise and interpret their meanings accurately. Many organizations outsource threat hunting because it requires a specialized skill set and qualified cybersecurity professionals are in high demand.

When developing threat hunting processes, consider the following issues:

- Software and licensing costs

- Third-party vendor contracts

- Testing frequency

- Training time and costs

- Acceptable software use

Threat hunting should be a routine part of your cybersecurity program. For an in-depth discussion of threat hunting in cyber extortion cases, see Chapter 5.

10.3.4   Continuous Monitoring Processes

More than three-fourths of all cyberattacks happen outside of normal business hours, according to a 2020 study by FireEye.[15] The reasoning behind this strategy is obvious: If there is nobody around to notice or respond to an attack, then the adversary has a much higher chance of fully deploying ransomware or stealing data without interruption.

Of course, IT staff need to sleep at some point or another. Adversaries are aware of this, which is why they frequently target victims during times and days when IT staff may be limited in numbers or not on the clock at all.

Continuous monitoring is critical for ensuring that detection and response can occur consistently, regardless of when attackers strike. A large enterprise with rotating shifts of cybersecurity staff *might* be able to accomplish this, but small to midsized (and many large) organizations don't have sufficient staff to implement effective 24/7 monitoring.

Outsourced monitoring services can be invaluable for ensuring 24/7 coverage, particularly at times when adversaries are most likely to strike—outside normal business hours, including weekends and holidays. This coverage can facilitate early detection of malicious activity and prevent serious cybersecurity incidents. In addition, outsourced monitoring providers can identify trends and patterns across a wide range of customer environments, benefiting even large organizations.

Effective continuous monitoring programs are carefully integrated into the organization's incident response procedures, ensuring that all qualified indicators of attack or compromise elicit an appropriate response within the expected time frame.

Importantly, continuous monitoring programs should be tested routinely to ensure that they are effective and to identify any weaknesses. This is typically accomplished by using attack simulation and response testing, in which a team of trained cybersecurity professionals conduct planned, timed testing designed to trigger various aspects of the detection and response processes. In this manner, gaps can be identified and addressed.

10.4   Operational Resilience

Boosting operational resilience is key to weathering a cyber extortion attack. When a cyber extortionist strikes, victims need to maintain their operations and regain normal functionality quickly. The following resources can dramatically reduce damage and facilitate a quick response in cyber extortion cases:

- Business continuity plan
- Disaster recovery processes
- Backups

15. Kelli Vanderlee, "They Come in the Night: Ransomware Deployment Trends," Mandiant, March 18, 2020, www.mandiant.com/resources/they-come-in-the-night-ransomware-deployment-trends.

In this section, we discuss each of these resources, including common pitfalls and tips for success.

10.4.1   Business Continuity Plan

An effective business continuity plan (BCP) can avert a potential disaster. In a cyber extortion attack, one of the first steps is to assess the functionality of information systems and identify which services have been impacted. The results of this evaluation then inform the response processes and influence the negotiations.

The BCP outlines how your organization will maintain operations when critical elements of the organization's normal systems are not functioning properly. This can occur because of natural disasters, service outages, cyberattacks, or other scenarios where normal operations are not possible for an extended period. At minimum, a BCP should include these elements:

- **Alternate contact information** for members of the response team and organization's leadership. This can include phone numbers, backup email addresses, physical locations, and more.

- **Out-of-band communication methods** for distributing information quickly in the event that normal communications channels are compromised or unavailable. Given the myriad of cloud-based communication options available today, many choices are possible, including chat platforms such as Slack, videoconference platforms, encrypted communication apps such as Signal or Telegram, third-party notification systems, and communications systems that do not involve the organization's infrastructure.

- **Current and complete inventory of information systems**, including physical locations, the purpose of each asset, and the specific software installed. This can help recovery teams quickly assess which services are unavailable and what their priority is during restoration.

- **Alternate workflows for critical processes**, including steps such as utilizing cloud infrastructure as a failover, redirecting traffic to a colocation facility, manual data recovery, and more. Consider how to maintain continuity when it comes to key processes such as invoicing, payroll, client management, and communications.

- **Process documentation** (including incident response procedures) stored in an alternate location so that if normal systems are impacted, the response team can still access them.

- **Credential repositories for key systems**, so that responders can recover and reconfigure them in the event of a disaster. Password vaults, such as LastPass and Dashlane, can be integrated into BCP workflows.

- **Training processes for responders and leadership** who may need to implement and execute the BCP. The response team needs to be familiar with the BCP and efficiently execute the playbook to minimize downtime and negative impacts.

Most importantly, the BCP needs to be established long before an incident takes place. An effective BCP is not something that can be created on the fly. A trusted security partner can help you get started, and ongoing testing of the plan using activities such as tabletop exercises will help an organization fine-tune the plan for its environment.

10.4.2 Disaster Recovery

The disaster recovery (DR) plan is your roadmap for restoring functionality after an impactful event such as a ransomware attack. Your choices in the response process can significantly impact the time to reach recovery milestones, which in turn impacts the potential damage. By following an established roadmap, responders can minimize downtime and avoid costly slowdowns.

Key components of a DR plan include the following:

- Contact information for recovery team members

- Critical data locations

- Infrastructure and software inventory

- Backup and recovery instructions

- Recovery time objective (RTO) and recovery point objective (RPO) (See Chapter 4 for details.)

- Resources such as instructions for gaining access, keys, and credentials

Technology infrastructures evolve quickly, as do threats. As a result, DR plans need to be tested, reviewed, and adjusted on an ongoing basis. Even small changes in configuration and software usage can be important when it comes time to recover.

When developing your DR plans, consider your recovery environment. Certain environments can be designed to support instant failover to a separate network infrastructure, or to support immediate deployment of clean virtualized environments that can facilitate fast recovery of operations even while the original environment is unavailable.

Case Study: Back That Truck Up!

In early 2017, the authors were called to assist a large transportation company that had suffered a ransomware infection. All of its systems were down, and the criminals had deleted the company's backups. The company had hundreds of trucks out on the road. The trucks were all outfitted with GPS transponders and laptops; this was how dispatchers communicated with drivers and tracked their progress. They sent the address, date, and time to the trucks via their online routing system and monitored their status in real time.

With their servers down, the company had no idea where the trucks were. They didn't even know where the trucks were supposed to be, and when. Their email was down, their bookkeeping system was down, and all their file shares were locked up. Staff could make phone calls, but they had no contact information for drivers or customers. A few drivers would call to ask where they were supposed to go, but the company didn't have answers.

The organization's leaders said at the time that if they couldn't get their systems back up and running, fast, they would go out of business.

The first question we asked was, "Do you have backups?" The staff explained that they had backups (offsite) but that unfortunately the server was in a remote data center attached to the company's primary domain, which meant it was inaccessible with the rest of the network down. Moreover, IT staff determined that the adversary had found the backup server, completely erased the hard drive, and then encrypted it for good measure to make recovery from backups impossible.

The victim requested that we begin negotiating with the criminals. The demand was approximately $10,000, which seemed large at the time. (How times have changed!) After receiving payment, the criminals sent the decryption utility, along with screenshots that they provided as a guide. We tested the decryptor and then helped the victim bring its servers online. All told, the trucking company was back up and running a few days after its systems were first taken down (albeit with a skeleton infrastructure). It was able to resume business quickly and was fully recovered within 2–3 weeks.

10.4.3 Backups

Backups are a critical component of cyber extortion response processes. The availability of effective backups can reduce an adversary's leverage and obviate the need for a victim to pay a ransom demand. In this section, we review the key components of a backup solution, the importance of testing backups, the emergence of "immutable" backups, and key issues involving offsite backup restoration.

10.4.3.1 Key Services and Data

An effective backup solution for an environment should include as many critical infrastructure components as possible in case an emergency requires a substantial rebuild. A well-designed and -configured backup system can also act as a significant time-saver in some cases, allowing a responder to rebuild specific components of critical systems without performing a full restoration. This can be very helpful if your operating system backups are infected or compromised.

Of course, all organizations face a tradeoff between functionality and cost. The more data you back up, the more you will pay to store that data, and the longer it will take to restore the data in a crisis.

Key services and data to consider including in backups include the following:

- Server operating systems

- Data repositories

- Proprietary applications

- Active Directory configurations

- Group policies

- Firewall and router configurations

- VLAN configurations

- Other critical network components

10.4.3.2 Test Your Backups (or Else You Don't Have Backups)

Backups need to be maintained, updated, and—most importantly—tested. IT staff should also be trained on how to access and execute recoveries without delay. A scripted and rehearsed recovery procedure should be included as part of the organization's response planning and tested periodically to ensure that restoration procedures do not become an unnecessary roadblock.

As a perfect example, consider Arizona Beverages and the ransomware attack it suffered in 2019.[16] After being severely impacted by an iEncrypt ransomware attack (linked to the infamous BitPayment gang), the company attempted to recover its network using the Cisco backup system connected to its network. Unfortunately, IT staff discovered that backups had not been configured properly and they could not immediately begin restoring data. The recovery process was delayed for days until Arizona Beverages signed an "expensive" service contract with Cisco. "Once the backups didn't work, they started throwing

---

16. Zack Whittaker, "Arizona Beverages Knocked Offline by Ransomware Attack," TechCrunch, April 2, 2019, https://techcrunch.com/2019/04/02/arizona-beverages-ransomware.

money at the problem," reported an unnamed source, according to TechCrunch, which first reported the attack.[17] This undoubtedly added a substantial expense to the recovery cost.

10.4.3.3 Immutable Backups

The term *immutable backups*, meaning backups that cannot be changed or deleted, has gained popularity as the number of ransomware attacks has increased. As ransomware gained momentum, defenders began implementing backup solutions more consistently, in an effort to prevent adversaries from holding the upper hand in the event of an attack. Victims that could quickly restore from backups were in a much stronger position because they could recover their data without paying for a decryption utility.

In response, adversaries began targeting backup solutions, deliberately seeking them out and destroying backups before detonating ransomware. After all, once the adversary gained administrative control over a network, they could often leverage this access to destroy the backup system as well.

Immutable backups, in contrast, cannot be deleted, even by an administrator. While the precise implementation varies by vendor, typically there is a time frame (e.g., 7 days) during which a backup cannot be modified.

Because of their built-in tamper protection, immutable backups are much more likely to survive an incident than their counterparts. It is important, however, that security staff verify that their backups are truly immutable. In some cases, products marketed as "immutable" can still be altered with an administrator account. If an adversary compromises the account, then the backups will likely be impacted along with the rest of the environment.

10.4.3.4 Offsite Backups

There are many benefits to storing backups offsite, including redundancy in the event of a physical disaster, as well as facilitating remote access. Today, many providers offer cloud-based backup services that facilitate quick and easy-to-use deployment and recovery.

The downside is that retrieving and restoring offsite backups can take a long time and eat up bandwidth. Often, IT staff test backups by restoring individual systems, and rarely have an opportunity to attempt a full, system-wide restoration process.

In the event of a major disaster, responders are often shocked by the length of time required to restore data even from offsite backup systems that are fully functional. In some cases, it is faster and cheaper to drive the data over in a station wagon than download it via the Internet (depending on available download speeds and usage pricing). It's important to ensure that actual recovery times are aligned with the organization's objectives when selecting backup solutions and developing restoration processes.

---

17. Whittaker, "Arizona Beverages Knocked Offline by Ransomware Attack."

10.5   Reducing Risk of Data Theft

Many cyber extortionists steal data, which they then threaten to publish or sell unless the victim pays a ransom. It's relatively easy to exfiltrate data, and the tools required to engage in data theft often do not trigger antivirus software and network monitoring alerts. As a result, exposure extortion is on the rise, and this trend shows no signs of stopping.

Organizations can quickly and effectively reduce the risk of data theft—and therefore the risk of exposure extortion—by employing the following:

- Data reduction

- Data-loss prevention systems

We will discuss each of these in turn.

10.5.1   Data Reduction

When cyber extortionists start to publish data, victims are often shocked at the volumes of data exposed. It is frequently an eye-opening experience, in part because they didn't realize they were storing such a vast volume of sensitive data to begin with.

The first step in reducing the risk of data theft is simple: Store less of it. Reductions in the amount of data held by an organization correlates with reduced risk. In 2019, Cisco's Data Privacy Benchmark Study showed that "GDPR-ready" organizations had an average of 79,000 records impacted in breaches with a 37% probability of a high-dollar data breach loss (exceeding $500,000), compared with organizations furthest from GDPR readiness, which had an average of 212,000 records impacted in breaches and a 64% probability of a high-dollar data breach loss. "With fewer records impacted … it is not surprising that the GDPR-ready companies experienced lower overall costs associated with data breaches."[18]

A strong data and asset inventory process is essential for accomplishing data reduction. "Organizations which have done the work to inventory their data have much better visibility to their data, how it is used, and the associated risks," said Robert Waitman, a director at Cisco's Security and Trust Office.[19] See Section 10.1.1 for more details on conducting an inventory.

Once the data inventory process is conducted, organizations are better positioned to reduce their inherent risk of data exposure by reducing the amount of unnecessary

---

18. "Maximizing the Value of Your Data Privacy Investments: Data Privacy Benchmark Study," Cisco, 2019, www. cisco.com/c/dam/en_us/about/doing_business/trust-center/docs/dpbs-2019.pdf.

19. Dan Swinhoe, "Does GDPR Compliance Reduce Breach Risk?," CSO, March 19, 2019, www.csoonline.com/article/3369461/does-gdpr-compliance-reduce-breach-risk.html.

sensitive data they retain. This, in turn, enables defenders to invest in securing a smaller volume of data.

Three key tactics may be used to reduce the volume of stored data:

- **Abstain:** Refrain from collecting sensitive data in the first place. To accomplish this, organizations need to understand how data enters their information systems. This typically requires interviews with personnel, data mapping, and process review. Then, identify opportunities for eliminating data collection.

- **Devalue:** Replace sensitive information with less hazardous data. Often, this is accomplished using *tokenization*, such as when payment card numbers in a merchant's systems are replaced with random strings that cannot be used to make purchases elsewhere.

- **Dispose:** Once sensitive data is no longer needed, purge it from the organization's systems. This seemingly simple activity can be surprisingly challenging to accomplish regularly. It requires that organizations routinely track data, assign responsibility for its disposal, identify information that is no longer needed, create a deletion process for various systems (including hard drives, databases, cloud repositories, and more), and then implement, track, and audit disposal activities.

By reducing the volume of data stored, organizations increase the per-record budget for information security and reduce cyber extortionists' potential leverage.

Heads Up! Data Is Hazardous Material

Data is a powerful resource that can be used to help or hurt people. Some types of data are sensitive yet commonly used, like oil and gas. Other types of data are practically radioactive.

For decades, organizations around the world have been stockpiling data in enormous quantities, without investing in significant controls. However, most organizations are overwhelmed and don't have the resources to control the vast quantities of data that they hold, or even know what exactly they are storing. It's no wonder that huge data leaks hit the headlines on a daily basis—and cyber extortionists take advantage.

10.5.2   Data-Loss Prevention Systems

Data-loss prevention (DLP) tools are software applications designed to identify, track, and protect sensitive data within an organization's environment. For example, a DLP tool may be configured to identify Social Security numbers in email and block any unencrypted emails from leaving the organization's network if they contain this type of sensitive information.

DLP solutions can reduce the risk of a cyber extortion event, or even prevent it altogether, by blocking an adversary from exfiltrating sensitive information and generating an alert. Effective DLP solutions come in many varieties, and normally fall into one of three categories:

- **Endpoint:** Protects information stored on workstations and servers

- **Network:** Monitors data in transit on the network

- **Cloud:** Protects data stored in cloud applications

DLP tools are very effective at protecting structured data with a clear and easily recognizable format, but can be less effective for protecting unstructured data such as sensitive, scanned information; intellectual property; or other information that can't quickly and accurately be identified through automated means.

Consider where your data is stored when selecting and configuring DLP software. For example, data stored in AWS needs to be protected and audited very differently than data stored on a locally accessible file server. While many DLP solutions are designed to operate in one type of environment, other tools can monitor endpoints, the network, and the cloud simultaneously. Prior to implementing a DLP solution, make sure to conduct a data inventory so that you can select the appropriate software and implement it effectively.

10.6 Solving the Cyber Extortion Problem

Cyber extortion is a systemic, widespread issue that can be successfully addressed only through corresponding large-scale changes. Individual organizations can reduce their risk of cyber extortion by employing the prevention and detection measures detailed in this chapter, but certain risks simply cannot be mitigated at an individual level.

It is no wonder that IT staff, security teams, and executives alike often feel discouraged. The problem not only *seems* far too large for one organization to tackle—it truly *is*.

In this section, we discuss the large-scale, macro changes that need to occur (and *can* occur) for cyber extortion to be relegated to the dustbins of history. These measures include the following initiatives:

- Get visibility.

- Incentivize early detection.

- Encourage proactive solutions.

- Reduce the attackers' leverage.

- Increase risk for the adversary.
- Minimize the adversary's payoff.

10.6.1 Get Visibility

Only a small percentage of cyber extortion cases ever become known to the public or law enforcement. Extortion cases that have an extreme impact on the public—such as those involving hospitals, schools, and municipalities—might make the news, but (based on the authors' firsthand experience) a huge number of cases are simply not of great interest to the media or are quietly resolved and fly under the radar. Even when cyber extortion cases are reported, the root cause is rarely publicly identified (and is often unknown), making it difficult to pinpoint widespread risk factors or implement truly effective solutions.

Victims of cyber extortion attacks justifiably fear their cases becoming public, lest they suffer reputational damage, lawsuits, regulatory investigations and fines, or other unhappy consequences. Quite often, victims take great pains to keep their attack quiet, making ransom payments through trusted third parties and hiding behind a veil of secrecy.

There might be legal or regulatory requirements for victims to report, in some cases, but victims are not always aware of these mandates. Reporting requirements vary based on jurisdictions—even within the same country—and might be specific only to industries such as healthcare or banking. Most organizational leaders have little to no experience in managing cybersecurity incidents. As a result, it can be challenging for organizations to understand their reporting obligations on a good day, let alone their worst. In cyber extortion cases, victims are under enormous stress and typically experiencing cash flow difficulties, and leaders are overwhelmed and unprepared. Unless they have access to expertise (through a cyber insurer or experienced IT firm), they often prioritize emergency recovery efforts and never report a cyber extortion event, even if doing so is encouraged or required.

To get visibility into the problem, it's essential to establish clear, easy-to-understand, widely applicable cyber extortion reporting requirements that are carefully designed so as to not overly burden victims. Everyday leaders need to clearly understand their reporting obligations even in the midst of a cyber extortion attack. Consider including incentives for conducting a root-cause analysis, so that proactive security measures can be appropriately prioritized.

10.6.2 Incentivize Detection and Monitoring

Victims rarely detect cyber intrusions in the early stages. Why? In the physical world, it's easy to tell that a burglar has entered. A window is broken; drawers have been opened; jewelry is gone. When a thief steals a car, the victim notices it's missing.

Not so with data. Hackers can quietly gain access to the victim's network with no obvious signs, and copy information without that action immediately impacting the victim. To trace the hackers' footsteps, victims have to record their activity. They also have to pay for someone to review the records of activity, which takes time and expertise.

Many organizations do not see strong reasons to invest in effective detection or monitoring. As a result, they don't have visibility into their own environments. They have no way of detecting a potential cyber extortion incident in the early stages, so they cannot shut down these attacks before large volumes of data are stolen and/or ransomware is deployed. The lack of detection capabilities contributes to the epidemic of cyber extortion incidents.

Certain organizations have more incentive than others to invest in logging and monitoring. For example, in the United States, healthcare providers are incentivized to investigate cyber extortion cases more fully and are more likely to collect evidence since it can be used to "rule out" a breach. In late 2016, the Department of Health and Human Services clarified that for healthcare providers and other covered entities, ransomware cases should be considered a potential data breach unless the victim conducts a risk assessment and demonstrates otherwise.

Incentivize investment in detection and monitoring to nip cyber extortion attacks in the bud and facilitate investigations when they do occur.

10.6.3   Encourage Proactive Solutions

As discussed earlier in this chapter, many cyber extortion attacks are preventable. Looking to public health as a model, risks can be mitigated throughout entire communities with a combination of education, incentives, and direct funding. These are typically implemented as a collaborative effort among government agencies, insurers, and nonprofit organizations. The same type of collaboration needs to occur with cybersecurity to reduce the number of victims and ensure that all organizations have access to knowledge, funds, and resources that can proactively reduce their risk.

Proactive prevention measures are key. Policymakers can, and should, work collaboratively with government agencies, cyber insurers, response firms, IT companies, cloud providers, and more to reduce the risk of cyber extortion attacks.

10.6.4   Reduce Adversaries' Leverage

As previously discussed, victims can reduce attackers' leverage in many ways:

- Develop BCPs to maintain operations during crises (see Section 10.4.1)
- Roll out disaster recovery processes to mitigate threats to availability (see Section 10.4.2)
- Implement backups to ensure availability of data (see Section 10.4.3)
- Reduce the volume of sensitive data stored (see Section 10.5.1)
- Implement DLP solutions (see Section 10.5.2) to reduce the risk of data exfiltration

All of these strategies can be reinforced and encouraged on a macro scale through government policies, funding, and insurer requirements, among other methods.

That said, one major strategy for reducing adversaries' leverage cannot be implemented on an organizational level: providing a path to mitigate harm after sensitive information has been leaked. Today, adversaries dangle sensitive information over the cliff of the Internet, threatening to release it to the public unless the victim pays a ransom demand. Frequently, the stolen data includes customer, patient, student, or employee personal information.

Once information is leaked, it may be downloaded, shared, analyzed, leveraged for commercial purposes, and distilled into data products. In many countries, data subjects have little to no control over the use of their personal information once it is leaked.

Lack of consistent regulation over data exchange and use gives cyber extortionists enormous leverage over the victims that they hold hostage. Once sensitive information is released, there is no way to control or undo the damage. When the stolen data affects third parties such as patients, students, and clients, this puts additional pressure on the hacked organization, because victims do not have a way to mitigate harm to these third parties except by paying the ransom demand.

Track and regulate how sensitive data is *used*, and give people opportunities to control the use of data that affects them. Taking this step would empower society to mitigate the harm of data exposure even after an adversary publishes stolen data, which in turn would reduce cyber extortionists' leverage over their victims.

10.6.5   Increase Risk for the Adversary

Throughout the history of cyber extortion, adversaries have rarely suffered consequences. When ransomware and cyber extortion attacks began hitting the headlines in 2016, law enforcement agencies were largely stymied by cryptocurrency and the dark web, which enabled cybercriminals to hide their identities and evade apprehension.

As public attention increased, however, so did funding and international coordination. Over time, law enforcement agencies began to make progress in tracking down high-profile cyber extortion groups. For example, in 2021, an international law enforcement operation took down the infamous and prolific REvil ransomware gang's servers. Other cyber extortionists clearly took note. The Conti ransomware gang issued a public statement on their data leak website about the REvil takedown, complaining: "Is server hacking suddenly legal in the United States or in any of the US jurisdictions?"[20]

Despite the irony of the Conti gang's outrage, the subtext was clear: Law enforcement actions against high-profile cyber extortion groups had been noticed, and the criminals weren't happy. Around the same time, cyber extortionists were ramping up their recruitment efforts, hiring affiliates and contractors to support their burgeoning industry.

---

20. Brian Krebs, "Conti Ransom Gang Starts Selling Access to Victims," Krebs on Security, October 25, 2021, https://krebsonsecurity.com/2021/10/conti-ransom-gang-starts-selling-access-to-victims/.

Public reward programs further increased the risk for adversaries. For example, the United States' Transnational Organized Crime Rewards Program (TOCRP) incentivized reporting.[21] Under this program, the U.S. government offered up to $10 million rewards for information about the REvil and Darkside cyber extortion gangs. It is not difficult to imagine that a cybercriminal might be motivated to betray their associates in exchange for millions of dollars.

In early 2022, 14 REvil members were reportedly arrested in Russia, resulting in a major public relations blitz that further shook the cybercriminal underground.

It's important to continue to increase risk (and perceived risk) for adversaries and their ecosystem. By publicly bringing cyber extortionists to justice, law enforcement agencies foster a perception of risk that can deter cyber extortion.

10.6.6 Decrease Adversary Revenue

Cutting off cyber extortionists' payments has the potential to kneecap their criminal enterprises. This can be accomplished in many ways. For example, there has been much debate about whether ransom payments should simply be outlawed. While this approach might seem straightforward, and therefore attractive, it can have devastating consequences for victims and the communities they serve, as discussed in Chapter 8.

In recent years, law enforcement agencies have successfully clawed ransom payments back from cybercriminals by seizing cryptocurrency wallet keys during raids and intercepting funds stored in cryptocurrency exchanges. For example, in the infamous 2021 Colonial Pipeline case, the U.S. Justice Department seized 63.7 Bitcoins (approximately $2.3 million at the time). "The extortionists will never see this money," said Stephanie Hinds, acting U.S. attorney for California's Northern District. "This case demonstrates our resolve to develop methods to prevent evildoers from converting new methods of payment into tools and extortion for undeserved profits."[22]

Sanctions are another effective tool used to disrupt the flow of money throughout the cyber extortion industry. For example, in 2021, the U.S. Office of Foreign Asset Control (OFAC) ramped up efforts to regulate and penalize cryptocurrency exchanges that cyber extortionists use to store and transfer their ill-gotten gains. While the designation and imposition of sanctions against these types of organizations does not directly solve the cyber extortion problem, it makes it more difficult for adversaries to transfer, launder, and most importantly cash out their ransom payments.

For all these reasons, efforts are needed to further disrupt cyber extortionists' revenue streams, through payment tracking, identification of illicit intermediaries, sanctions, and other methods.

---

21. "Transnational Organized Crime Rewards Program," U.S. Department of State, Bureau of International Narcotics and Law Enforcement Affairs, August 25, 2020, www.state.gov/transnational-organized-crime-rewards-program-2/.

22. Dustin Volz, Sadie Gurman, and David Uberti, "U.S. Retrieves Millions in Ransom Paid to Colonial Pipeline Hackers," *The Wall Street Journal*, June 7, 2021, www.wsj.com/articles/u-s-retrieves-millions-paid-to-colonial-pipeline-hackers-11623094399.

10.7 Conclusion

Cyber extortion teaches us that we are all connected—for better and for worse. In an instant, a hacker on the other side of the globe can hold a victim hostage. Just as quickly, the hacker's grip can be released.

The future of cyber extortion will be determined not just by the adversary, but also by society's reaction. As described in this chapter, there exist effective security tools and techniques that can prevent cyber extortion attacks. Organizations can dramatically reduce their risk by implementing a strong cybersecurity program, deploying security technologies, investing in detection and monitoring, reducing the risk of data theft, and increasing operational resilience.

All of this requires knowledge and funding beyond what most organizations have available today. This is in part due to the rapid adoption of technology throughout every corner of our economy, and a corresponding rush to collect and horde data without fully assessing the risks of doing so. Compounding this challenge is the nascent cybersecurity industry, in which standard best practices are constantly evolving and training programs are not yet mature.

While individual organizations can reduce their risk of cyber extortion by investing in the tools and techniques described in this chapter, the reality is that no one organization can successfully address the problem of cyber extortion alone. Truly mitigating the global cyber extortion crisis will require systemic changes that can only be addressed on a macro scale. Governments need to enact smart, consistent policies to encourage accurate reporting and incentivize positive change. Insurers need to incentivize adoption of effective risk-reduction techniques. Law enforcement agencies need to collaborate globally to dismantle cybercriminal operations and disrupt revenue streams. Everyone must work together to raise awareness and make effective tools and techniques accessible to organizations of all sizes around the globe.

While cyber extortion will never entirely disappear, we can work together to relegate it to the footnotes of our daily lives.

10.8 Your Turn!

Every cyber extortion incident is unique. The response team's options and priorities will vary depending on the victim organization's industry, size, and location, as well as the details of the incident itself.

Based on what you learned in this chapter, let's think through key elements of prevention.

Step 1: Build Your Victim

Choose one characteristic from each of the three columns to describe your victim's organization:

Industry	Size	Location
Hospital	Large	Global
Financial institution	Midsized	United States
Manufacturer	Small	European Union
Law firm		Australia
University		India
Cloud service provider		Country/location of your choice
Organization of your choice		

Step 2: Choose Your Incident Scenario

Select from one of the following incident scenarios:

A	Ransomware strikes! All of the victim's files have been locked up, including central data repositories, servers, and workstations.
B	A well-known cyber extortion gang claims to have stolen all of the victim's most sensitive data and threatens to release it unless the victim pays a very large ransom demand. The gang posts the victim's name on their dark web leaks site, along with samples of supposedly stolen data.
C	Double extortion! Both A and B occur at the same time.
D	The victim is hit with a denial-of-service attack on its Internet-facing infrastructure that slows its access and services to a crawl. The adversary threatens to continue and even escalate the attack unless a ransom is paid.

Step 3: Discussion Time

After the cyber extortion crisis has been resolved, you are asked to advise the victim's leadership on how they can prevent similar attacks in the future. Given what you know about the victim and the scenario, answer the following questions:

1. How is a data and asset inventory useful for reducing the risk of cyber extortion incidents such as the one your victim experienced?

2. Name one preventive measure that you recommend for the victim and explain why it is important.

3. What does the term "immutable backups" mean, and why is it important?

4. Name three elements of an effective business continuity plan.

5. Why is it important to consider cyber insurance coverage when developing incident response plans, training, and tabletop exercises? Provide at least one example.

Afterword

Cyber extortion attacks are a symptom of a much bigger problem: Our society's technology infrastructure is permeated by weaknesses and vulnerabilities, which adversaries exploit on a regular basis. Much of the time, adversaries remain invisible, lurking undetected in victims' systems. Their crimes may be silent—quietly stealing data, selling access on the dark web, or leveraging their foothold to compromise more organizations. Even when these crimes are detected, victims rarely report them to authorities, choosing instead to keep quiet and avoid the potential shame and liability of a breach.

In a perverse way, cyber extortionists have done us a favor. By making the problem visible, they have incentivized investment in solutions. Never before has society invested more in the war against hackers. Cyber extortion has caught the attention of executives and boards, spurred international cooperation among law enforcement, and driven cyber insurance companies to incentivize widespread risk mitigation. Above all, it has provided clear justification and spurred investment in cybersecurity.

This brief moment of visibility will not last. As the perceived risks associated with cyber extortion increase, adversaries will shift back to less visible tactics and retreat into the darkness. We have seen this before. For example, in the early 2000s, "noisy" worms suddenly caused massive network takedowns. Blaster, Slammer, Code Red, Nimda, and others replicated across victim networks so quickly that they impacted operations and caused widespread damage. In response, organizations invested in patching, firewalls, security policies, and more. But adversaries didn't give up and go away: They merely adapted and shifted to stealthier tactics, honing and improving their malicious techniques away from the public eye.

History may well repeat itself. In response to ransomware, today's defenders have invested in backups and endpoint protection utilities. Adversaries, in turn, have already shifted their tactics, de-emphasizing ransomware in favor of simple data theft and threats of exposure.

What happens next will depend on society's reaction. A much-needed crackdown on cyber extortion gangs may drive adversaries back underground, back to techniques that carry less perceived risk. Instead of notifying victims and the public that they've been hacked, adversaries may choose to leverage their access in other ways. For example, dark data marketplaces are more mature than ever before, and make it easy for adversaries to monetize stolen data with little risk.

Every crisis is an opportunity, and the global epidemic of cyber extortion is no exception. We can leverage this moment to incentivize early detection and reporting and finally gain visibility into the true scope and scale of our cybersecurity challenge. We can increase funding for development and implementation of security tools, which will help organizations of all sizes thwart adversaries. We can work together to launch awareness campaigns, so as to educate our communities and encourage implementation of effective security programs. However, if we don't act quickly, the criminals will shift to quieter tactics that will undermine the current political and social momentum. Now is the time to take action and build a stronger, more secure world.

Checklist A

Cyber Extortion Response

Here is a quick, high-level checklist for responding to a cyber extortion incident. The steps are meant as a guide; specific response needs will vary from case to case. Tasks in this checklist often occur simultaneously and should not be taken as a linear process. Immediately following each item on the checklist, you'll find the section number (in parentheses) where you can find more detailed information. Note that this checklist will evolve over time; see the authors' website for the latest version.

The Crisis Begins

The following activities are normally initiated immediately after an incident is discovered.

☑ **Activate incident response processes.** (4.2)

☑ **Involve the appropriate people** and appoint an incident manager who will maintain responsibility for oversight of the response, communication, and status. (4.3)

☑ **Conduct triage** to evaluate and assess the current state, understand the victim's recovery objectives, and determine appropriate next steps. (4.4)

☑ **Assess your resources**, including budget, insurance coverage, sources of evidence, staff, technology, and documentation. (4.5)

☑ **Develop an initial response strategy**, a living document that will guide your process. (4.6)

- **Establish goals** that are realistic and aligned with the organization's priorities. (4.6.1)

- **Create an action plan**, by enumerating key milestones and tasks. (4.6.2)

- **Assign responsibilities** for each task in the action plan. (4.6.3)

- **Estimate timing, work effort, and costs** and share these with the leadership team. (4.6.4)

☑ **Communicate with stakeholders** including the response team, affected parties, and the public. (4.7)

Containment

During the containment phase, responders need to halt malicious activities and ensure the adversary is locked out of the environment as quickly as possible. Here are common actions taken during the containment process:

- ☑ **Gain access to the environment**, either through physical means or carefully restricted remote access.

- ☑ **Halt malicious encryption/data deletion.**
    - Change file access permissions. (5.3.2.1)
    - Remove power from the impacted hosts. (5.3.2.2)
    - Kill the malicious processes. (5.3.2.3)

- ☑ **Disable persistence mechanisms** such as monitoring processes, scheduled tasks, and automatic startup scripts. (5.4)

- ☑ **Halt data exfiltration.** (5.5)
    - Check alerts, logs, and outbound network traffic for signs of suspicious outbound communications.
    - Block suspicious outbound network traffic at the perimeter firewall, or an intermediary internal firewall if available.
    - Block access to any cloud services or file-sharing sites used by the adversary to transfer data.
    - Disallow the use of utilities such as FTP applications, PowerShell, and Win-SCP if not necessary.
    - Restrict data repository access by modifying permissions, roles, and application configurations as appropriate.
    - Remove any email forwarding rules that were created by an adversary.
    - Consider cutting off all network traffic as a temporary measure.
    - Take other steps to block data exfiltration as appropriate.

- ☑ **Resolve denial-of-service attacks.** (5.6)

- ☑ **Lock out the hackers.** (5.7)
    - Kill remote connection services. (5.7.1)
    - Reset passwords for local and cloud accounts. (5.7.3)

- Audit and remove any newly created accounts. (5.7.3)

- Roll out multifactor authentication. (5.7.4)

- Restrict perimeter communications. (5.7.5)

- Minimize third-party access. (5.7.6)

- Mitigate risks of compromised software. (5.7.7)

☑ **Hunt for threats.** (5.8)

- Use threat hunting tools such as endpoint detection and response (EDR), security information and event management (SIEM), and vulnerability scanners to hunt for signs of suspicious activity.

- Remove suspicious hosts or virtual machines (VMs) from the environment.

- Deactivate unexplained or malicious user accounts.

- Disable newly installed or suspicious software applications.

- Eradicate any other sources of potential threats.

- Generate signature data for any identified threats and update security solutions to leverage new information.

Investigation

"Investigation" refers to the process of systematically uncovering facts about the incident, so as to inform response processes, reduce risk, and ensure that the victim meets obligations. In cyber extortion cases, this typically includes the following tasks:

☑ **Research the adversary** to gather actionable intelligence that may guide the response. (6.1)

☑ **Scope the incident** to understand the full extent and impact; document your findings for use by the team and third parties involved in the response. (6.2)

☑ **Determine if a formal breach investigation** will be required, based on legal, regulatory, and contractual obligations. (6.3)

☑ **Preserve evidence** from sources such as security software and devices, ransom notes, system artifacts, and authentication logs. (6.4)

Negotiation

Victims might decide to communicate with the adversary in an effort to reduce ransom amounts, buy time to recover data, reveal information about the adversary, and bring the extortion attack to a resolution. Here is a guide to the negotiation process, along with tips for the negotiator:

- ☑ **Establish negotiation goals** before you start so that communications are aligned with your budget, timeline, and information security needs. (7.2)

- ☑ **Consider possible outcomes** and how you would respond to each. (7.3)

- ☑ **Identify and prepare the communication medium(s)** you will be using, based on the information shared by the adversary. (7.4)

- ☑ **Understand common pressure tactics** and prepare stakeholders for possible communications from the adversary outside of normal channels. (7.5)

- ☑ **Choose an experienced negotiator** who understands the importance of tone, timeliness, and trust. (7.6)

- ☑ **Make first contact** with the adversary. (7.7)

- ☑ **Identify which information** the victim will (and will not) share with the adversary. (7.8)

- ☑ **Review and avoid common mistakes.** (7.9)

- ☑ **Obtain "proof of life"** that demonstrates the adversary is able to deliver on their promises. (7.10)

- ☑ **Ask for discounts** (respectfully). Most cyber extortionists expect to haggle over the price. (7.11)

- ☑ **Close the deal**, by agreeing on a price, form of payment, timing, and deliverables received in return. (7.12)

TIP: Tips for Cyber Extortion Negotiators

- Maintain a neutral professional tone throughout all communications.
- Provide brief but factual information.
- Require "proof of life."
- Don't pretend the victim is someone they are not.
- Don't try to trick the adversary.
- Don't respond with anger or blame.
- Don't make unrealistic promises.

Payment

If the victim considers making a payment, here is a general overview of the process:

- ☑ **Decide whether to pay**, considering the pros and cons of both. (8.1)

- ☑ **Notify the appropriate parties of a potential ransom payment**, such as the victim's insurance company, and identify any requirements or constraints. (8.1)

- ☑ **Understand the forms of payment** accepted by the adversary, as well as any surcharges for nonpreferred currency types. (8.2)

- ☑ **Ensure payment is not prohibited.** Conduct due diligence to determine whether the recipient is associated with a sanctions nexus, and document carefully. (8.3)

- ☑ **Engage a payment intermediary** to facilitate the ransom payment. (8.4)

- ☑ **Be aware of common timing issues**, including funds transfer delays, insurance approval hurdles, and fluctuating cryptocurrency prices. Plan carefully to minimize the risk of timing impacts. (8.5)

- ☑ **After the payment is made**, confirm receipt, request the promised deliverables, notify government agencies or other parties as appropriate, and properly account for the payment. (8.6)

Recovery

As the victim restores their environment, it's important to follow a carefully planned process to prevent permanent loss of data or reinfection. These steps are a guide to work toward fully restored operations:

- ☑ **Back up important data**, such as configuration files and data repositories (including encrypted data in ransomware cases). (9.1)

- ☑ **Build your recovery environment** using a segmented network to avoid cross-contamination. (9.2)

- ☑ **Set up monitoring and logging** to ensure that you have visibility to detect signs of malicious activity, both during the recovery process and long term. (9.3)

- ☑ **Establish your process** for restoring individual computers, making sure to address evidence preservation, restoration of functionality, malware eradication, risk mitigation, and monitoring. (9.4)

☑ **Restore the production environment** based on a prioritized plan. (9.5)

☑ **Restore data (carefully),** whether from backups, collection from production systems, re-creation, or decrypted files. (9.6)

☑ **Decrypt encrypted data** if necessary, using a methodical process designed to minimize risk. (9.7)

☑ **Maintain an effective response on a long-term basis as needed**, to address lawsuits, regulatory investigations, public relations needs, and other chronic effects. (9.8)

☑ **Adapt** by conducting a postmortem, updating documentation, and improving the cybersecurity program. (9.9)

Checklist B

Resources to Create in Advance

The following sections outline a general checklist for resources to have available before a cyber extortion crisis, so that you can make informed decisions and implement an effective response. These include plans, procedures, contact information, templates, technology, credentials, and reference materials.

Full response programs are ideal, but if you have not had time to create these, start with the items listed in the checklist that follows. These are simply general guidelines; modify and adapt them to suit your environment.

Note that you will almost certainly need to call in outside help during your recovery process. Make sure to have documentation for key activities that *outside parties* can follow, even if they aren't intimately familiar with your environment.

> **Tip**
>
> Make sure response plans and documents are available even if your entire technology environment is down. The best methods for doing this vary depending on the organization, but it can be as simple as copying the information to encrypted USBs and storing them offline at different locations. Review your options and consider how you will access information in the worst-case scenarios.

Response plans that clearly delineate:

☑ **Roles and responsibilities** (described in Section 4.3), with key details such as:

- Who coordinates the response and is empowered to make decisions?

- Who can make financial decisions in a crisis (such as whether to purchase new equipment/software, pay a ransom, etc.)?

- Who will decide which evidence to preserve, and which *not* to preserve?

- Who drafts and approves internal and external communications, such as statements to the media, key stakeholders, regulators, and more? (Typically, public relations and your breach coach should be involved, at a minimum.)

- Who is responsible for notifying responders and stakeholders, from outside IT consultants to the board of directors? (You may want to establish a phone tree.)

- Backup assignments for each task (in case a person is out or there is a need for schedule rotation).

☑ **Triage guidelines for first responders**, such as:

- Triage framework (Section 4.4.2)

- Diagnostic questions for assessing the current state (Section 4.4.3)

- Recovery objectives (Section 4.4.4)

☑ **Defined incident management and escalation processes**

☑ **Documentation processes for responders**

☑ **Notification obligations**, including requirements for contacting insurers, regulators, government agencies, and other parties

---

Crisis communications plans that address:

☑ Response team communications (Section 4.7.1)

☑ Affected parties (Section 4.7.2)

☑ Public relations (Section 4.7.3)

Specific procedures for tasks such as:

☑ Evidence collection, including clear, specific steps for gathering and preserving evidence

☑ Backing up various device configurations, and rolling back changes if needed

☑ Restoration of data and systems (It's important to test this in advance and keep it up to date!)

☑ Conducting an investigation, including adversary research, scoping, and breach investigation

Contact information for the response team, leadership, and third parties:

Internal staff

- ☑ IT
- ☑ Legal
- ☑ Cybersecurity
- ☑ Finance
- ☑ Executive team
- ☑ Public relations
- ☑ Board of directors contact

External parties

- ☑ Managed services providers (MSPs) and technology vendors
- ☑ Cyber insurance claims hotline/form
- ☑ Breach coach/cyber attorney
- ☑ Incident response/forensics firm
- ☑ Ransom negotiator
- ☑ Bank
- ☑ Public relations firm
- ☑ Law enforcement (FBI, Secret Service, police department)
- ☑ Regulators

Make sure to include after-hours contact information in case it is needed and keep the contact list up-to-date.

Templates for use throughout the response:

- ☑ **Response strategy templates** to be filled out and periodically updated during the crisis.
- ☑ **Communications templates** that have been preapproved by legal counsel, public relations specialists, and the leadership team. These may include public notification

templates to use in the event of a potential cybersecurity incident, sample communications for human resources personnel to use with employees, templates for regulator notifications, and more.

Technology to support response efforts:

☑ **Effective detection systems.** The earlier an incident is detected, the easier it is to minimize damage. Ensure that the organization has detection mechanisms in place, such as endpoint detection and response (EDR), network detection and response (NDR), antivirus, and more. Note that adversaries often strike after normal business hours, on holidays, and on weekends. It is not enough to simply have detection systems installed; today's organizations need 24/7 monitoring for potential incidents.

☑ **Centralized incident documentation system**, such as ticketing software

☑ **Centralized monitoring and logging systems**

☑ **Threat hunting software**, such as EDR, security information and event management (SIEM), vulnerability scanners, and other tools

☑ **Evidence preservation tools** appropriate for the types of systems in use, such as imaging software/hardware and cloud-based log export utilities

☑ **Backup and restoration tools**

☑ **Credentials and methodology for accessing:**

- Monitoring and logging systems

- Threat hunting software

- Backup and restoration tools

- Network equipment

- Cloud applications

- Workstations, servers, and other infrastructure

Reference materials:

☑ Network diagrams that illustrate key servers, network devices, cloud repositories, and interconnections

☑ Inventory of servers, cloud assets, and key data repositories, along with information about who has administrative access

☑ Data and asset classification policy

☑ Accurate, up-to-date list of all employees, users, roles, and accounts

☑ List of available sources of evidence, along with retention times and prioritization guidelines for various types of incidents (Make sure to get input from the organization's selected breach coach ahead of time.)

☑ Documentation describing any key dependencies or the order of operations that would be important for restoring the technology environment and access to data

☑ Backups and documentation of network device and server configurations, account lists, domain structure, etc.

☑ "Gold standard" images of workstations, servers, and network devices, to facilitate quick redeployment

☑ Prioritized list of business functions and systems needed to support them, reviewed and approved by the organization's leadership in advance

☑ Copy of the cyber insurance policy, including a summary of key requirements that may affect the response

Checklist C

Planning Your Response

Your cyber extortion response capability must evolve over time to meet current threats, adapt to changing resources, and fit the needs of your technology environment. As a result, response process development must be an ongoing routine within every organization. Here is a checklist for building and maintaining an effective response process.

- ☑ **Assign responsibility for planning.** Make sure one person is clearly assigned responsibility for cyber extortion response planning, and delegates tasks as needed. Since cyber extortion is a crisis, this individual should ideally be involved in crisis response planning for the organization as a whole and be empowered to coordinate across business units. Revisit and refresh responsibilities on a routine basis.

- ☑ **Establish an approval process.** It's important to establish the process for approving updates to your response program. This will help to ensure that new processes can actually be put into practice, and do not linger in limbo.

- ☑ **Prioritize based on risk.** Make sure your response processes are aligned to address your high-risk scenarios. Ideally, your organization should routinely conduct cyber-security risk assessments, which you can leverage for this purpose.

- ☑ **Involve key stakeholders.** While the response planning process should be led by one person, it is important to involve key stakeholders throughout the organization. Consider who will be involved in a cyber extortion response effort, and ensure they are consulted in the planning phase.

- ☑ **Conduct planning sessions.** This is where the rubber hits the road. Schedule workshops or other planning exercises as needed in which you step through the response process, make decisions, and identify documentation and resources to develop.

- ☑ **Create documentation and resources.** Develop documentation and resources needed to support an effective response.

- ☑ **Conduct training and awareness campaigns.** Responders must understand their roles, know to access key resources, and recognize how to make decisions, communicate, and take action in a crisis. To accomplish this, it's important to routinely conduct training and awareness campaigns. This can include a range of activities, from short reminders during meetings to more in-depth live training events. Tabletop exercises, in which participants practice responding to crises, can be especially valuable for practicing communication strategies, identifying gaps, and understanding roles.

☑ **Revise and update.** Cyber extortion is constantly evolving. Make sure to regularly review and update response processes based on the latest threats, risk assessments, postmortem analyses of crises, and other developments.

Checklist D

Running an Effective Cybersecurity Program

Cyber extortion techniques and tactics vary widely. To defend against cyber extortion, organizations need to guard against all types of cybersecurity incidents by building and maintaining a strong cybersecurity program. To accomplish this, organizations need to know what they are trying to protect, understand their obligations, manage risk, and monitor risk.

Here is a checklist that organizations can use as a foundation for a strong cybersecurity program.

Know What You're Trying to Protect

(Section 10.1.1)

Understanding the scope of your information resources is critical for maintaining an effective cybersecurity program and preparing for response.

☑ **Inventory data and assets.** Take an inventory of the sensitive data that the organization stores, along with where it is stored and who may access it. To simplify this process, the organization can classify data into categories based on regulatory requirements and security risks.

Understand Your Obligations

(Section 10.1.2)

Cybersecurity-related laws are emerging rapidly, the regulatory landscape is constantly evolving, and new contracts increasingly include cybersecurity-related clauses. All organizations should have a process for continuously tracking laws, regulations, and contractual obligations, and updating policies and procedures as needed.

☑ **Maintain a statement of applicable laws, regulations, and obligations.** A qualified cyber attorney should evaluate your organization's regulatory and contractual obligations with respect to cybersecurity and produce a written statement, which should be reviewed and updated annually.

☑ **Know your oversight responsibilities.** Your minimum responsibilities are often defined by law, regulatory guidance, or industry standards. Assign a qualified team member to research and document your organization's responsibilities and ensure that the oversight processes are aligned with requirements, with input from an experienced cyber attorney as needed.

Manage Your Risk

(Section 10.1.3)

Every organization is unique, and therefore every cybersecurity program is different. Across the board, however, a proactive and methodical approach is key. Here are high-level steps that every organization should take to effectively manage cybersecurity risks.

☑ **Assign roles and responsibilities.** Ultimately, it is people who design, build, and implement your cybersecurity program. Ensure that you have an experienced cybersecurity professional leading your program, and budget for appropriate staffing at all levels. Outsource as needed to ensure that you have qualified and trained personnel responsible for each component.

☑ **Build your cybersecurity program.** Every organization should have a formal, written cybersecurity program that is designed to comply with relevant laws, regulations, and other obligations. The program should be reviewed and updated at least annually, or more frequently as needed.

☑ **Choose and use a cybersecurity controls framework.** Use a reputable cybersecurity controls framework as the foundation for your cybersecurity program, such as the NIST Cybersecurity Framework or ISO 27001. Customize it as needed for your organization.

☑ **Develop your risk management plan.** Create, implement, and maintain a plan for prioritizing and addressing cybersecurity risks. Make sure to prioritize security technologies that will effectively reduce risk. Update this plan as often as practical, and proactively include supplier risks.

☑ **Engage in training and awareness.** Routinely communicate cybersecurity policies, procedures, and threat updates to stakeholders, including IT staff, security team members, legal counsel, general employees, and the leadership team. Popular formats include on-demand training platforms, live webinars, and awareness campaigns.

☑ **Fund your cybersecurity program.** No cybersecurity program can address every risk. Make sure to prioritize investments in cybersecurity so that they are aligned with risk. This may include allocating budget for human resources, equipment, services, and more.

☑ **Get cyber insurance.** Select cyber insurance coverage based on the anticipated residual risks to ensure that appropriate risks are transferred. Coverage should be aligned with your leadership's risk appetite. Maximize the value of your policy by ensuring you fulfill all the requirements and integrate it into your incident response programs.

Monitor Your Risk

(Section 10.1.4)

It's important for every organization to maintain an accurate understanding of current risks, so that it can effectively protect its information resources.

☑ **Perform a cybersecurity controls assessment.** Routinely evaluate the organization's cybersecurity program by assessing controls in place and comparing the results with a widely accepted framework, such as the NIST Cybersecurity Framework or ISO 27001.

☑ **Conduct technical security testing.** Regularly check your systems for known vulnerabilities, configuration weaknesses, policy gaps, and more. Tests should be selected to fit each organization's unique and ever-changing technology environment.

☑ **Obtain a risk assessment report.** Identify potential threats and vulnerabilities, map these to controls in place, and determine the residual risk to the organization. Ideally, the risk assessment should incorporate the results of the controls assessment and technical testing. By accurately understanding the organization's risk profile, leadership can effectively invest funds where they are needed most and make efficient use of limited resources.

☑ **Track and analyze cybersecurity incidents.** Keep track of cybersecurity incidents, analyze root causes, and provide reports and metrics to leadership. This way, the organization can learn from incidents and identify effective measures for reducing the risk of future issues.

Cause we know reality is crazy
That's why nothin amaze me
Look in the past
You might have to go farther than the book in your class
—Deltron 3030, "Memory Loss," May 23, 2000

Index

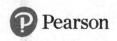